The

DIVIDED

MIND

of the

BLACK

CHURCH

RELIGION, RACE, AND ETHNICITY
General Editor: Peter J. Paris

Beyond Christianity: African Americans
in a New Thought Church
Darnise C. Martin

Deeper Shades of Purple: Womanism
in Religion and Society
Edited by Stacey M. Floyd-Thomas

Daddy Grace: A Celebrity Preacher
and His House of Prayer
Marie W. Dallam

The Methodist Unification: Christianity and
the Politics of Race in the Jim Crow Era
Morris L. Davis

Watch This! The Ethics and Aesthetics
of Black Televangelism
Jonathan L. Walton

American Muslim Women: Negotiating Race,
Class, and Gender within the Ummah
Jamillah Karim

Embodiment and the New Shape of Black
Theological Thought
Anthony B. Pinn

From Africa to America: Religion and
Adaptation among Ghanaian Immigrants
in New York
Moses O. Biney

Afropentacostalism: The Changing
Discourses of Black Pentecostal and
Charismatic Christianity
Edited by Amos Yong and
Estrelda Y. Alexander

Creole Religions of the Caribbean:
An Introduction from Vodou and Santería
to Obeah and Espiritismo, Second Edition
Margarite Fernández Olmos and
Lizabeth Paravisini-Gebert

The Divided Mind of the Black Church:
Theology, Piety, and Public Witness
Raphael G. Warnock

For a complete list of titles in the series,
please visit the New York University Press website at
www.nyupress.org.

The

DIVIDED

MIND

of the

BLACK

CHURCH

THEOLOGY, PIETY, AND PUBLIC WITNESS

RAPHAEL G. WARNOCK

NEW YORK UNIVERSITY PRESS

New York and London

NEW YORK UNIVERSITY PRESS
New York and London
www.nyupress.org

First published in paperback in 2020

References to Internet websites (URLs) were accurate at the time of writing.
Neither the author nor New York University Press is responsible for URLs
that may have expired or changed since the manuscript was prepared.

Library of Congress Cataloging-in-Publication Data
Warnock, Raphael G.
The divided mind of the Black church : theology, piety, and public witness /
Raphael G. Warnock.
pages   cm. — (Religion, race, and ethnicity)
Includes bibliographical references and index.
ISBN 978-0-8147-9446-3 (alk. paper)
ISBN 978-1-4798-0600-3 (alk. paper)
1. African American churches. 2. Black theology. I. Title.
BR563.N4W28 2013
277.3'08308996073—dc23   2013017725

New York University Press books are printed on acid-free paper,
and their binding materials are chosen for strength and durability.
We strive to use environmentally responsible suppliers and materials
to the greatest extent possible in publishing our books.

Manufactured in the United States of America

10 9 8 7 6 5 4 3 2 1

Also available as an ebook

In honor of my wonderful parents,
the late Reverend Jonathan Warnock and the Reverend Verlene Warnock

To all of my beloved siblings and to those whom I am blessed
to serve as pastor at the Ebenezer Baptist Church

CONTENTS

ACKNOWLEDGMENTS

Writing is at root a solitary undertaking. But it is greatly aided by the support, honest input, and constructive criticisms of colleagues, family, and friends. That is why I am so very grateful for the many people who have helped to make this a stronger project and with small and sometimes random acts of kindness and grace transformed even the tedious side of writing into a labor of love.

First, I am grateful for my parents, the late Jonathan Warnock and Verlene Warnock, my first pastors and teachers, from whose mouths I first heard the gospel of liberation and through whose example my siblings and I were inspired to embody its implications in personal conduct and communal commitment. Their fervor for the gospel was significantly deepened by my introduction to rigorous inquiry into the content and meaning of the church's proclamation. This occurred first during my years as a student at Morehouse College, under the tutelage of great teachers like Lawrence Edward Carter, Sr., dean of the Martin Luther King, Jr., International Chapel, Aaron Parker, Duane Jackson, and Roswell Jackson.

Then at Union Theological Seminary, I met James H. Cone, whose text *For My People: Black Theology and the Black Church*, I first encountered while working on a paper during my senior year in high school. Little did I know then that he would become my academic adviser and mentor. Cone taught me much about the rigor of intellectual inquiry, both as an act of faith and as a gift of "tough love" for the church. Still other professors teaching during my matriculation, including Christopher Morse, Emilie Townes, Delores Williams, Gary Dorrien, Vincent Wimbush, and the late church historian James Melvin Washington, affirmed and challenged my bivocational commitment as scholar and preacher and helped to create, at Union, a critical context for my growth.

But that context was expanded and continually tested in the laboratory of my active and simultaneous ministry on the staff of Birmingham's Sixth Avenue Baptist Church and Harlem's Abyssinian Baptist Church. I thank those congregations and their respective pastors, the late John Porter and Calvin O. Butts III, for their deep investment in me across the years. This work began as my dissertation while serving as pastor of Baltimore's Douglas Memorial Community Church, and by the time of my graduation, I was also beginning my pastorate at the Ebenezer Baptist Church. I thank the people of those congregations for giving me time and space to think and write. That time and space was greatly facilitated by the work of pastoral and administrative staff members at Douglas and Ebenezer, assisting and attending to the daily operations and pastoral concerns of congregational life. I offer my heartfelt thanks to Calvin Mitchell, Catherine Luckett, Rhonda Boozer, Vernard Caples, Mark Wainwright, Darryl Roberts, Shanan Jones, Michael Wortham, Frank Brown, Selina Smith, Walter Hughes, Natosha Rice, Wilbur Willis, Bobbie James, Clevette Ingram, and Jason Myers for their faithful service as associate pastors and to Glenda Boone, Esther Harris, Marvel Leverett, Mary Kay Williams, Rosalyn Barnes, Andrea Darden, Susan White, Atiba Nkrumah, Willie Lyons, Evelyn Prettyman, and April Lopez for their attention to the daily administrative operations of church life.

It was Peter Paris of Princeton University who suggested that the dissertation should become a book. I am proud that this work is a part of the Religion, Race, and Ethnicity series of which he serves as series editor, and I thank him and my editor, Jennifer Hammer, for their encouragement and advice through this process. Finally, I want to thank a host of colleagues and friends, whom I met during my matriculation through three degrees at Union Theological Seminary and whose sharp questions and challenges, across the years, have made me a better scholar, pastor, and person. Among them are JoAnne Terrell, Mark Chapman, Leslie Callahan, Joy Bostic, Diane Stewart, Clarence Hardy, Sylvester Jones, Jonathan Cutler, Adam Clark, Kanyere Eaton, Lorena Parrish, Mark Kellar, and Adolphus Lacey. Additionally, Gayraud Wilmore, Obery Hendricks, Randall Bailey, Dennis and Christine Wiley, Monica Coleman, and J. Alfred Smith provided more encouragement, support, and insight than they know. To them and so many others, I owe my sincere thanks and gratitude. All errors and limitations are mine alone. All glory belongs to God.

Introduction

WHAT IS THE true nature and mission of the church? As a community formed in memory of Jesus Christ and informed by the gospels, what is it that makes it a faithful and authentic witness, and what exactly is it called to do? Indeed, all Christian communities must ask and try to answer that question. From the fledgling communities behind the gospels to the classic debates of Nicea and Chalcedon through the Reformation until now, christology and ecclesiology have always been done together so that those who are informed by a memory of Jesus must wrestle simultaneously with the implications of that memory for their own mission. That is the church's burden. Yet, for reasons of history and theology, the burden carries with it an extraordinary freight, and the question has itself a distinctive resonance when the church is one built by slaves and formed, from its beginning, at the center of an oppressed community's fight for personhood and freedom. That is the history of the black church in America and the theological prism through which any authentic inquiry into its essential mission must be raised.

As a group of researchers discovered while making their way through the community of Bronzeville during the Great Depression, hardly any question is more vociferously argued in the black community, even among those who do not attend, than the meaning, message, and mission of the black church.[1] Indeed, because so much is at stake in the viability of a community's oldest and most enduring indigenous institution, black intellectuals, W. E. B. Du Bois,[2] Carter G. Woodson,[3] Benjamin E. Mays,[4] and E. Franklin Frazier[5] among them, have agonized, often with great consternation, over the purpose and the promise of the black church.

In more contemporary times, Eddie Glaude, professor of religion and chair of the Center for African American Studies at Princeton University, re-presented this classic genre of scholarship, recapitulating some old themes in a new era when he created a storm of controversy by declaring in the *Huffington Post* that "the black church is dead."[6] Ironically, both the exasperated, hyperbolic character of his assertion and the ensuing conversation and controversy that it created, on all sides of the debate, bespeak the enduring significance of the institution in question. If the black church *is* dead, as Glaude asserts, concern over its prospects for resuscitation and role as an instrument of liberation is very much alive.

In important ways, it is this enduring concern for the relationship between black religion and black resistance—piety and public witness —that helps to account for the origins and development of black theology. From the very moment of its emergence from the fiery tumult of riot-torn cities and heated national debate regarding the meaning of a new and rising black consciousness, captured in the expression "black power," black theology has been careful to situate its own self-understanding within the larger historical narrative of black religion and black resistance. Because of the black church's central, though not exclusive, place in this narrative, it has been, for black theologians, a primary focus of historical interpretation and theological reflection.

To be sure, white churches have always been a critical part of the analysis. This is so because of their complicity and active participation in slavery, segregation, and other manifestations of white supremacy. But they have also been engaged by the discussion because black theology, even while focused sharply on black suffering, has endeavored to take seriously ecumenical Christianity's claims regarding the marks of the true church, that is, a body that is one, holy, catholic, and apostolic.[7] Yet, owing to the centrality of black churches' historical location in the story of African American resistance, their cultural and institutional prominence within black life, and the theological questions raised by their legacy of separatist existence, black churches—their origins, development, and mission—have occupied a central place in the discussion and, as they emerge within the critical reflections of black and womanist theologians, are central to this investigation.

Purpose

I AIM IN this book to analyze what black and womanist theologians have had to say regarding the essential mission of the black church and to critically examine what black churches and their pastors have had to say in response. Admittedly, the issue seems, at face value, rather broad and perhaps unwieldy. However, the double-consciousness of black Christianity—that is, a faith profoundly shaped by white evangelicalism's focus on individual salvation (piety) yet conscious of the contradictions of slavery and therefore focused also on sociopolitical freedom (protest)—provides a meaningful angle and a conceptual framework through which to inquire into the black church's sense of vocation and a basis for teasing out the nuances of a meaningful theology of the church.

By examining the historical significance of the rise and development of black theology, a self-conscious discourse of critical theological reflection and an important conversation partner with the black church regarding the meaning of Christian faith, this book asks the following: As an instrument of salvation through Jesus Christ, is the mission of the black church to save souls or to transform the social order? Or is it both? As it would seek to be faithful to the gospel message and mission of Jesus Christ, is it called to be an evangelical church or a liberationist church? Can it truly be an evangelical church without also being a liberationist church? Can it be a liberationist church without also being an evangelical church? Put another way, does the gospel mandate insist that the church organize its institutional life so as to address itself primarily to "the slavery of sin" or to "the sin of slavery"? And in that vein, as an ecclesial community, profoundly shaped by a memory of the cross and the tragedy of human brokenness, how ought it to understand its own role in the protracted work of atonement? Is it called to give its life over to a freedom known *outside* history or *within* history? Moreover, might one characterize the former orientation as *otherworldliness* and the latter as *this-worldliness*? Or does the New Testament message itself render such neat distinctions too facile, calling the church to faithfulness by maintaining a critical and dialectical connection between historical witness and eschatological consciousness? In summary, as the church of Jesus Christ seeks to bear witness to the "kin-dom" of God imbued with love and justice, does it do that best by giving itself over to the work of personal piety or of social protest? And what is the relationship between the two?

I argue here that on these fundamental questions the black church has had a divided mind which has in turn shaped its ambiguous history. But that divided sense of vocation and the questions lodged therein resurfaces with new meaning during the era of the civil rights and black power movements and is given, for the first time, sustained and systematic theological treatment with the birth of black theology. With the rise of black theology, a profoundly evangelical church with a distinctive liberationist heritage and a peculiar eschatological consciousness was confronted with the theological complexities of its own self-understanding and asked what kind of church it desired to be. It is to that issue, as it is shaped by the early context of black theology and emerges in the writings of black and womanist theologians and black pastors up to the present, that we give our attention.

Why This Project?

A FEW TEXTS, such as Dale P. Andrews's *Practical Theology for Black Churches: Bridging Black Theology and African American Folk Religion,*[8] James H. Harris's *Pastoral Theology: A Black Church Perspective,*[9] and Forrest Harris's *What Does It Mean to Be Black and Christian? Pulpit, Pew, and Academy in Dialogue,*[10] have addressed themselves to the problematic relationship between the systematic reflections of black theologians and the actual institutional life of the black churches.[11] Moreover, it is a problem that has been acknowledged at least as early as the mid 1970s—a time when black theology was beginning to gain some traction in the academy, even as it engaged other theologies at home and abroad.[12]

However, I provide here, as no one else has, a theological treatment of this problem that takes into account the *full historical development* of black theology, including its first-generation interlocutors, current voices, and the work of womanist theologians, as they urge the black church to consider its mission in relation to the meaning of the gospel. Moreover, this work endeavors to situate the conversation between black theologians and black pastors as a distinctive moment within the larger historical narrative of black Christian faith. With the rise of black theology, black Christians, both in the black caucuses of white denominations and in black denominations, understanding themselves to be heirs to the independent black church movement, initiated for the first time a self-conscious project of independent theological reflection about the meaning of Christian faith, taking stock of the problem of racism as *heresy* and declaring war against its maintenance and sacralization in orthodox Christian speech.

But it was the civil rights movement, centered in the churches and led by a son of the black church, Martin Luther King, Jr., and the black power movement, as it raised sharp questions about the meaning of black identity and the relevance of Christian faith for the suffering black masses, that provided a necessary historical context. The radical implications of these two movements have clearly been formative for the development of black theology as an intellectual discipline. However, what is not altogether clear is the extent to which the black church has fully integrated the theological meaning of black power and the epoch-making implications of King's ministry into its very self-understanding nearly two generations after his death. This question, I argue, must be at the center of the discussion, and I aim through succeeding chapters to develop a heuristic framework that accomplishes that end.

Interpretations of the relationship between black theology and the black church have not sought to chart the full historical development and dynamism of that relationship as evidenced in the documents of black theology's earliest institutional manifestation within the black church (i.e., the National Committee of Negro Churchmen) and in the discussions between black and womanist theologians and the dialogue between the theologians and black pastors regarding the meaning of the faith and the mission of the church.[13] The work of Dale Andrews, who has contributed much to the conversation as a practical theologian, is a good example. His *Practical Theology for Black Churches* offers the most explicit and sustained treatment of the problem to date. However, his analysis is limited by a cursory view and summary judgment of black theology that does not adequately engage the history and substance of the conversation that has actually taken place between black theologians and the black pastors who have actually written about it. In that sense, some of the complexity of the actual discussion is lost.

Andrews's work does not acknowledge, for example, that black theology actually emerged *not* among trained academics but *from within* the black church itself and that it had its earliest articulation among pastors in search of the church's more radical side. Moreover, Andrews's summary judgment of black theology, focused on the first generation of academic theologians, offers precious little engagement of second-generation black theologians and virtually no treatment of womanist God-talk and ecclesiology, even as it purports to explain what Andrews sees as a chasm between "the black theology project," a misleading reference,[14] and the black church. Accordingly, the considerable efforts of womanist theologians to speak directly to the black church and the challenges that they are raising regarding the implications of the liberation ethics of black theology and pastoral care of the black church for women, gays, and lesbians sitting in the pews is left untreated.[15] On the other hand, monographs by second-wave black and womanist theologians that offer some treatment of the full development of black theology as a discipline have not given especial attention to the black church.[16] The absence of such a work represents, in my view, a critical gap in the literature with serious implications for the future of black theology and the mission of the black church.

Moreover, as theology always emerges from life itself, the pursuit of this topic is consistent with my own vocational identity and commitments as one who was trained in black theology and is attentive to its prophetic challenge to the churches and the society while also seeking to make use of its insights in my own ministry as pastor of Atlanta's historic Ebenezer Baptist Church. My doctoral adviser in systematic theology at Union Theological Seminary was James Cone, the father of black theology, and I serve as senior pastor in the spiritual home and pulpit of Martin Luther King, Jr.

Ebenezer Baptist Church, founded in 1886, amid the broken promises of Reconstruction, has long been an activist Christian community baptized in the spirit of enslaved ancestors who came to Jesus during the revivalistic preaching of the Second Great Awakening. Martin Luther King, Jr., following that tradition and, more immediately, his older sister, Christine, whom he would not let "get ahead" of him, reports that as a young child, he responded to the invitation to "join the church" one Sunday morning in 1936: "[A guest revivalist] came into our Sunday School to talk to us about salvation."[17] That was his first conversion experience, not an abrupt crisis moment but a gradual coming into consciousness in the context of a Christian family and church where his father served as pastor. The second conversion was indeed a crisis moment, a "kitchen experience," that brought him face-to-face with his own doubts and fears during the dangerous days of the Montgomery Bus Boycott, grounding him in personal faith in a sovereign God and catapulting him into the ministry of public witness and social transformation.[18] As he pursued the latter, as leader of the Southern Christian Leadership Conference (SCLC) and copastor of the Ebenezer Baptist Church, he extended and expanded the prophetic tradition of his father, Martin Luther King, Sr., who led a voting-rights campaign through the streets of Atlanta in 1935, and his grandfather A. D. Williams, Ebenezer's second pastor, who led the fight for the first "colored" high school in Atlanta and was a leader in the Atlanta branch of the National Association for the Advancement of Colored People (NAACP). It is in that historical and moral continuum that I seek humbly to be faithful to my own charge of pastoral care and public witness in a new moment.

But long before my pastorate at Ebenezer and my training at Union, I grew up in Savannah, Georgia, the son of two pastors in the Pentecostal Holiness tradition, or as Zora Neale Hurston and others have characterized it, the "Sanctified Church." Therein I was exposed to the liberating power, profound joy, and practical dilemmas posed by its doctrine of a transformative personal piety that emphasizes the sanctity of one's own relationship with the sovereign God and spiritual gifts expressed passionately in worship and translated clearly in a strict and meticulous ethic of personal holiness. To be sure, it is basically an evangelical piety with both continuities and differences with that in most black churches. Shaped by this sharp emphasis on personal piety, I was yet drawn to the prophetic protest strand of black Christian witness—not prominent and, when present, not always obvious —in the churches in which I grew up. In that sense, the black Christian dilemma I describe here and the tensions I examine are ecclesial and personal, historical and autobiographical. I reside at the intersection, moving regularly between "Jerusalem and Athens," ivory towers and ebony trenches. I am a child of Pentecostal Holiness parents, raised in the "Sanctified Church," trained in systematic theology by black theologians and privileged to serve in the pulpit of Martin Luther King, Jr.

Taking note of Martin King's prophetic challenge to the American churches, black and white, regarding their mission and commitment to freedom, informed by the distinctive critique and contribution of black theologians as they carry out this basic thesis of liberation, and shaped by the strange interior freedom and personal piety of the "Sanctified Church" with its exuberant spirituality, I have long been interested in exploring black theology's gospel of liberation in relationship to the radical heritage, peculiar spirituality, and ambiguous political reality of the black church.

Scope

THIS WORK PROCEEDS in full knowledge that the precise definition of the black church, and whether the complex and heterogeneous character of black ecclesial groupings in the North American context even allows for such a designation, has been contested terrain. In C. Eric Lincoln and Lawrence Mamiya's groundbreaking text *The Black Church in the African American Experience*, the authors limit their operational definition, for the purposes of a sociological study, to three Methodist and three Baptist communions and one Pentecostal communion, constituting seven historic black mainline denominations and, at the time of the study, about 80 percent of all African American Christians.[19]

While recognizing that in general usage the term "the black church" may include black congregations in white denominations, they limit the scope of their examination to the large independent black denominations, also excluding black Christians in smaller black denominations and in independent, nondenominational churches. In the end, such a limited designation is too narrow, given the current reality of black Christianity and given the development of independent black Christian reflection (black theology) among black people and black caucuses in predominantly white denominations.

Recognizing this complexity and the painful irony of deep gender contradictions in a church founded for freedom, womanist theologian Delores Williams has argued that "the black church is invisible, but we know it when we see it." While endeavoring to stand in solidarity with the principle that challenges "black denominational churches,"[20] as she calls them, to live up to the promise of their highest liberationist ideals, I argue that the concept of an "invisible black church" is too elusive to address the historical meaning and oppositional witness of a separatist black Christian response to racism in the nineteenth century, its *theological* reemergence in the twentieth century, and the implications of both for all the American churches in the twenty-first century.

Thus, when I refer to the black church, I speak of the varied ecclesial groupings of Christians of African descent, inside and outside black and white denominations, imbued with the memory of a suffering Jesus and informed by the legacy of slavery and segregation in America. While this historical phenomenon has its deep roots in the independent black church movement, the tragedy and depth of racism ensures the relevance of such a designation for black congregations and caucuses of various configurations who, consciously and unconsciously, live within the conflicting intersectionality of being black and Christian in America.

At the center of that struggle is the tension between the pietistic and liberationist strands in African American Christianity. Chapter 1 of this book accounts for the historical roots of that tension in a faith formed within the fires of revivalistic piety, primarily during the Second Great Awakening, but distinctively shaped by the fight against white-supremacist notions ensconced in the faith that the slaveholders shared. Thus, as scholars such as Albert J. Raboteau[21] and others have shown, what black Christians received was something other than what they were given. This phenomenon, *the formation of a liberationist faith* (the invisible institution) was, I argue, the first moment in a complex continuum of historical moments in which black people have endeavored to work out an antiracist and holistically salvific appropriation of Christian faith and black churches have wrestled through the dilemmas of theological double-consciousness in search of their distinctive mission. The second moment, covered also in chapter 1, is *the founding of a liberationist church* (the independent black church movement). The theological meaning of the separatist identity of the black church is examined, followed by an analysis of the third moment, the *fomenting of a church-led liberationist movement* (the civil rights movement) and the implications of Martin Luther King, Jr.'s ministry for the discussion between black theologians and black pastors regarding the black church's essential mission.

Chapter 1 is a critical engagement of the Christian identity of black churches and the significance of the rise of black theology for that discussion. Central to the discussion is the 1964 publication of a book by Joseph R. Washington titled *Black Religion: The Negro and Christianity in the United States*.[22] It is a pivotal piece that unwittingly underscored the need for a self-conscious theology of black liberation. Washington, a black scholar, characterized black Protestantism in America as a kind of distorted folk religion, disconnected from historical Christianity and essentially bereft of a genuine theology or an enlightened understanding of the faith. Moreover, he argued that the public theology of King, America's most well-known systematic theologian, with his leveraging of the New Testament message of the gospel ethic of love for the tactical purposes of a movement, actually embodied the problem of a religion long centered in protest but lacking in any critical dimension for apprehending Christian doctrine or Christian Tradition.

An emerging generation of black clergy and black theologians sought then to counter Washington's thesis, underscoring the crucial theological link between faith and social transformation and connecting that to an African American legacy of prophetic religion and principled resistance. Black theology emerged in the work of what became the National Committee of Black Churchmen (eventually, the National Conference of Black Christians) and in black caucuses. It was the context for a principled challenge to the black church to consider its mission, one issued in the constructive work of academic black theologians. I characterize their work as the fourth moment in the development of black Christian resistance to racism and the appropriation of a holistic understanding of salvation's work. It is *the forging of a liberationist theology* (black theology).

Chapter 3 examines that discussion in the writing of key texts by black theologians, showing both its continuities and discontinuities with the work of previous interpreters of the black church. Chapter 4 examines varying pastoral responses of black pastors who have actually written about black theology in the period of its nascence up until the contemporary moment. Emmanuel McCall, a leading black evangelical, for example, has argued that black theology is utterly disconnected from the black church and that by no means do "black liberation theologians represent the thinking and attitudes of the 'rank and file.'"[23] This chapter examines varying pastoral responses to the substance of black theologian Gayraud Wilmore's rejoinder that if McCall is correct, it is "because the majority of Black preachers confuse themselves with Billy Graham and the most unenlightened versions of White evangelicalism. Because they do not know *the rock from which they were hewn*" (emphasis mine).[24] The gender contradictions on both sides of the discussion are briefly taken up in this portion of the discussion.

Chapter 5 explores womanist responses to questions regarding the mission of the black church. Womanists have had to challenge the deradicalization of the black church while also providing a historical corrective to what I call the dewomanization of black radicalism. In this way, they are bridging many gaps, with important implications for how one understands the relationship between liberation and survival, political activism and spiritual militancy. The book ends with a call to black pastors and black and womanist theologians to commence, in view of this retrospective analysis, a fifth and new moment in the development of black Christian faith. This new and integrative moment, *the flowering of a self-critical liberationist community*, calls for honest, risk-taking dialogue and critical self-reflection that collates the pietistic and liberationist dimensions of black faith and marshals them in concert with other voices, in a bold, public theology that calls all freedom-loving people together for the fostering of a sustainable planet and a more just and peaceful world.

1

THE GOSPEL OF LIBERATION

BLACK CHRISTIAN RESISTANCE
PRIOR TO BLACK THEOLOGY

The Black Church

THE BLACK CHURCH was born fighting for freedom. That fact is evidenced by the resistance and testimony of slaves,[1] signified in the oppositional witness of pioneers of the independent black church movement,[2] and confirmed by the work of scholars across disciplines.[3] The freedom for which the black church has fought has always been both internal and external, expressing itself politically and spiritually, embracing black bodies and souls. This is so because historically the faith of the black church has been shaped and characterized by two complementary yet competing sensibilities: revivalistic piety and radical protest. In the North American context, both have been present from the beginning, and it is the dialogue and *differences* between the two that constitute the central tension in African American Christian faith. Moreover, it is this tension, more than anything else, that plays itself out in the divided mind of the black church and in the dialogue between black pastors and black theologians regarding the church's essential mission.

Many black pastors, some even while very much engaged politically, have tended to emphasize in their preachments and privilege in their ministry the pietistic side of black faith aimed at the freedom of the soul, in this world and the next. On the other hand, black theologians, informed by a distinctive and undeniable trajectory in black faith, have focused primarily on the political side, radical protest aimed at the freedom of the body in this world, expressed eschatologically by slaves who bore witness to it in their subtle songs about the next world. Historically, both the pietistic and the political side of black faith have been prominent, and each has made its own assertions about the character and meaning of freedom.

Black theologian Gayraud Wilmore explains the political character of black faith when, in his classic text *Black Religion and Black Radicalism*, he rightly asserts that "there has been and continues to be a significant difference between black religion and white religion in their approaches to social reality and social change—whether in reference to theological liberalism or to fundamentalism." Based on that fact alone, Wilmore persuasively argues, "black faith has been 'more radical' in the proper sense of that much maligned term."[4]

Owing to a unique political consciousness that was shaped in the brutal context of chattel slavery, racial oppression, and state-sanctioned terrorism in North America, this fundamental posture of resistance applies to black religion in general and, notwithstanding its "ambiguous politics,"[5] the black church in particular. For in a racist context, even the black church's pietistic proclamation has often, though not always, represented resistance through its assertion of black personhood, an egalitarian ethic and inclusive claim running through black faith that "all of God's children got shoes."[6] Moreover, this ecclesiology of personhood expressed in its piety and its politics is, more than anything else, the single, unifying strand historically setting the black church apart as the conscience of the American churches.

That is to say, of the American churches, the black church has clearly offered the most radical and sustained response to racism, what theologian James Cone has rightly called *"America's original sin and . . . its most persistent and intractable evil"* (emphasis mine).[7] This response has manifested itself in the establishment of independent churches and denominations, as African Americans refused to accept segregation and second-class citizenship within Christian communions, and culminated with the civil rights movement, during which they organized effective challenges to similar conditions within the society in general. Pioneers of the African Methodist Episcopal Church, the oldest of the independent denominations, offered in 1817 this rationale and raison d'être:

> We have deemed it expedient to have a form of Discipline, whereby we may guide our people in the fear of God, in the unity of the Spirit, and in the bonds of peace, and preserve us from that spiritual despotism which we have so recently experienced—remembering, that we are not to Lord it over God's heritage, as greedy dogs, that can never have enough; but with longsuffering, and bowels of compassion, to bear each other's burdens, and so fulfill the law of Christ.[8]

As eloquently expressed by these pioneers of African Methodism, the black churches and denominations insisted from the beginning on "a form of Discipline" that is egalitarian and inclusive, irrespective of race. Actively resisting the "spiritual despotism" of racial apartheid within the church, they have sought to signify their commitment to the unity of the Spirit and a radical understanding of the freedom of the Christian, *even* if that could only be done within the confines of a separatist institutional identity. In the black church's piety and through its politics, it is with the mission of liberation that the black church emerged.

The Black Church and White Theology

DESPITE THE BLACK church's distinctive emphasis on the gospel message of salvation and a creative hermeneutics of freedom shaped by the experience of engaging biblical texts through the lens of slavery and segregation, the circumscriptions of that experience ensured that it would be well within the twentieth century before the black church had the benefit of trained theologians providing *systematic theological reflection* on the significance of its witness among the churches and their varying theological claims. As the bishops made bold to establish in 1817 a new "form of discipline," most of them, like Richard Allen, did not have the benefit of theological training or, for that matter, formal education. Thus, the limits of their bold enterprise had to do with the formation of an egalitarian communion that did not discriminate against members of the church. Their statement, both literal and institutional, to the meaning of their separatist existence commended an egalitarian ethic to the American churches and to the larger society. But owing to practical limitations and political possibilities, the new discipline argued for no new theology.[9]

Thus, historically the official documents of the AME Church and other mainline, independent black denominations have included no new creeds or church documents representing a systematic challenge to the fundamental assumptions of Western Christian orthodoxy and, more germane to our discussion, no ecclesiological statements offering a countervailing view of the essential mission of the true church. The political reality discussed earlier makes this quite understandable for most of the black church's history.

Yet, as Christian ethicist Peter Paris has noted, even after the civil rights movement and the birth of black theology, black churches and the theological schools sponsored by black denominations have been slow to recognize the value of systematic theological reflection on their own history and distinctive commitment to justice and the extent to which therein is a faith that sets black Christianity radically apart from the theology of white churches.[10] Rather, seeing Protestant Christian doctrine as something *fixed* and caught up in the public rhetoric of a struggle that, quite understandably, emphasizes the quest for justice and humanity as something *universal*, black church leadership has too easily conflated Western Christian doctrine with its own sensibilities about freedom. The controlling assumption has been that whites simply failed to live up to the ethical mandates of Christian faith but that their understanding of the God of Christian faith was essentially correct. Paris astutely observes that the problem with this assumption is that it fails to acknowledge that

> white churches actually experienced no alienation between their thought and practice. This is evidenced by the fact that any attempt to preach racial equality in the pulpit has always been viewed as an act of hostility against the prevailing ethos. Since blacks assumed a static theology that transcended both races, they inevitably concluded

that racist activities were deliberate violations of professed theological beliefs. They had forgotten that the Christian churches ostensibly
had no difficulty with slavery for centuries prior to the abolitionism of
the nineteenth century. In fact, it is highly doubtful that the New Testament itself offers unequivocal opposition to slavery. Thus, if slavery
had such a long history among Christians, one should not suppose that
Christians would necessarily believe themselves to be under religious
obligation to treat ex-slaves as first-class citizens.[11]

Indeed, as black theologians have consistently pointed out and as a
handful of white theologians have acknowledged in print, the European and American theology that informs the work of white churches,
in much of its evangelical, liberal, and neo-orthodox variations, has
reinforced the status quo of a racist society, has marginalized black
people, and has largely ignored their struggle as a *theological* problem.[12] Decades after the rise of black theology, few white theologians
have taken seriously black theology's claims regarding the centrality
of the black struggle for understanding the meaning of the gospel in
our times. Most have been conspicuously silent regarding what James
Cone calls "America's central theological problem" in their work.
Indeed Cone's earliest work and his entire career have represented, in
part, a response to this deep contradiction in theological discourse. He
argues, for example, in *God of the Oppressed*,

> The history of white American theology illustrates the concept of the
> *social a priori* asserted by Werner Stark and the other sociologists of
> knowledge. . . . The social environment functions as a "mental grid,"
> deciding what will be considered as relevant data in a given inquiry.
> For example, because white theologians are not the sons and daugh-
> ters of black slaves but the descendants of white slave masters, their
> theological grid automatically excludes from the field of perception
> the data of Richard Allen, Henry H. Garnet, and Nathaniel Paul, David
> Walker, and Henry M. Turner. This same axiological grid accounts for
> the absence of the apocalyptic expectations of the spirituals among the
> so-called "hope theologians"; and the same explanation can be given
> why the white existentialists do not say anything about absurdity in

the blues. . . . It is obvious that because white theologians were not
enslaved and lynched and are not ghettoized because of color, they do
not think that color is an important point of departure for theological discourse.[13]

While this is clearly the case, there have been a few exceptions. The
political theology of Frederick Herzog represented one such exception during the nascence period of black theology. His *Liberation Theology*, based on the Gospel of John, was the first book-length response
to black theology by a white American theologian.[14] Among the
Europeans, Theo Witvliet's insightful work demonstrates a rigorous
engagement not only of the constructive work of black theologians
but a critical analysis of its roots in slave religion and in the faith of
the black church. For example, he observes the ambiguous role that
the spirituality of black institutional churches has played in black liberation, inasmuch as it is "an expression both of liberating protest
and revolutionary élan and of escapism and alienation." Moreover, he
criticizes black theologians for giving little attention to the pneumatological side of a faith where the power of the Spirit is prominent and,
with the global phenomenon of Pentecostalism, increasingly so.[15]

Finally, Helmut Gollwitzer is one European theologian who, even
while leveraging his own Barthian critique and caution to what he
sees as the ideological preoccupations of black theology, actually sums
up the deep theological contradictions that necessitated black theology very well. Reflecting on the world out of which the central doctrines of the Reformation emerged and the political backdrop against
which heated debates between Calvinists, Lutherans, and Arminians
took place, Gollwitzer observes that "no uneasiness evolved in regard
to colonial exploitation, manhunt, shipment of humans across the
Atlantic, and the degradation of human beings to beasts of burden, a
million times over, systematically and with a vengeance."[16] Succinctly
put, centuries of Western reflection and debate about the meaning of
Christian faith and the mission of the churches did precious little to
undermine slavery and segregation but offered much in support of it.
Often through the complicity of silence and sometimes through a con-
spicuous biblical hermeneutics of white supremacy,[17] the theological

thinking of white Christians actually emerged from their actions, and their actions have reinforced their thinking.

This is why black theology is important both in the history of black struggle and in the larger history of Christian theological reflection. Black theology, since its emergence in the 1960s, has endeavored to give substance and systematic expression to a theological perspective that sees the work of salvation in the broadest of terms, both underscoring and explicating the theme of liberation as the central message of the gospel and the essential mission of the church. In that regard, James Cone and other leading interpreters of the black theology movement called on black Christians and their churches to make a decisive theological break with white Christianity and, for the first time, do theology for themselves.

Yet this theological movement and the challenge that it represents would have far-reaching implications for the black churches' own self-understanding, and it would animate an important internal debate about the essential mission of the church. But its challenge is best understood within the larger historical narrative of black religious resistance to racism. For the radical roots of the black church and the academic reflections of black theologians are inextricably linked by a certain set of claims regarding the holistic character of salvation in the biblical witness, by the reality of racial oppression in America, and by an identifiable trajectory of black religious resistance to that oppression from slavery to the contemporary moment.[18] What I aim to do in this chapter is to highlight three particular moments that signify critical turning points in the black Christian narrative prior to the rise of black theology, the fourth moment. For the theological claims of black theology are rooted both in scripture and in the experience of black people's struggle for freedom. One cannot account fully for their distinctive hermeneutical insight into the former without reference to the latter.

Black Christian Resistance: Four Moments

WHILE BLACK THEOLOGY came to voice on the heels of the civil rights and black power movements of the 1960s, its systematic explication of the liberationist demands of the gospel and its simultaneous defense and critique of the black church can best be understood in the light of the continuing project of black religious resistance to racism in North America from the Middle Passage to the present moment. My argument is that the *systematic* project of black theology came as a logical *next step* along a complex continuum of moments in which black people have endeavored to work out an antiracist appropriation of the Christian faith and black churches have wrestled through the dilemmas of their own theological double-consciousness in search of their distinctive mission.

To be sure, while there is a necessary historical development in the way my argument proceeds, I do not mean that these are moments in a strictly chronological sense. Clearly, there is overlap. With the first two moments I discuss, there is some overlap in terms of historical chronology. But beyond that, it will be obvious that there is a certain conceptual continuity that resists the notion that each moment is hermetically sealed. Indeed the way in which the four moments are interlocking steps, nuanced and inextricably linked by a subterranean unity of black resistance to racism, will prove integral to the development of my case. Yet highlighting the *differences* as distinct moments does provide an apt heuristic device for situating the emergence of black theology as a discourse, for understanding the dilemmas through which the black church in search of its mission has had to wrestle, and ultimately for proposing some broad outlines for further constructive work by black and womanist theologians and black pastors. I would broadly outline these salient moments in the history of African American Christian resistance in this way: (1) *the formation of a liberationist faith* (invisible institution); (2) *the founding of a liberationist church* (independent black church movement); (3) *the fomenting of a church-led liberationist movement* (civil rights movement); and (4) *the forging of a self-conscious liberationist theology* (black theology). Put another way, each of the four steps respectively represent (1) Christianization, (2) institutionalization, (3) conscientization, and (4) systematization.

Integration, or a fifth moment representing *the flowering of a self-critical liberationist community*, is much needed in this postmodern era. It calls for deeper, sustained, and more intentional collaboration between black theologians and pastors committed to new, risk-taking dialogue with each other. Because of the inextricable relationship between proclamation, praxis, and critical reflection for any faith community, the effectiveness of the black pastoral and theological communities is each tied to the other. A fifth moment has the potential to be a salvific moment because it would involve the "broadening of communal space" (the ancient Hebraic definition for salvation) for challenging together structures of systemic sin and injustice in the social order and in the churches; probing together the complex connections between racism and topics much neglected by black theology and the black church such as ecology; and for developing together a public and pastoral theology of liberation, healing, and wholeness.

As interlocking steps in a stairwell, the four moments are inextricably connected, and each moment is best understood in relationship to the others. For example, because theological reflection tends to come subsequent to *praxis* and usually as the result of some deep historical contradiction or methodological problem, it is difficult to imagine a systematic black theology of liberation, as we now know it, that would have emerged *prior* to the first three moments. Other than the obvious lack of trained theologians and research scholars prior to the rise of black theology, it is the complex narrative of black religious resistance, culminating with the civil rights and black power movements, that accounts for the what and the when of black theology's emergence.

Specifically, it was the radical ministry of Martin Luther King, Jr., pastor and public theologian, that opened the way. Standing within the long protest tradition of the black church[19] and heading the Southern Christian Leadership Conference, a radical outpost of the black church whose mantra and mission was "To Redeem the Soul of America,"[20] King's ministry embodied the clearest American version of a gospel emphasizing social transformation and a vision of a church surrendered to that work. As a pastor and theologian, he understood it to be none other than the work of salvation. In fact, Martin Luther King, Jr., came to see the work of racial justice and social transformation not merely as the work of a movement but fundamentally as the church's reason for being. As we shall see, black theologians and the ministers involved in the black theology movement were both conscientized by this movement and critical of its limitations. This is why neither the emergence of black theology nor its critique of the black church can be accounted for apart from the ministry of King and its implications regarding the character of the work of the church as an instrument of salvation.

Moreover, I argue that if it is true that the black church's own commitment to freedom has not been adequately sustained, some four decades after the civil rights movement, then it is due, in large measure, to its failure to integrate within its self-understanding and sense of vocation the third and fourth moments in the history of black religious resistance. Thus, the black church, born in radical protest and shaped by revivalistic piety, has had, even at its best, a *divided mind*, that is, an ambiguous relationship with the radical *theological* implications of its long witness against the sins of the social order. Let us now examine each moment as it sheds light on this problem and provides a historical context for understanding the reflections of black theologians and their contemporary claims regarding the essential mission of the church.

1. A LIBERATIONIST FAITH (THE INVISIBLE INSTITUTION) / CHRISTIANIZATION

Albert J. Raboteau, historian and author of the seminal work *Slave Religion: The "Invisible Institution" in the Antebellum South*, has persuasively argued that "slaves did not simply *become Christians*; they *fashioned Christianity* to fit their own peculiar experience of enslavement in America" (emphasis mine).[21] Along the same lines, Howard Thurman observes that "by some amazing but vastly creative spiritual insight the slave *undertook the redemption* of a religion that the master had profaned in his midst."[22] Both Raboteau and Thurman provide important insight. For to "fashion Christianity" to suit African Americans' "peculiar experience" underscores the ways in which slaves were not simply passive recipients of missionary preaching but active and creative agents in the development of a religious self-understanding that had pragmatic and life-sustaining value for those in bondage. And to undertake "the redemption of a religion . . . profaned," as "pre–black power theologian"[23] Thurman suggests, bespeaks the subtle and unsystematic workings of a theological corrective to the faith with implications for slaves and slaveholders alike.

In that sense, while black theology represents the first, self-conscious effort of black Christians to do theology with reference to their own experience, a systematic treatment of a clear break from the theology of white churches, it stands within the trajectory of a long line of Christian protest against racism. For in testimony and independent institutional praxis, black Christians of the eighteenth and nineteenth centuries challenged the heresy of the premise that slavery and Christian faith were compatible. While the incompatibility of the two may be a tacit assumption today, as the works of Orlando Patterson and others have clearly demonstrated, that has not been the case for most of the history of Christianity in the West.[24] This refashioning, indeed redemption, of a faith introduced to them by the missionary effort of a Christian slavocracy and the forging of their own perspective within the "invisible institution"—clandestine spaces of worship carved out within the hush harbors—may be regarded as the first moment in a long trajectory of critical turning points prior to the emergence of black theology.

Ironically, the creative witness of black slaves was informed both by the piety of the Great American Revivals[25] and the politics of the American Revolution.[26] The former emphasized an individual conversion experience as the pathway to an internal freedom. The latter involved a political revolution based on what the Declaration of Independence calls "inalienable rights" and armed resistance as the means to an external freedom. Indeed, slaveholders recognized the dangerous implications in each for those who were determined to maintain the status quo. Hence, there was initially considerable resistance from planters to introducing slaves to Christian faith for fear of what it might suggest about their own worth and status in the divine economy.[27] Likewise, the high egalitarian principles of the American Revolution and the glaring hypocrisy of fighting the British for freedom from tyranny while subjecting black people to chattel slavery was not lost on many in the colonies, black and white.[28] With the implications of a revivalistic piety and revolutionary politics each being dangerous and potentially subversive in its own right, it is not difficult to see how both freedoms held together, each informing the other, provide a recipe for abolition and slave rebellions. Therefore, the task of a so-called Christian slaveholding society became the construction and maintenance of a distorted theology that kept internal freedom and external freedom—piety and protest—wholly separate, while also holding at bay the revolutionary implications of each for a people in bondage.

This is why the lower house of Maryland asked the upper house in 1664 "to draw up an Act obliging negroes to serve *durante vita* . . . for the prevencion of the dammage Masters of such Slaves must susteyne by such Slaves pretending to be Christ[e]ned[;] And soe pleade the lawe of England."[29] Similarly, the Bishop of London opined, "And so far is Christianity from discharging men from the duties of the station and condition in which it found them, that it lays them under stronger obligations to perform those duties . . . not only from the fear of men, but from a sense of duty to God, and the belief and expectation of a future account."[30]

By contrast, black Christians saw clearly the contradiction between their status and worth in the divine economy and their social status in a so-called Christian nation. No one embodied this belief more clearly and courageously than Harriet Tubman, abolitionist, liberator, and member of the AME Zion Church who escaped slavery and risked her own life during some nineteen return trips to the South in order to free hundreds of slaves.[31] Reflecting on the theological meaning of her witness, pastoral theologians Edward and Ann Wimberly have observed that "the desire for social deliverance burned deep in her breast along with the desire for personal salvation. Personal and social salvation mutually influenced each other in the slave tradition."[32]

Indeed, it is the relationship between personal and social salvation, revivalistic piety and radical protest, that sits at the heart of our concern, as we examine the double-consciousness and divided mind of the black church and how that informs the debate between black theologians and black pastors regarding the essential mission of the church. As the Wimberlys point out, both orientations have been integral to black Christians' understanding of the faith. The former represents the profound influence and evangelical consciousness of the

First and Second Great Awakenings in the eighteenth and nineteenth centuries and the influence of the Azusa Street Revival and the global movement of Pentecostalism in the twentieth century.[33]

But if the evangelical piety of the black church emerges from a distinctive encounter during the revivalistic fervor of the Great Awakenings, the latter orientation of radical protest emerges from the tragic historical experience of racial oppression and collective struggle for survival and liberation. But each influences the other. Furthermore, as C. Eric Lincoln and Lawrence Mamiya have observed, they operate in a complex dialectic in which one or the other may function more dominantly within a particular black church or church tradition or at a particular moment within black church history.[34]

Yet it is the peculiar genius of slave religion that within the invisible institution the two were held together in tandem and in a remarkably creative tension. In that sense, slave religion actually evinced an oppositional piety. Resisting all truncated notions of salvation that would separate "the slavery of sin" from "the sin of slavery," black Christian slaves gave voice to their own version of the faith through (1) a biblical hermeneutics of freedom (e.g., the Exodus motif), (2) freedom songs (the spirituals), and (3) an underground ethic of freedom and survival (e.g., insurrection, running away, stealing, "puttin' on ol' massa").

Regarding the hermeneutics of freedom, there is widespread agreement among interpreters of black religion that central to the difference between slave Christianity and slaveholding Christianity was their respective appropriation of the Exodus motif of the Old Testament.[35] Vincent Harding observes that one of the abiding and tragic ironies of American history is that while European colonists conceived of their adventure in the New World as the establishment of the New Israel, black slaves came to think of themselves as the Old Israel, enslaved by Pharaoh and awaiting their liberation from Egypt.[36] This sentiment they expressed, sometimes with double meaning,[37] in the spirituals, and they lived it out through varying strategies of resistance and a complex ethic of survival that included insurrection, running away, stealing, and other forms of subversion.[38]

In this way, the difference between the slaves' view of the faith and its ethical requirements on them and that of whites was "wide and deep."[39] A "Christian" slavocracy sought to reconcile the irreconcilable, by separating in both ecclesiastical and civic law, personal salvation and social salvation. Tragically, the same system extended to black converts the promise of eternal life and the tragic imposition of "social death."[40] Moreover, this theological construction was further reinforced by a pietistic rhetoric of petty moralisms that ignored the fundamental absurdity and inescapable moral quagmire of existing as human chattel. That black slaves rejected the contradiction, positing their own oppositional piety, is summarized well by Lucretia Alexander, a former slave:

> The preacher came and . . . he'd just say, "Serve your masters. Don't steal your master's turkey. Don't steal your master's chickens. Don't steal your master's hawgs. . . . Don't steal your master's meat. Do whatsomever your master tell you to do." Same old thing all the time. My father would have church in dwelling houses and they had to whisper. . . . Sometimes they would have church at his house. *That would be when they want a real meetin' with some real preachin'.* . . . They used to sing their songs in a whisper. That was a prayer meeting from house to house . . . once or twice a week. (Emphasis mine)[41]

2. A LIBERATIONIST CHURCH (THE INDEPENDENT BLACK CHURCH MOVEMENT) / INSTITUTIONALIZATION

The independent black church movement of the late eighteenth and nineteenth centuries is the second of three critical moments, distinct turning points in the development of African American religious resistance to racism prior to the emergence of black theology. This church was none other than the institutional expression of the desire of black slaves in the South and free blacks in the North to have what Lucretia Alexander termed *"a real meetin' with some real preachin'."* For while the oppositional witness of black Christianity had its genesis in the clandestine spaces of the invisible institution of the antebellum South, it raised its first visible protests against racism with the establishment of independent black churches.

Gayraud Wilmore, a pioneer of the black theology movement, has aptly designated this moment in the continuing project of black religious resistance to racism "The Black Church Freedom Movement." He rightly argues that it "must be regarded as the prime expression of resistance to slavery, . . . a form of rebellion against the most accessible and vulnerable expression of white oppression and institutional racism in the nation: the American churches."[42] Inasmuch as it offered a countervailing response to racism in the church and the larger society, one can say that its message was *political*. But by opting to separate rather than to accept the racialized polity, seating patterns, preaching, and practices of white churches, black Christians were also positing an egalitarian understanding of the church, exposing by contrast the contradictions of a white church that was just as racist as the society in general. In that sense, one can say that implicit in the praxis of the pioneers of independent black churches was an *ecclesiological* statement against the heresy of a racialized hierarchy within the Body of Christ.

Through the nineteenth-century black church's primary function as *refuge*—providing a spiritual respite and safe harbor from the violence and terror of white supremacy—and through its *antislavery* efforts, among black Baptists, for example, at the level of the local congregation, association, and denomination,[43] it embodied, in my view, what James Cone identifies as the threefold task of the church.[44] First, it proclaimed the reality of divine liberation. This is evident in the bold proclamation and praxis of men such as Bishop Henry McNeal Turner,[45] Nathaniel Paul,[46] and Harvey Johnson.[47] And, even while circumscribed by deep gender contradictions within a church formed for freedom, nineteenth-century black preaching women such as Jarena Lee,[48] Sophie Murray, Elizabeth Cole, Rachel Evans, Harriet Felson Taylor, Zilpha Elaw,[49] and the internationally traveled AME evangelist Amanda Berry Smith[50] proclaimed their version of divine liberation without a license or ordination.[51]

Second, the black church of the nineteenth century actively participated in the struggle for liberation. This is evident in its thrust toward independence, participation in the work of abolitionism, involvement in the development and maintenance of the Underground Railroad, missionary work among freedmen and freedwomen in the South, and the founding of black schools. While there has been much scholarly work covering these domestic activities, less known are its endeavors to globalize issues of oppression. But as Lawrence Little's work demonstrates, even when the black church's global efforts were contradictory, given the severe limitations imposed by white-supremacist structures, the black church did provide a distinctive voice on behalf of other voiceless peoples around the world, even while black people were negotiating overwhelming odds stacked against their own lives within the American empire.[52]

Third, even with the nineteenth-century black church's contradictions, particularly with respect to issues of gender, it did provide "a visible manifestation that the gospel is a reality."[53] This it did by providing a subjugated people an antiracist institutional alternative, a church where they knew themselves to be the people of God. Furthermore, by separating themselves from the racialized congregational structure of white churches, black churchmen and churchwomen of the eighteenth and nineteenth centuries evinced, through their actions, a holistic and embodied view of salvation and of the church as an instrument of the same.

Indeed, how a church conceives the work of salvation and consequently the nature of its vocation as salvation's instrument will determine the character of its witness and the depth of its involvement in the hard and elusive work of social transformation. White churches, with few exceptions,[54] posited a decidedly truncated soteriology aimed at the saving of individual souls and the maintenance of the social order, inside and outside the church. Black churches provided an oppositional witness carried in defense of a freedom that had both evangelical and political dimensions. Hence, the very emergence of these churches represents a critical moment both in the history of black religious resistance and in the history of American religion. For black churches, at their best, evinced, through their actions, an alternative ecclesiology, that is, a radical understanding of the church and of its salvific work, that brought together issues that a so-called Christian slavocracy had endeavored so hard to keep apart—baptism and freedom; bodies and souls; social deliverance and personal salvation; the slavery of sin and the sin of slavery.

Yet the oppositional witness of the black church against racism and on behalf of justice has not always been consistent, nor has the nature of its response been the same. Because it is still a participant in and a product of the American Protestant ethos, with its attending theological assumptions and cultural secretions, the black church, the church born fighting for freedom, has had a divided mind. This is why the radicalism of the black church has ebbed and flowed in dialectical fashion in the face of varying political and socioeconomic challenges before and after the Civil War. While it has been more radical than its white counterparts and has more clearly embodied the vision of an egalitarian church, focused on the gospel themes of freedom and hope, its total institutional life has represented what Hans Baer and Merrill Singer aptly describe as "a sometimes stormy admixture of diverse responses to oppression"[55] and what Manning Marable terms "the ambiguous politics of the black church."[56] This is to say that the black church has been both radical and unradical, the most prominent instrument of liberation within the African American community *and* the foremost conservative custodian of an uncritical evangelical piety that undermines the aims of liberation.

Owing to the black church's own theological double-consciousness and the intractable character of white supremacy, the proclamation and praxis of the black church has evinced competing notions of freedom. It has crafted both (1) a creative counterworldliness or eschatological consciousness that has empowered its people to fight as hopeful agents of freedom against the overwhelming tide of history *and* (2) an uncritical otherworldliness that has endeavored simply to avoid the contradictions of history, holding out for freedom in the world to come. To be sure, liberation, as black theologians have emphasized it, has been a prominent theme. Moreover, the black church's own emphasis on liberation represents, within a very complicated story, an identifiable trajectory which, more than anything else, distinguishes its historical witness from that of white churches. Yet it must be understood that in terms of the content of its proclamation and the nature and scope of its sociopolitical praxis, the black church has been, within every period of its history, a mixed bag.

This is so for at least two reasons. First, the black church, notwithstanding its separatist identity, has been clearly formed and decidedly influenced by the revivalistic piety and evangelical consciousness of the great American revivals. The global explosion of Pentecostalism in the late twentieth century coupled with the growing influence and social upward mobility of the once marginalized "Sanctified Church"[57] would clearly require today's student of African American religious history to add to the First and Second Great Awakenings of the eighteenth and nineteenth centuries the legacy of the Azusa Street Revival in the early twentieth century. African American Christianity was born in the fires of the former two revivals, and African American churches were the primary creative agents in the emergence and formation of the latter.[58]

Hence, the evangelical consciousness and revivalistic sensibilities of America's foremost ecclesiastical advocate for freedom have emphasized the primacy of individual conversion experience and the interiority of the spiritual life. When the black church is at its best, the quest for external freedom and the hunger for internal freedom emerge from the very same root. Yet when it has come to African Americans and the issue of race, white evangelicalism has always privileged internal freedom while diminishing the importance of external freedom or dismissing it altogether. George Whitefield, a prominent preacher and leading figure during the First Great Awakening and a strong advocate of Christianizing slaves even while maintaining them in bondage, gloats in a letter to a friend, regarding his revivalistic efforts in Philadelphia, "near fifty negroes came to give me thanks for what God had done to their souls. . . . I believe masters and mistresses will shortly see that Christianity will not make their negroes worse slaves."[59] While the black church has never embraced such a truncated understanding of salvation, it has nonetheless been informed and, in some ways, claimed by it. One might call this the theological double-consciousness of the black church. In this way, the reactionary, wholly otherworldly, and conservative side of the black church's ambiguous politics is best understood as that which emerges when the black church, informed by the sensibilities of its white evangelical counterpart, has seen social transformation as significant but not central to the divine work of salvation.

The second reason for the black church's ambiguous understanding of its own mission and mixed response to the forces of oppression is related to the first. For most of its history, the black church has not had the benefit of a self-conscious theology of liberation capable of explicating the theological meaning of its historical identity. Indeed, it would be difficult for any manifestation of the church to give its life completely over to sustained struggle against the overwhelming forces of oppression without the concomitant benefit of critical reflection on the meaning of that struggle and a systematic understanding of its own identity and mission. Given the inherent double-consciousness of black Christianity, profoundly influenced by white evangelicalism yet shaped by the distinctive history of black struggle, how does one keep the black church clear about its mission and honest about the depth of its own commitment to the work of freedom and justice in the society? This is a problem that has plagued the black church for all of its history. And it is within the light of this problem that one sees the importance of the emergence of an independent black theology within the history of black religious resistance. Yet it was the ministry of Martin Luther King, Jr., that provided the historical and cultural bridge. For without the conscientizing impact of his ministry on a new and radical breed of black clergy, it is difficult to imagine the emergence of what we now know as black theology.[60]

3. A Liberationist Movement: Martin Luther King, Jr., and the Civil Rights Movement / Conscientization

No single factor has contributed more to the rising political consciousness of the black church and the search for the radical side of its mission than the ministry of Martin Luther King, Jr.[61] To be sure, his ministry stands within and not apart from the long saga of black struggle and the cultural history of the black church. But within the twentieth century, King's prophetic voice and public theology raised and refocused the latent theme of liberation prominent among certain nineteenth- and twentieth-century figures of the black church,[62] and his praxis so crystallized the radical side of the black church's mission that it unwittingly laid the necessary foundation for the emergence of a new phenomenon in black religious history—a black theology of liberation.[63]

My argument may be summarized in this way. If within the history of black religious resistance the invisible institution represents the formation of a *liberationist faith*, and the rise of independent black churches and denominations constitutes the founding of a *liberationist church*, then King's movement, under the auspices of the SCLC, signifies the fomenting of a church-led *liberationist movement*. SCLC, a clergy-centered organization that functioned as a radical arm of the black church, had an unapologetic mantra and unabashed mission: "To Redeem the Soul of America." And it is this third moment, embodied in the ministry of King, that provides, in the twentieth century, the clearest manifestation of the church as an instrument for social transformation. King's ministry and movement represented the most significant challenge to the conservative and accommodationist side of the black church *from within* its own institutional life. To the degree that the institutional churches, black and white, shied away from the work of confronting the political power structure, not seeing this as central to the work of divine salvation, his approach represents the *ecclesiola en ecclesia*, the church over against church. Perhaps this is why he asks in his "Letter from Birmingham Jail" (an epistolary response to clergy who found his actions "unwise and untimely") the following question: "Is organized religion too inextricably bound to the status quo to save our nation and the world? Perhaps I must turn my faith to the inner spiritual church, the church within the church, as the true *ekklesia* and the hope of the world."[64] In this way, King's ministry pushed the boundaries of the American churches' self-understanding, insisting that they see the work of social transformation as essential to their identity and mission, indeed their very raison d'être.

Yet it was nascent black theologians—conscientized by the activist ministry of Martin King, challenged by the critique of King by the Muslim cleric Malcolm X and the young black power activists whom he had politically influenced,[65] informed by the claims of a rising black consciousness, and led primarily by the constructive theological work of James Cone—who would begin to develop a self-conscious and *systematic* understanding of the black church as an instrument of liberation. This was a mission that, in their view and contrary to that of King, demanded a radical separation from the theological assumptions of white Christianity.

Like King, particularly in his sermons to black audiences, the black theologians will emphasize the liberationist heritage and mission of the black church. But unlike King, they will insist that sustaining a mission that is radically different from that embraced by white churches requires a theology that is decidedly different from that of white churches. Thus, if King's movement, writings, and public theology provided a conscientious praxis, the black theology movement came to provide self-conscious and independent reflection on the meaning of that praxis in the divine work of black liberation. As we shall see in the next chapter, black theology is the fourth moment in the history of black religious resistance to racism.

Each of these four moments in the development of black Christian resistance to racism is inextricably connected to the others, and it is not possible to fully understand one without reference to its counterparts. The first moment, the formation of a liberationist faith, might be characterized as African American *Christianization*. It represents the complex and creative ways in which slaves, stripped of all rights and human dignity, found ways to "co-constitute the black self,"[66] receiving unto their African selves a faith that was significantly different from the one given to them. The second moment, the founding of a liberationist church, represents the *institutionalization* of black Christian resistance manifested in the work of abolitionism, the maintenance of the Underground Railroad, the founding of black schools, leadership in movements such as the Negro Convention movement, and the provision of a refuge from the incessant storms of white supremacy.

But King's movement, rooted, as it was, in a certain liberationist trajectory that reaches back through both of the two preceding moments, is yet the clearest and most impactful moment of *conscientization*. Unlike any moment before or after it, the civil rights movement provided the black church, America's "nation within a nation,"[67] a distinctive opportunity in which to consider on a *national* scale the meaning of its collective identity, as black people in the South and the North fought alongside others to transform the whole society. Unavoidably, the broad and national scope of this integrationist movement, formally and informally sourced by old networks of black church culture, carried with it certain nationalistic implications, some of which King himself embraced, regarding the distinctive meaning of the black church, black people's peculiar history of suffering, and their messianic mission in American culture. Finally, serving as the conscientizing influence on a whole new breed of young clergy, the ministry of civil rights activism provided the social and ecclesial context out of which *systematization* could emerge, that is, a radical and independent theology focused on the mission of liberation as that which defines the true church in American society. But let us say more now about Martin Luther King, Jr., the implications of his activist ministry for the mission of the black church, and the impact of his ecclesiological vision on those who would be the leading interpreters of an emerging black theology.

Martin Luther King, Jr., Revivalistic Piety, and Social Transformation

IT IS UNNECESSARY and clearly beyond the scope of our discussion to summarize here the history of the civil rights movement from Montgomery to Memphis. Several other works do that very well.[68] My aim is simply to underscore the significance of King's ministry, both its strengths and limitations, for the consciousness of nascent black theologians and to tease out some of the ways in which the content of his proclamation and the challenge of his public theology reveal certain issues and tensions within the divided mind of the black church.

David L. Chappell provides in his brilliant book *A Stone of Hope: Prophetic Religion and the Death of Jim Crow* a sharp analysis and contributes much to our deeper understanding of how the civil rights movement achieved historically improbable victories which we now take for granted and the central role that the hope resident in a peculiar religious consciousness played in sustaining those who struggled against overwhelming odds. He persuasively argues, among other things, that the civil rights movement was a religious revival, a time character- ized by those who were at its center as "a heady, life-transforming era touched with divine significance." Chappell argues that the testimony of the ordinary people involved suggests "that it may be misleading to view the civil rights movement as a social and political event that had religious overtones. . . . It was, for them, *primarily a religious event.* . . . To take the testimony of intense religious transformation seriously is to consider the civil rights movement as part of the historical tradi- tion of religious revivals, such as the so-called First and Second Great Awakenings, as much as it is part of the tradition of protest move- ments such as abolitionism, populism, feminism, and the labor move- ment" (emphasis mine).[69]

With solid research and deft historical analysis, Chappell's reflec- tions on the civil rights movement as a revival offer a sustained treat- ment of an idea touched on by previous interpreters. For in *The Origins of the Civil Rights Movement: Black Communities Organizing for Change,* sociologist Aldon Morris discusses the way in which the SCLC, as the radical wing of the black church, organized itself across the South for the purpose of "refocusing the cultural content of the religion of the black masses" for the work of political deliverance.[70] Albert J. Rabo- teau also suggests that the movement was a revival,[71] and Richard King in *Civil Rights and the Idea of Freedom* draws a similar parallel.[72]

Moreover, with historical imagination and insight into the creative interplay between the rationalistic framework of the God of Person- alism that Martin King had studied in graduate school and the per- sonal God of the black folk religion to which he had been exposed as a child but had held at arm's length, Stewart Burns discusses the way in which the revivalistic piety of the masses evangelized the young pas- tor and theologian, even as both he and they were evangelized by the movement. Hearing King's sermon at the Holt Street Baptist Church mass meeting over against the text of King's own spiritual biography —from the black church to elite northeastern seminary and univer- sity training back to the black church—Burns describes the moment in this way:

On the night of December 5, 1955, he was thrust into presiding over a church mass meeting that was a supercharged melting pot of black spirituality of all shades, . . . poor working people who, unlike King, talked to God everyday and lived their toilsome lives in an elevated world of Spirit. He stood face-to-face with the fierce raw emotionality of black church culture, a volcanic congregation believing itself in the presence of the Lord. As many participants later testified, the holy spirit was alive that night, and in a hundred such nights to come, with a palpable power and crystal clarity that overwhelmed the freshly minted doctor of theology. Yet by some uncanny act of grace, the breath of Spirit that he drew in that evening burst out of him in a jeweled torrent of unscripted words, a Lincoln-like synthesis of the rational and emotional, the secular and sacred. The faithful, King now among them, had conjured the kingdom of God in that place."[73]

As Chappell points out, revivals, presumably he means on a massive or national scale (e.g., the Great Awakenings), do tend to bring about a shift in the foci or emphases of church doctrine.[74] And King's mass meetings and impassioned preachments to a wayward nation and an apostate church, like those of the revivalists before him, served as a catalyst for a tectonic shift in theological emphasis. I agree generally with Chappell's assessment. Moreover, I argue that the heart of the theological shift occasioned by the civil rights movement, particularly as it pertains to the culture and agenda of the black church, had to do with a sea change in the critical nexus and creative tension between individual conversion and social transformation. For informed by the revivalistic piety of the great revivals yet shaped by the struggle against political oppression, the critical nexus between individual conversion and social transformation sits at the very heart of black faith. Moreover, both the strengths and limitations, the character and the content, of the black church's response to structural evil, in a given moment, proceeds directly from the nature of the theological tension between the two. Indeed, the faith and praxis of the black church has moved dialectically through history between both poles.[75]

This is to say that, on the one hand, black churches have evinced an evangelical piety that emphasizes individual conversion for the purposes of survival in this world and salvation in the next. On the other hand, they have also manifested a revolutionary faith that unapologetically sees the church as an instrument for social transformation. It should be emphasized that the relationship is indeed dialectical and not one of mutually exclusive categories. For the historical picture of black faith is quite complicated. And the impulse to transform the society, whenever it does emerge, tends to proceed both from and in concert with the piety. As Larry Murphy has suggested regarding the history of African American religion in general, "Piety was not one thing and liberation its antithesis. Rather, the latter derived its motive power and its transcendent validation from the former."[76] Along these same lines, one might further observe that an eschatological view that appears prima facie to be "otherworldly" may actually be what I prefer to call "counterworldly," that is, standing radically over against the severe limits of the current world order while "hoping against hope,"[77] holding out amid the dismal prospects of a given moment, for a firmer foundation within the world.[78]

As the best interpreters of King have come to increasingly understand, Martin Luther King, Jr., was very much a child of the black church, its faith, its language, and its culture.[79] Hence, quite conversant in the hope resident in black eschatological faith, King awakened through his preaching and praxis its activist side, creatively giving voice to a doctrine of the church that emphasized its mission as an instrument of radical protest and social transformation. In this way, his activist orientation trails through every area of his theology, including his theology of the cross, a prominent theme in black faith, and an eschatological hope captured in his public references to "the beloved community" and "the promised land."

Yet, as a social revivalist who remained a pastor and copastor throughout the years of the movement, King's emphasis on social transformation was organically and creatively connected to the evangelical piety of the black church that tends to emphasize individual conversion. Often, it is embodied in the centrality given in evangelical testimony to the occurrence of a "crisis moment," a palpable encounter and ongoing personal experience with God. For black Christians have always insisted that "you've got to know the Lord for yourself."

Remarkably, and with a kind of Hegelian synthesis that King interpreters have observed in other areas of his thinking and praxis but have
overlooked with respect to his faith itself, King embodied and commu-
nicated with credibility the dialectical tension between the evangelical
and liberationist poles of black faith, individual conversion and social
transformation. But the creative synthesis and revivalistic effectiveness
of his public pronouncements on this score represent the culmination
of a personal theological trek, a development, along with others, in
his own spiritual biography.

For King, who at age seven "joined the church not out of any dynamic conviction, but out of a childhood desire to keep up with [his]
sister," confesses in a 1950 essay written for Professor George Washington Davis, "I have never had an abrupt conversion experience."[80]
Even while situated in the evangelical ethos of black Baptist faith, with
its emphasis on the "crisis moment," a decisive and divine encounter
to which preachers and other believers often testify, the preacher confesses in a sermon toward the end of his life that prior to the Montgomery Bus Boycott he "had never felt an experience with God in the
way that you must have it if you're going to walk the lonely paths
of this life."[81] To be sure, I am not arguing for the absolute necessity
of a singular, definitive moment in order "to walk the lonely paths of
this life," nor would I want to diminish the religious significance of
King's childhood conversion, which he described simply this way: "the
gradual intaking of the noble (ideals?) set forth in my family and my
environment."[82] Indeed, that would be an apt description of the spiritual biography of many Christians, particularly those in nonevangeli-
cal traditions.

Even so, the interpreter is compelled, it seems to me, to hear King's
autobiographical description of his spiritual development within the
context of his own spiritual tradition and in relation to his own apprehension of the same. Given the fact that he understood, in a way that
few ever will, the piercing loneliness that comes with public acclaim
and severe criticism and because he faced the likelihood of martyr-
dom on a daily basis, there is much to be gained by an interpretation
that takes seriously King's own words (a hermeneutics of suspicion
notwithstanding) regarding that which anchored his own sense of

vocation in the world. In that regard, there is a deep continuity yet a qualitative *difference* between the faith he claimed in his childhood and the faith that would (re)claim him within the context of the movement. Over and again, and in a way quite consistent with evangelical testimony to one's conversion experience, King, the social revivalist, would testify in his sermons regarding a certain metanoia, a "kitchen experience" at the beginning of the movement in Montgomery.[83]

King's personal encounter with the God whom black Christians insist "you've got to know for yourself" occurred on January 27, 1956, as he endeavored to find peace and reassurance in the midst of a tense environment of racial strife and phone calls threatening his life and that of his wife and firstborn infant child. Although he had received threatening calls before, this one got his attention. After getting home very late following a steering committee meeting, the hate-filled voice on the other end of a telephone call which came after midnight said, "Nigger, we are tired of you and your mess now, and if you are not out of this town in three days, we're going to blow your brains out and blow up your house."[84] Although he had already by then become accustomed to about forty such phone calls a day, he was shaken by this one. He was concerned about his safety and that of his family. Attempting first to find "a little relief" over a cup of coffee and then reflecting on what his graduate theological studies had suggested to him regarding the "philosophical and theological reasons for the existence and reality of evil," he said he was left feeling weak.[85]

Realizing that his mother and father could not help him, it occurred to him that he had to turn to the God of his parents, "that something in that person that your daddy used to tell you about." "And I discovered then that religion had to become real to me and I had to know God for myself." It is there, while in prayer, that King "heard a voice," saying, "Martin Luther, stand up for justice. Stand up for truth. And lo, I will be with you, even until the end of the world."[86]

Previous interpreters of King have observed the significance of this moment in his life. Because he would often think back to it in the midst of overwhelming stress and strain as a kind of existential anchor, David Garrow opines that "it was the most important night of his life."[87] Similarly, Stewart Burns observes that it was on the one-year anniversary of this spiritual encounter that King's home "was nearly blown to kingdom come" and that it is then that he speaks publicly for the first time about how this "kitchen conversion" anchored him in the face of death.[88] James Cone notes the significance of the encounter as that which reconnected King to "the God of the black experience"[89] and "the faith of the black church."[90]

I, too, see this *metanoia* or conversion experience as very significant for the reasons mentioned by King and discussed among his interpreters. It grounded his philosophical understanding of personalism in the existential reality of a personal God whom he could claim and who claimed him as he walked "the lonely paths." Also, it afforded him the courage to face death.[91] Moreover, it both reconnected and deepened his connection to the faith experience of African Americans, those for whom he would provide a public voice.[92]

But in addition to these reasons, I argue that this conversion experience is both striking and significant for the organic and sublime way in which it collates the two primary strands in black people's understanding of salvation and of their own salvation history: individual conversion experience and social transformation, personal piety and communal liberation. For while "personal and social salvation mutually influenced each other in the slave tradition,"[93] black churches, like their white counterparts, have often been guilty of a bifurcated understanding of their mission that diminishes the church's role as an instrument of social salvation or of a truncated theology that dismisses that role altogether.

Perhaps because King's most dramatic conversion experience occurred within the context of social struggle, never would he separate the two or privilege one over the other. It is precisely his piety and personal encounter with the God whom he needed to know for himself that demanded that he "stand up for justice . . . [and] truth." Conversely, as one dares to stand up for justice and truth in the face of a determined, organized, and incorrigible evil, good intentions will never suffice for an authentic encounter with God. "You'd better know him," he says in a sermon after referring to his kitchen encounter, "and know his name, and know how to call his name!"[94] In another sermon preached at the Ebenezer Baptist Church, he counsels his congregation, "When you know God, you can stand up amid the agonies and burdens of life and not despair. When you know God, you can stand up amid tension and tribulation and yet smile in the process. . . . When you know God, you can have on some shoes that can help you walk through any muddy place."[95] In this way, personal piety and the struggle for liberation are, to appropriate words King used to reference our common humanity, "caught up in an inescapable network of mutuality," and it is difficult to see where one begins and the other ends. I argue that this is the key to understanding King and his ministry and that it is both the existential basis and conceptual foundation for what Luther D. Ivory aptly calls "a theology of radical involvement."[96]

Hence, with sharp theological acumen and with the fervor and mass appeal of a great revivalist who had been converted himself and would be continually evangelized and radicalized by the movement, King would facilitate, over a thirteen-year journey, a major social impact on the laws and culture of the entire nation and, more germane to our discussion, a *conscientizing* impact on a whole new generation of black clergy. As we will see, it is largely because of the conscientizing impact of King's ministry and theology that black theology emerges.

But the immediate issue here is that King was effective in evangelizing and conscientizing the black church, in large measure, because he spoke a language that resonated with both the evangelical and liberationist strands in its heritage and self-understanding. Unlike anyone before or after him, King gave creative voice to a dialectical appropriation of the personal and social dimensions of salvation. In fact, this serves, in my judgment, as the *cohesive thread* running through every area of his theology. The key to King's ecclesiology, his understanding of the cross and of the mission of the church as the community of the cross as well as his eschatological vision, is this dialectical relationship between the personal and social dimensions of salvation and his effort to encourage *both black and white churches* to fully embrace the latter as integral to their mission.

Thus, he challenged the West's post-Constantinian privatization of Christian faith, insisting that the cross, for example, not only signifies freedom from the alienation of individual sin and reconciliation with God but also provides "an eternal expression of the length to which

God is willing to go to restore broken communities."[97] In that sense, the church, as community of the cross, is called to bear creative witness against the sin that alienates the individual self from God *and* to go the length of giving its life over to the struggle of dismantling sinful structures that calcify patterns of human alienation in the society in general. In a speech titled "Revolution and Redemption," given before an assembly of Baptists in Amsterdam, Holland, King connects the suffering of Jesus with the collective resistance and reconciling work of churches in a broken world. "Jesus Christ gave his life for the redemption of this world, and as his followers, we are called to give our lives continuing the reconciling work of Christ in this world." It is important to emphasize that the redemptive work and suffering vocation about which King spoke was not simply one of individual conscience and commitment but one in which "whole churches may be crucified."[98]

When King was asked by the editors of the *Christian Century* to comment on his own view of suffering in light of the constant death threats that he received, one hears again the way in which this Hegelian synthesis of the personal and social dimensions of faith is the controlling category that informs his theology of the cross:

> My personal trials have also taught me the value of unmerited suffering. . . . I have attempted to see my personal ordeals as an opportunity to transform myself and heal the people involved in the tragic situation which now obtains. . . . Unearned suffering is redemptive. There are some who still find the cross a stumbling block, and others consider it foolishness, but I am more convinced than ever before that it is the power of God *unto social and individual salvation.* So like the Apostle Paul I can now humbly yet proudly say, "I bear in my body the marks of the Lord Jesus." The suffering and agonizing moments through which I have passed over the last few years have also drawn me closer to God. *More than ever before I am convinced of the reality of a personal God.* (Emphasis mine)[99]

These hurried remarks of a man caught up in the lived experience of the question that was put to him show again the profound way in which King's biblical understanding of the social and individual dimensions of the saving work of Jesus on the cross inhered almost seamlessly in his thought and in his life. Informed by this fundamental understanding, King would endure the "stations of the cross" that took him from reformer to revolutionary, bearing the marks of criticism, death threats, and increasing loneliness through public leadership and private travail.

But so too did this collation of souls and society, individual piety and liberationist struggle, inform King's eschatological vision of the coming kingdom of God. Synthesizing the evangelical and revolutionary strands of black Christian understanding, King posited a radical vision of history that transcended the limits of history, buoying King's own sense of determination and emboldening black people's willingness to fight in the face of bleak prospects and overwhelming opposition. It was best captured in a favorite rhetorical phrase, variations of which are found in his writings and in his sermons before various congregations:

> The preacher must be concerned about the whole man. Not merely his soul but his body. It's all right to talk about heaven. I talk about it because I believe firmly in immortality. But you've got to talk about the earth. It's all right to talk about long white robes over yonder, but I want a suit and some shoes to wear down here. It's all right to talk about the streets flowing with milk and honey in heaven, but I want some food to eat down here. It's even all right to talk about the new Jerusalem. But one day we must begin to talk about the new Chicago, the new Atlanta, the new New York, the new America. And any religion that professes to be concerned about the souls of men and is not concerned about the slums that cripple the souls—the economic conditions that stagnate the soul and the city governments that may damn the soul—is a dry, dead do-nothing religion in need of new blood.[100]

Although this collation of the gospel's concern for souls and society was crystallized and deepened for King by the work of the movement, it actually serves very early on as a working theological norm for King.[101] Thus, arguing that "the gospel of Jesus is a social gospel as well as a personal gospel seeking to save the whole man," the establishment of a "Social and Political Action Committee" "for the purpose of keeping the congregation intelligently informed concerning the social, political and economic situation" is prominently listed among several recommendations made to the Dexter Avenue Baptist Church immediately upon his call as its new pastor.[102]

But King was to have ample opportunities to test this theological hypothesis and to articulate his holistic view of the church's work as an instrument of salvation over against the truncated, pietistic pronouncements of his white clergy colleagues in the heat of battle in Montgomery, Alabama. For as King and members of the Montgomery Improvement Association (MIA) negotiated with the mayor, the mayor's "citizens committee," and city bus officials, he was upbraided by Dr. E. Stanley Frazier, minister of the St. James Methodist Church. Frazier was "a tall, distinguished-looking man, the quintessence of dignity," and one of the most eloquent spokespersons for segregation in the Methodist Church. He informed the MIA members that not only were they wrong for conducting a bus boycott, but what made the situation even more egregious was the prominence of ministers of the gospel in the movement's leadership. A minister "is to lead the souls of men to God," avoiding all entanglements with "transitory social problems." Speaking eloquently of "God's unspeakable gift," he reminded them of the Christmas story and pointed their attention, during the season of Christmas, "toward the Babe of Bethlehem" and "a glorious experience of the Christian faith." King rejoined, "We too know the Jesus that the minister just referred to. We have had an experience with him, and we believe firmly in the revelation of God in Jesus Christ." Arguing that there is no conflict between piety and protest, King insisted that, in fact, "if one is truly devoted to the religion of Jesus he will seek to rid the earth of social evils. The gospel is social as well as personal."[103]

Following the challenges and victory of the Montgomery Bus Boycott, King summarized the same theological point in his first book, *Stride toward Freedom*:

Religion deals with both earth and heaven, both time and eternity. . . . It seeks not only to integrate men with God but to integrate men with men and each man with himself. This means, at bottom, that the Christian gospel is a two-way road. On the one hand it seeks to change the souls of men, and thereby unite them with God; on the other hand it seeks to change the environmental conditions of men so that the soul will have a chance after it is changed. Any religion that professes to be concerned with the souls of men and is not concerned with the slums that damn them, the economic conditions that strangle them, and the social conditions that cripple them is a dry-as-dust religion.[104]

I argue that this really is the heart of King's conscientizing message to the American churches, *black and white*, regarding their mission. It gathers together the pietistic and liberationist strands of black faith and weaves them through every area of a public theology, including his ecclesiology, his theology of the cross and of the church as the community of the cross. Moreover, it is a theology that expresses itself in a militant adventism, signaling "the glory of the coming of the Lord," "a new heaven and a new earth." But it is deeply grounded in *King's own faith experience*, as one reared and shaped by the faith context of the black church; intellectually disciplined by the theoretical frameworks to which he was introduced in college and graduate school; transformed by the suffering of the masses; and converted by his own protracted spiritual struggle, signified in a crisis moment, a "kitchen experience" in which he is urged to "Stand up!" Thus begins the journey of coming to terms with the vastness of his global vocation and the revolutionary character of the church's true mission.

Martin Luther, Martin Luther King, Jr., and the American Churches

YET IT SHOULD be said that it is quite ironic that as King retells, late in his career, the story of his dramatic kitchen encounter in a 1967 sermon,[105] he invokes, with the thunderous oratory of the black preacher, his historical sixteenth-century namesake: Martin Luther. With rhetorical and narrative embellishments not unusual for preachers and not present in the earlier written account found in *Stride toward Freedom*,[106] it is now to the man whose name is Martin Luther, a twentieth-century reformer who is both historically conscious and self-aware, that the Spirit directs its urgings. Indeed, Luther was among those whom King had celebrated as "creative extremists" in the "Letter from Birmingham Jail," his brilliant *apologia* for the movement and powerful response to eight white clergymen critical of his actions. In the letter, King had declared with Luther, "Here I stand; I cannot do otherwise, so help me God,"[107] and in the sermon before a black congregation, "Martin Luther" is urged to "Stand up!" In this way, King summons in defense of his movement the heroic genius of the Protestant reformer and what he invariably saw as a basic understanding of the gospel, irrespective of the ethical contradictions of race, shared by both blacks and whites alike.

To be sure, Martin Luther, like Martin Luther King, Jr., was an extremist. For in Luther's context, the revolting peasants had sensed the radical implications of his version of the gospel. It was a new gospel that dared to circumvent the sacramental requirements and excesses of those in power, insisting on "justification by faith" alone. The "Lutheran assault"[108] on clerical and ecclesiastical authority, as well as the social and political import of Luther's arguments regarding "The Freedom of the Christian,"[109] captured the imagination of those who were struggling at the bottom rung of a feudalistic society. As they stated their demands in the "Twelve Articles," they not only used scripture but attached to their demands names from both of the major camps within the Reformation. At the top of the list were Melanchthon and Luther. Inspired by Luther's radical stance vis-à-vis the powers, they asked him to offer his response to the "Twelve Articles," offering that they would withdraw from any demand that proved to be inconsistent with scripture. The preface to the "Twelve Articles" appealed to the biblical story of the Exodus, a prominent theme in black faith and in the public ministry of Martin King, as the theological basis for their struggle against tyranny and abuse. Moreover, informed by Luther's "Two Kingdoms" doctrine,[110] they proffered a plan of redemption, as it were, that would combine dimensions of both what Luther called the Kingdom on the Right and the Kingdom on the Left.[111]

Agreeing that many of the demands made by the peasants were, in fact, reasonable and just, Luther repudiated the practices of the princes and lords whom he regarded as "wild and dictatorial tyrants." Yet he felt bound by scripture to insist that insurrection against temporal authority (the Left Kingdom), insofar as that authority did not traverse its civic boundaries, interfering with spiritual authority (the Right Kingdom), was indeed insurrection against the God who was Lord over both. In this way, he argued, on the basis of his "Two Kingdoms" doctrine and an interiorized understanding of salvation, that the social and economic concerns pressed by the peasants in the name of "divine law" and in memory of the Exodus were "carnal" and "misguided." He later deepened his resistance to the peasants, actually encouraging their massacre. Sharpening his rhetoric against them, he submits in a railing polemic, "Against the Robbing and Murdering Hordes of Peasants," that "baptism does not make men free in body and property, but in soul." Over against the peasants who, not unlike black slaves within the North American context, appealed to the Exodus motif as the basis for a freedom known within history, Luther opines that they were "making freedom a completely physical matter. . . . A worldly kingdom cannot exist without an inequality of persons, some being free, some imprisoned, some lords, some subjects."[112]

Such is an understanding of the work of salvation and of the church's role as salvation's instrument that stands in stark and marked contrast to the theological assumptions behind the civil rights movement. For King's ministry emerges from the experience of a black church shaped in the cauldron of American chattel slavery, and it represents a radical trajectory of unapologetic political resistance to racism that white versions of the gospel, in their evangelical, liberal, and neo-orthodox manifestations, have been hard-pressed to support. And, although King does wonder aloud regarding the white churches "Who is their God?"[113] he never fully acknowledges or explicates in a systematic way the depth of the *theological* difference that emerged among those who were the heirs to the Lutheran theological legacy and of slaveholding Christianity and those who were the descendants of a slave Christianity shaped on the underside of the same history. For

King, black Christian faith and white Christian faith were the same, and he appealed to a common Christian tradition as the basis for both the methods and the aims of the movement. King critiqued white Christians in the light of their theology. Never did he reject white theology itself.

Yet, as a creative theologian and social revivalist, King manages to shift the salvific emphases of the black church's self-understanding more toward its radical tradition, deepening its commitment to the ministry of social witness by making the social transformative work of the civil rights movement an indelible part of the church's memory of itself. Because of King, the black church can never again reject or diminish the work of liberation as central to its vocation without also rejecting or diminishing its own history, including the civil rights movement. Nor can it emphasize the pietistic dimension of its self-understanding while minimizing the work of liberation. For King offered a compelling theological articulation of the inextricable connection between the two.

King's most important theological contribution is the profound way in which he made the work of addressing the sins of racism and redeeming the soul of the social order with respect to its interconnecting evils such as militarism and poverty central to the church's claim to be an authentic witness to the One who called it into being. For King, the work of social transformation and bearing witness against the social sin of racism is not only appropriate for the church but mandatory if it would truly be the church. In this way, it can be said that a new understanding of the church's mission and the seeds for theological renewal were proleptically present in the civil rights movement and in the ministry of Martin King. He informs and, in important ways, anticipates the claims made by black theology. But was he a black theologian?

Was King a Black Theologian?

AS EARLY AS 1975, Paul Garber, a white theologian, suggested that King was not just a theologian who happened to be black but that in a way akin to James Cone, J. Deotis Roberts, and Joseph R. Washington,

"King was a black theologian."[114] To be sure, there is value in Garber's effort. For, as Cone has observed, few white theologians have engaged King's theological thinking at all.[115] Moreover, Garber is among the earliest of interpreters to suggest that King's cultural identity as a black man, standing "in the venerable tradition of Black preachers in America," should not be marginalized as "non-intellectual" and cannot be bracketed in any credible effort to truly understand his theology.[116] David Garrow,[117] James Cone,[118] and Lewis Baldwin[119] offer the most sustained analysis of this issue, and their respective works proceed from the premise that the biblical faith of the black church was the most important source in King's intellectual development as a theologian, preacher, and activist. As their work demonstrates, King was a black theologian, in the sense that it is artificial and absurd to separate his blackness, the most persistent and pervasive fact of his social existence, from the process and content of his thinking.

Yet Garber's argument that King was, in the order of Cone, Roberts, Washington, and other interpreters of the black theology movement, a black theologian is problematic. The problem with the argument is that it does not adequately engage the difference that black power and black consciousness made, a social development that came toward the end of King's life and one whose principles of self-empowerment and self-love he increasingly embraced but whose nationalistic politics he handled with suspicion, criticism, and distance. Moreover, while King's theology shares with black theology a similar emphasis on the importance of social salvation, his relationship to the theme of blackness is thornier and more complex than Garber's thesis allows. In essence, Garber's argument does not take into full account the degree to which the rise of black theology constitutes *a new moment*, the fourth moment, I argue, in a distinctive trajectory of black religious resistance yet inextricably connected to the one that preceded it.

As the civil rights movement, sourced by the religio-cultural capital of the black church, gained ascendancy in American life and culture, the ground was laid for new and critical discussions within the black community regarding the mission of liberation and *the meaning of the gospel*. To what extent are they related? Did the demands of justice for black people require a decisive break from white theology? Was it possible for any church in America to claim an authentic Christian identity without an active commitment to the struggle against racial injustice? Could King's nonviolent movement, and by extension the black church itself, claim an authentic connection to the Protestant Christian tradition which King referenced, or was it a social movement with a Christian veneer? Over against King's integrationist tendency to emphasize a common Christian tradition among blacks and whites alike, another integrationist and Boston University–trained academic, by the name of Joseph Washington, an associate professor of religion at Albion College, argued to the contrary that "if Protestantism involves identification with the Reformers and their post-Reformation interpreters, it is not helpful to call Negroes Protestants in this historical and theological sense. The fact that Negroes form congregations called by the same denominational nomenclature as White Americans remains the extent of their common ground."[120] With this rather provocative claim and challenging critique, Washington's published work served as part of the context for the emergence of black theology.[121] If King's ministry marks the third moment in the development of black Christian resistance to racism, the questions raised by Washington's book, the response that he received from the white and black church communities, and the rise of the black power movement helped to underscore the need for the fourth moment: *the formation of a self-conscious theology of black liberation (systematization).*

Although the publication of Washington's first book, *Black Religion: The Negro and Christianity in the United States*, provides only one of "three contexts of the origins of black theology,"[122] the book, its preceding essay, and the hard questions raised by each provide an important segue into our understanding of the significance of the rise of black theology and its relationship to the three moments, including the civil rights movement, that preceded it. To be sure, the civil rights movement and the black power movement represent the larger social context for the emergence of black theology. Moreover, there is no evidence that Washington's work was central to the discussions of the National Conference of Black Christians and other major players in the development of nascent black theology. Yet the book did throw into bold relief sharp questions regarding the theological character and authenticity of the black church's distinctive witness. These were questions regarding the historical meaning and appropriate mission of the black church to which only a self-conscious black theology could respond. That response represents a fourth moment in the history of black Christian resistance to racism.

2

THE GOSPEL'S MEANING AND THE BLACK CHURCH'S MISSION

Are Black Churches Christian?

OBSERVING, IN THE light of history and Martin Luther King, Jr.'s movement, the marked differences between the social agenda and overall religious orientation of white churches and black churches, Joseph Washington dared in a 1963 essay to ask, "Are American Negro Churches Christian?" As he reflected on the black church's "past alienation from the theological roots of Protestantism" and a tradition of protest that he judged to be "based upon influences external to the Christian faith, if not in contradiction with the faith," Washington concluded that "Negro religious institutions have developed a pattern of life totally irrelevant to the Christian faith."[1]

Washington offers a sustained treatment of this issue first raised in the 1963 essay in his 1964 text *Black Religion: The Negro and Christianity in the United States.* He argues there that while black churches carried the nomenclature of the Christian communions from which they separated, they lacked the following: "a sense of the historic church, authentic roots in the Christian tradition, a meaningful theological frame of reference, a search for renewal, an ecumenical spirit, and a commitment to an inclusive church."[2] But above all, Washington was concerned that black churches and denominations lacked what he had identified in the 1963 essay as "a dynamic theology" capable of explicating for black Christians the meaning of the faith and serving as a corrective for theological error regarding the church's reason for being.[3] Theology is faith's critical and questioning side, and without it,

Washington reasoned, there could be no guard against heresy and no guarantee of an authentic connection to Christian Tradition.

Moreover, despite the amazing and admirable impact of the civil rights movement on the social order, it and King's ostensibly Christian rhetoric as its leader and symbol was a glaring example, in Washington's view, of this persistent lack of a critical dimension for testing the validity of various faith claims over against the doctrines of the faith as worked out across the centuries. Specifically, while Washington understood the goal of integration, justice, and equality in the civic realm to be "Christian and human," he judged the means to the goal, namely, "massive and militant noncooperation in nonviolence," to be "Unchristian and inhuman."[4] Washington argued that while King referenced Christian language, namely, the Sermon on the Mount, as his rationale in the articulation of the movement's public theology, it had the import of a utilitarian choice that had more to do with maintaining social control and morale among his foot soldiers than any genuine or wholesale assent by those involved to the revelation of God made manifest in the death and resurrection of Jesus Christ.

Moreover, Washington observed that the very aspect of Christian faith that was most marginalized by a movement, judged by many observers to be Christian simply because of the involvement of black congregations, is precisely where Christian faith begins. It begins with the christological affirmation that "Jesus Christ is Lord." Thus, love of neighbor, centered around the Sermon on the Mount and emphasized by King as a universal principle, should be seen rather as the ethical extension of the more essential truth that God acted in Christ.[5] In this way, America's most well-known systematic theologian had erroneously conflated Gandhian principles with the unique Personality behind the New Testament message and had confused the christological essence of the faith with the ethics of faith, leveraging the latter in an activist methodology that actually distorted the meaning of the faith. Washington chides King as a public theologian, critiquing this ethical preoccupation which he observes not only in King's movement but as a theme running throughout the history of black churches. Over against this, he argues that the Christian is not motivated primarily by principles but is compelled to "respond to God" through faith alone and in view of the revelation of God in the Christ Event.[6]

> The teachings of Jesus are readily available to anyone who wishes to live by them as a basis for principles to spark action in the realm of civil liberties or rights. Commitment to the Christian faith is not required for response to Christian principles. . . . The Negro has grounded his belief in Christianity in an ethical code, the principles of which are not founded in an enduring faith and therefore devoid of content and the refreshment of a critical dimension. The principles he esteems are not relevant to his contemporary needs. *Thus the Negro is forced to depend upon civil rights, religious feeling, sentiment, and color as substitutes for faith.* (Emphasis mine)[7]

What is quite evident is that Washington did not see the concern and struggle for justice in society as *central* to one's Christian identity or essential to the mission of the Church in the world. In that sense, his views are quite consistent with those of Martin Luther and the denominational variations of the mainline Protestant Tradition, of which he sees black congregations as, at best, orphaned stepchildren.

Washington's devastating critique of the religion found in black churches was met with fierce objections from clergy and religious intellectuals within the black community. We shall explore those objections later in this chapter. But what is important to see at this juncture is the extent to which Washington saw clearly, as no one else had, the profound depth of the *theological difference* between the gospel of liberation preached by King and ensconced as a distinctive strand within the fabric of black church history and the presuppositions of white Christianity. King, ever the universalist, did not. Seeing the difference between the religion of black churches and white churches, Washington assumed that while the segregationist actions of whites in the society and in the church were wrong, the theology that both he and King had studied and embraced in graduate school was essentially correct. Therefore, he reasoned, King's theology—his militant understanding of the church's essential mission and his use of the gospel message as a theological principle for massive nonviolent resistance, irrespective of his intentions or the social impact of the movement —had to be wrong. This is why Washington accused King in the *Black Religion* text of making out of the civil rights movement "a faith."[8] As he pushes his argument, he correctly observes that the struggle for justice does not presuppose Christian faith. For Gandhi, like King, had struggled nonviolently for justice. Yet Gandhi was a Hindu and not a Christian.[9]

Yet for Washington, the reverse is also true. Christian faith does not presuppose struggle for justice in the social realm. Moreover, he intimates that King's appropriation of scripture (e.g., the love ethic of the Sermon on the Mount) as the basis for a social movement had the indirect effect of confusing social ethics with genuine faith in Jesus, Son of God. In this way, Washington privileges personal piety while diminishing the ministry of protest and the work of social transformation as integral to the work of salvation and thus the mission of the church. It is personal piety that really matters. For above all else, "faith demands a fundamental change in the individual."[10]

On the other hand, participation in the civil rights movement demanded only that one not retaliate in the face of violence. In this way, love is lifted out of its New Testament context and leveraged as a technique in service to a quasi-religion whose God is Justice and Equality under the law. The religion of the movement did not require, of the activist, assent to genuine faith in the true God fully revealed in Christ. Moreover, assent, by a white power structure, to the demands of the movement came as a result of coercion and not in response to the redemptive, reconciling, healing Christian love that was at the heart of King's rhetoric. In Washington's view, King's high theological credentials and his powerful rhetoric as a public theologian conflated and confused love as universal principle or social technique with love as an individual's genuine response in faith to the God revealed in the cross and the resurrection. Furthermore, the impact of King's public theology had the unfortunate effect of lending even more credence to a black folk religion rooted, since its inception, in protest and religious feeling rather than an enlightened understanding of the gospel of *sola gracie*—a gospel embodied in the legacy of King's own

namesake, Martin Luther, and the white churches that were the heirs
to this tradition.

But while King had unwittingly exacerbated this problem, as Washington saw it, he did not create it. Washington laid the blame for its
origins and maintenance at the feet of white Protestants. He pointed
to their failure and refusal, since the early days of the plantation missionaries, to religiously educate slaves, "telling the Negro a simple
story" rather than providing exposure to the theological insights of
the faith.[11]

According to Washington, from slavery through the rise of independent black churches on to the civil rights movement, this theological neglect had not been corrected, and the resulting handicaps to
black congregational life had yet to be overcome. In fact, because faith
was, for him, so inextricably connected to the "critical dimension"[12] of
self-conscious theological reflection and because, prior to the rise of
black and other liberation theologies, there was no critical alternative
to the academic hegemony of established modes of doing theology,
Washington concluded that blacks did not have an authentic theology but a folk religion. And bereft of an authentic theology for testing
the meaning of their ecclesial life together, they had no true church.
Rather, black people in America had "religious congregations," characterized by a "crass materialism . . . overlaid with theological terminology and a feeling for religion which when analyzed may now be
more liberally this-worldly than otherworldly."[13]

Thus, Washington concludes that the religious expression of the
black church was so distinctive that it might best be characterized as
the "fifth major religion" of American culture, alongside Judaism,
Protestantism, Roman Catholicism, and secularism. He argues that
"there are Negroes who are Protestants, there are Negroes who are
Christians, there are Negroes in churches—but there is no Negro
Protestantism, Negro Christianity, or Negro church."[14] Instead, what
is found in the black church might best be described as a "folk religion," uniting blacks across denominational lines in an essential theme
of racial unity and protest but bereft of any substantive understanding
or theological appreciation for the denominational nomenclature that
each of the churches bears.

Disconnected from the history of Protestantism and the debates that shaped its concerns and thus its fundamental character, black people were deprived access to the critical content of the Christian faith, as defined by white people and codified in their creeds. Black churches in America recited those same creeds and statements of faith while living out a countervailing religious tradition that addressed, in a distinctive way, their humanistic concerns for freedom, affirmation, and material survival. Washington correctly observes the dissonance between those creeds and black faith and praxis. Because the creeds, polity, and statements of faith were the result of Protestant history and sustained critical reflection, he reasoned that the dissonance represented a fundamental distortion of the faith on the part of black congregations and not the other way around.

In this way, Washington observed a qualitative difference between the Christianity that was passed onto African Americans and the Christianity they received unto themselves. Because he was the first to demonstrate this difference in a sustained way, connecting it to early American missionary efforts and black religious history, he actually deserves much credit. Measured up against the long history of black church interpretation, his rigorous engagement of black religion suggests that hardly any interpreter, up to that point, had taken it more seriously than he did.

Yet it is the next step in his logic that is the heart of the problem. He interprets black people's differing understanding of the faith to be a distortion of the faith. Hence, he offers this prescription: "The responsibility of white Protestantism is to create conditions wherein the Negro will realize assimilation is in his best interest and that of the Church," and "the responsibility of all Negro congregations which exist essentially because of racial ties is to go out of business."[15]

It is a view most poignantly expressed as he speaks analogously of the Negro as one who, like the Ethiopian Eunuch of the New Testament Book of Acts,[16] is in charge of a large treasure, that treasure being the "Negro church." That church, Washington argues, is a diversion. And although the Ethiopian may be vaguely familiar with the grammar and stories of the faith, he might rightly ask, "How can I understand unless someone will give me the clue?" The responsibility of the entire white community, Washington argues, is "to get in and sit beside him."[17]

Shapers and interpreters of black theology, including James Cone and Gayraud Wilmore, have identified this text and its thesis as part of what gave rise to black theology, helping to spur a new kind of independent and self-conscious reflection among black clergy and religious intellectuals regarding the theological identity of the black church and the meaning of the gospel. The book was well received among liberal, white religious intellectuals.[18] On the other hand, it did not receive a warm welcome among black scholars in the academy or in the church.[19] By raising the ire of black clergy and black religious intellectuals whose ecclesiology had been shaped by the activist orientation of the civil rights movement, Washington became part of nascent black theology's impetus and inspiration. As James Cone has put it,

> Indeed, black theology, in part, was created in order to refute Washington's book. The black clergy wanted to correct two flagrant misconceptions: (1) that black religion is not Christian and thus has no Christian theology, and (2) that the Christian gospel has nothing to do with the struggle for justice in society. The black clergy contended that Washington had everything backward. It was black religion that was truly Christian, and it was Christian precisely because it had identified the gospel with the struggle for justice in society. White churches were hypocritical: they said one thing but did another; they preached love but ignored justice, and then developed a theology that justified it.[20]

Black Theology: The Fourth Moment

THUS, IT IS in the light of the history of African American religious resistance to racism, from slavery to the civil rights movement, that one can best understand the significance of black theology and the claims that it has made regarding the essential mission of the black church. It is the fourth moment in the history of black religious resistance to racism. Informed by the gospel of liberation, ensconced in the long history of black resistance to racism, most clearly embodied in the twentieth century in the civil rights movement and the public ministry of Martin King, black theology emerged.

In King's theological thinking, struggling for the kingdom of God, or "the beloved community," as he often called it, was the Christian Church's own especial vocation and responsibility, making of it a credible manifestation of the truth of the gospel. Moreover, under the banner of the SCLC and its mantra "To Redeem the Soul of America," King was the first American theologian to effectively articulate a public theology that made it a fundamental contradiction to claim to be Christian while perpetuating or tolerating segregation at the same time. Because silence in the face of broken human community was, for him, a moral contradiction that belies any claim to be the true church, he could not help but ask, regarding white churches in the South with their "tall church spires and sprawling brick monuments dedicated to the glory of God, . . . What kind of people worship there? Who is their God?"[21] He claims elsewhere that "the broad universalism standing at the center of the Gospel makes brotherhood morally inescapable. Racial segregation is a blatant denial of the unity we have in Christ. Segregation is a tragic evil which is utterly *un-Christian*" (emphasis mine).[22]

But King employs theological imagination in "Paul's Letter to American Christians," as he dares to assume the identity of the Apostle himself, offering a clear challenge to "Christians among you who try to find biblical bases to justify segregation." Over against segregation's apologists, he argues that "the underlying philosophy of Christianity is diametrically opposed to the underlying philosophy of racial segregation."[23] In that sense, King understood segregation and its infrastructure of support within the church to be both a moral evil and a theological heresy.

Thus, conscientized by the theological claims and public ministry of Martin King as well as the devastating critique of black power advocates who were also challenging the society and the church, James Cone and other nascent black theologians launched a severe critique and full-fledged confrontation with the white church, calling it an apostate church. They began to raise, in a systematic way, new questions about the inextricable relationship between *knowing the faith and living the faith.* They remembered that black Christians were the heirs of slave Christianity while their white counterparts were the descendants of slaveholding Christianity. Therefore, they reasoned, if white Christians cannot manage to live out the meaning of the faith, perhaps they do not understand the faith. They began to ask, "How can one have a distorted view of humanity and a correct view of God?" Sensing what their slave ancestors seemed to intuitively know, they concluded, with Joseph Washington, that the faith of the black church is different from that of the white church. But in contradistinction to Washington, they argued that given the tragic history of slavery and segregation, indeed it should be. Thus, for the very first time, a group of black Christians set out to define and affirm the differences in a sustained and systematic way, both empowering a self-alienated black community and evangelizing an apostate white church.

Because these "theologians" were mostly pastors, a new black theology and the radical remnant of a new black church emerged *together*, declaring war and common cause against the complex dimensions of an ideological, ecclesiastical, and political culture that had left the masses of black people suffering and self-alienated. Notwithstanding differences among the theologians themselves, they were determined to speak with one voice about what it means to be black *and* Christian. But their unified voices came from at least three distinct loci: the National Conference of Black Christians; an emerging movement of black caucuses within white churches; and the voices of a new generation of black theologians. Among these new voices, none was more creative or influential than James Cone, and none was more unlikely than a transformed Joseph Washington.

NATIONAL CONFERENCE OF BLACK CHRISTIANS

Organized in 1966 and operated by black clergy, the National Conference of Black Christians (NCBC; originally the National Committee of Negro Churchmen and then the National Conference of Black Churchmen) served as a primary site for the emergence of nascent black theology. It was not initially established as a permanent organization. Rather, it began as an ad hoc group of ministers, primarily from the North, who came together for the purpose of publishing a statement that would begin to clear the air of controversy and confusion surrounding a new slogan, made popular by Stokely Carmichael, members of the Student Nonviolent Coordinating Committee (SNCC), and other youth in the civil rights movement, called "Black Power."[24] It should be noted that the Harlem pastor and congressman Adam Clayton Powell, Jr., was apparently the first to use the term in a speech, given at Howard University's commencement.[25] This created considerable energy around a new folk expression, the origins of which are always difficult, if not impossible, to identify.[26] However, the slogan represented the more secular and nationalistic wing of the movement and was most effectively punctuated by Carmichael during the continuation of the James Meredith "March Against Fear."[27]

Predictably, this paradigmatic shift from the slogan "Freedom Now" to "Black Power" was met with much confusion and consternation in the white community. Liberal whites felt betrayed, and such characterizations as "reverse racism" were the ringing response. "Black Power" was also rejected, at first, by many in the black community, most notably Dr. King, who tried unsuccessfully to convince Carmichael, Floyd McKissick, and others to abandon the slogan. To the chagrin of many, the concept took hold, particularly among the members of SNCC and black youth in riot-torn cities. And in July 1966, a group of five people came together at a meeting in the New York–based Interchurch Center, the administrative heart of American Protestantism, in order to fashion what they could not have known would lay the foundation for the development of a distinctive black theology.[28] Published July 31, 1966, as a full-page advertisement in the *New York Times*, the watershed document addresses several audiences.

For our purposes here, what is important to observe is the way in which this powerful statement, written by the Reverend Benjamin Payton[29] and subsequently revised and adopted by a total of forty-eight churchpersons, provides a thoughtful defense of black power, while also identifying the black church as its earliest antecedent and, given the black church's history of autonomy, its most logical ally. Moreover, the statement managed to publicly articulate a rationale for the existence of an independent black church, linking it to a discussion regarding the critical nexus between love and power as the basis for authentic human interaction. In language intended for popular consumption, the statement echoes, in some sense, the basic themes of a Niebuhrian Christian realism regarding the complex nature of power among groups[30] and anticipates theological assertions that James Cone will make regarding the significance of justice as a precondition for authentic reconciliation.[31]

> As black men who were long ago forced out of the white church to create and to wield "black power," we fail to understand the emotional quality of the outcry of some clergy against the use of the term today. It is not enough to answer that "integration" is the solution. For it is precisely the nature of the operation of power under some forms of integration which is being challenged. The Negro Church was created as a result of the refusal to submit to the indignities of a false kind of "integration" in which all power was in the hands of white people. A more equal sharing of power is precisely what is required as the precondition of authentic human interaction. . . . We regard as sheer hypocrisy or as a blind and dangerous illusion the view that opposes love to power. Love should be a controlling element in power, not power itself. So long as white churchmen continue to moralize and misinterpret Christian love, so long will justice continue to be subverted in this land.[32]

The Reverend Leon Watts, a prominent participant in the group, characterized the significance of the statement in this way: "This group of ecclesiastical renegades, denominational radicals and *mad* preachers, pushed by the wave of growing Black militancy and the unresponsiveness of the white denominations to the Black condition, continued to meet. . . . Standing between us and the Black community was 'white Christianity,' which we allegedly represented. That impression needed to be corrected posthaste."[33]

Moving in March 1967 to become a permanent organization, the National Committee of Negro Churchmen (NCNC) went through several name changes, eventually becoming the National Conference of Black Christians (NCBC). This group—led by outstanding pastors such as Edler Hawkins, pastor of the St. Augustine Presbyterian Church in the Bronx and leader of the Presbyterian Black Caucus and Nathan Wright of the Episcopal Church,[34] Baptists such as Kelly Miller Smith,[35] and Catholics such as Lawrence Lucas[36]—represents black theology in its earliest institutional incarnation. Professional theologians were scarce among the group. In fact, it was not until 1969 and with the publication of James Cone's *Black Theology and Black Power*, the first text to use the term "black theology," that Cone attended the first meeting of the NCBC. Joining its Committee on Theological Prospectus, he and other trained academics, including Preston N. Williams, Carleton Lee, Henry Mitchell, and J. Deotis Roberts, became the intellectual power behind the NCBC's statement on "Black Theology."

> Black Theology is a theology of black liberation. It seeks to plumb the black condition in the light of God's revelation in Jesus Christ, so that the black community can see that the gospel is commensurate with the achievement of black humanity. Black Theology is a theology of "blackness." . . . The message of liberation is the revelation of God as revealed in the incarnation of Jesus Christ. Freedom IS the gospel. Jesus is the Liberator![37]

Part of the power of the NCBC is that, for at least the first several years of its brief history,[38] its impact can be seen in both theological and programmatic terms. On the theological side, the NCBC gave public voice, in its various statements, to the earliest utterances of a creative and distinctive black theology, persuasively connecting it with the black power movement and the nineteenth-century black church freedom movement. On the programmatic side and with varying degrees of success and failure, it negotiated with the white church establishment, argued for reparations, coordinated some degree of cooperation and work between blacks in both black and white denominations, and became the catalyst for a growing movement of black caucuses within white denominations. In that sense, it embodied the need for a new theology and a new church.[39]

"A Summary Report" of the NCNC's first two years, written in the fall of 1968 by Gayraud Wilmore, then chairman of the NCNC Theological Commission, sheds light on the burgeoning of a new moment of self-conscious reflection about the precise meaning of Christian faith in the light of black struggle and self-awareness regarding the mission and liberating potential of the black church. Among a list of thirteen critical questions being raised in a survey sent to NCNC members, the following seem most significant for the emergence of a nascent black theology: (1) "Is our traditional assumption of the mystical unity of the church as the Body of Christ incompatible with the creation of NCNC as a separate organization of black churchmen? If not, why not? What is the relationship between the quest for true unity of the Body of Christ and the quest for racial justice?"; (2) "Is it theologically valid to speak of a black Christ or a white Christ? Whatever were the historic circumstances under which the Christ figure first appeared, must that historic situation and the elements with which it consists be considered eternally, universally authentic, valid and normative?"; (3) "If God acts in history do we know him within the history of the American experience as slanted by white people or should we seek to understand God in our history as black people? What is to be said about the moral integrity of the white interpretation of history?"; and (4) "Is there a Christian theory of violence and what would it say about the role of violence in effecting social change?"[40]

Thirteen members of the NCNC, mostly Protestant, with the one exception of a Catholic priest, Father Lawrence Lucas, responded to these questions. There are significant nuances and diversity of opinion in their responses. For example, the respondents were divided almost evenly around the question of violence as a valid Christian option for effecting social change. Charles Shelby Rooks opines that "to talk about a 'Christian' theory of violence is to distort the picture of Christ that has come down to us in the biblical account and in tradition." Another respondent agrees, echoing Luther's "Two Kingdoms" doctrine and his response to the Peasants Revolt as he writes, "I, myself, cannot condone violence as a means of effecting social change— except as employed legally by a representative, duly constituted government." On the other side, Father Lawrence Lucas speaks for other members when he observes that "the greater responsibility lies on those who are more responsible for the conditions under which black people are revolting. On the principles of legitimate self defense, I think the deliberate, planned type of violence can be morally justified and violence can be or play a role in effecting social change."[41]

Regarding the theological significance of the Black Christ, it is interesting that the scholars represented in this small survey were generally more conservative than the pastors. For example, Frank T. Wilson, former dean of Howard Divinity School, suggests that "imputation of blackness or whiteness to Christ seems to have no point. Where this has been invoked in support of racism it is sheer blasphemy." Yet Lucas represents the view of some of the more radical pastors in the group as he states that "the historic circumstances under which the Christ figure first appeared must be considered eternally, universally authentic, valid, normative, revelatory, etc." Yet "it is under the present circumstances" that Christ is being revealed. Thus, he continues, "in so far as white 'Christians' have distorted this Christ into a white Christ interested only in subjugating, exploiting black people, I think it is valid to speak in terms of present realities of a black Christ to correct this distortion."[42]

Within the diversity of this important dialogue, there was a general sense that a new black church was coming of age and "a sneaking suspicion . . . that something is stirring in parts of the black church; that there is a kind of 'black theology' aborning, equal to the budding renaissance in arts and letters which is heralded today in Harlem and other black communities across the nation." In the quest of the NCNC members for church renewal among black Christians themselves as the basis for authentic church renewal characterized by a commitment to justice within the larger ecumenical movement of the twentieth century, they asked, "What is the distinctive, unique, and authoritative meaning of 'blackness' in the context of historic Christianity? Put another way: Does the black church have 'anything going for it' (as does black music, humor, fiction, business, education, etc.) today that sets it apart as an indispensably viable institution, not only of the black community, but of American society generally?" As early as 1968, the NCNC already anticipates a turn within the movement that will come decisively in 1977 with the emergence of the

Black Theology Project, Theology in the Americas, and the dialogue between black theologians and other Third World theologians. It asks, "Can [the black church] be the primary instrument for the liberation of black people in this country and perhaps in Asia, Africa, and Latin America, . . . and if so, to what extent will this necessitate a break with the fundamental norms, styles and structures of mainline, white American Christianity?"[43] Indeed, the broad outlines of a decisive break, a creative rupture within American Christianity, pointing the way to a radical understanding of the church's mission in the world, was already under way with the birth of the Black Caucus Movement.

The Black Caucus Movement

In varying ways, black churchpersons were recognizing anew a common faith tradition characterized by principled protest against racism. Furthermore, they saw the need to create, whether through the work of independent black denominations or the development of black caucuses within white denominations, alternative ecclesial spaces for working out the meaning of the faith on their own terms.[44] The penetrating and pervasive impact of the black caucus movement on American Christianity really deserves a sustained study of its own. Catching hold among black Protestants, Catholics, and Evangelicals, it called on the American white churches to account for the heresy of racism manifested both within the church structures themselves and through the churches' uncritical support of white supremacy in the political and economic structures of the nation.

One of the most vocal and active of the groups was Black Methodists for Church Renewal. Illustrative of the liberationist spirit emerging from within that specific caucus and the caucuses in general is an article written by the Reverend Gilbert Caldwell. In the article, Caldwell, who had reached the status of becoming the first black superintendent in New England Methodist history and later went on to chair the NCBC board (1974–1976), shrugs at the tokenism apparent in being a "first" and wonders aloud about the future of "black folk in white churches." Although he is operating within the structure of a white denomination, his logic actually turns the argument of Joseph

Washington, who felt that blacks needed to be evangelized by whites, on its head. Caldwell spoke for many pastors involved in Black Methodists for Church Renewal and other black caucuses, as he asserted that the great question of the day was whether the white church was prepared to be evangelized by the insights and wisdom of black Christians and not the other way around. He opines, "The next few years will determine whether the predominantly white Christian church can receive the 'new wine' black Christians have to share. If it shows that it cannot, then we must modestly say, it has lost the chance of a lifetime. And some of us will begin to create the necessary new wineskins."[45]

JAMES CONE AND THE SYSTEMATIZATION OF BLACK THEOLOGY

Indeed, the ministers of the NCBC, the black caucuses, and a new breed of radical, religious intellectuals were already creating "new wineskins." One such intellectual was theologian and former pastor James H. Cone. Because of his contribution to the birth and development of the discourse, Cone is rightly regarded as the father of black theology. His singular impact in shaping the norms, sources, and contours of an emerging discourse is even more remarkable when one considers that he was a professor at a small Michigan college, relatively unknown to members of the NCNC when they published the "Black Power" statement in the *New York Times* in July 1966 and when he authored *Black Theology and Black Power*, the book that gave black theology a public identity in the churches and the academy in 1969.

We shall examine Cone's constructive contribution in more detail in chapter 3, but what is important for our argument at this juncture is the way in which his creative theological engagement of black power and his devastating critique of the white church undermined the latter's presumed status as a normative point of reference for the doing of theology. Rather, the struggle for liberation is the essential mark of the gospel of Jesus Christ. Criticizing white theologians' preoccupation with the "death of God" controversy and their continuing obsession with the problem of modernity while ignoring the problem of race, Cone argues,

If theology fails to re-evaluate its task in the light of Black Power, the emphasis on the death of God will not add the needed dimension. This will mean that the white church and white theology are dead, not God. It will mean that *God will choose another means of implementing his word of righteousness in the world*. It will mean also that the burden of the gospel is placed solely on the shoulders of the oppressed, without any clear word from the "church." This leads us to our last concern, *the black church. It is indeed possible that the only redemptive forces left in the denominational churches are to be found in the segregated black churches.* (Emphasis mine)[46]

Unoptimistic about the white church's willingness to divest itself of white privilege, to be exorcised of the demons of white supremacy, and to act as an instrument of God's liberation, Cone posits a hermeneutics of the streets which suggests that the advocates of black power might serve as "another means of implementing [God's] word of righteousness in the world." Furthermore, he holds out a tempered hope that if redemption is to be found within the institutional structures of American Christianity at all, it will "be found in the segregated black churches." As such, he expresses a black messianism, not completely new in the history of black religious thought[47] but characterized, in this instance, by the black consciousness movement of that era, signaling the birth of a self-conscious black theology and a radical black church.

The Politics of God: The Conversion of Joseph Washington (and Others)

THE RISE OF black theology on the American religious landscape represents, both for the black and white churches and the academy, a critical turning point in the history of their relationship between each other and the history of their respective engagement of the social order. Indeed, black theology must be regarded as the fourth moment or turning point in the history of African American Christian resistance to racism. The cohesive thread tying each moment together has to do with the distinctive character of the black church's ineluctable attention and response to racism, America's central theological problem, and the commitment of black Christians to the work of social transformation, even as it is linked to a basic pietistic impulse deep in the soul of black faith.

If Martin Luther King, Jr., set out to activate black churches whose mission would be "To Redeem the Soul of America," then a central part of black theology's mission would be to redeem the soul of the black church. This it would endeavor to do by providing the black church a systematic understanding of the biblical basis for the church's work of justice and reconnecting it to a memory of its liberating heritage. Operating, like all revolutionary discourse, on the ecclesiastical margins, it is nonetheless significant that black theology had its earliest incarnation among pastors in the NCBC and black caucuses in white denominations. As such, a new theology and a new church emerged together, emphasizing the creative tension between praxis and theory. Responding to Joseph Washington and others who shared his limited view of the church's work as a salvific instrument, nascent black theology advanced a view of salvation that sees the struggle for human liberation as absolutely central to the gospel and the meaning of Jesus's death on the cross. In so doing, it defended the alternative ecclesial witness and the strands of protest tradition that run throughout the black church's history.

As the voices of trained academics such as James Cone, J. Deotis Roberts, and Preston Williams were added to black theology's rising chorus, the attack against the hypocrisy of white churches and white theologians became even more strident, and its academic side grew to increasing prominence. As an intellectual discipline, it undermined at least four patent assumptions that had held sway in American religious life: (1) acknowledged European and white American theologians have an exclusive claim on defining the appropriate norms, sources, and grammar for authentic theological reflection; (2) the fight for justice and resistance to human oppression is not central to the gospel or essential to Christian identity; (3) churches representing the dominant culture are the natural plumb line or the most appropriate point of reference for the doing of ecclesiology; and (4) the black church and black religion are not to be taken seriously as subjects worthy of sustained and disciplined academic reflection.

That black theology did much to undermine all of these assumptions is seen in the writings of two generations of scholars who followed and in the work of pastors who claim its influence on their ministries. But one of the earliest indications of the way in which nascent black theology was shifting the center of gravity comes from Joseph Washington himself. Influenced by the times and the dialogue taking place among his colleagues, Washington begins to sound a significantly different note, although he does not fully acknowledge it as such. It is also very likely that he is transformed by the death of Martin Luther King, Jr., to whom he dedicates the second edition of his second book, *The Politics of God: The Future of the Black Churches*. Pushing toward the ideal of meaningful ecclesial integration while also conceding that black churches would likely remain prominent in black life for years to come, he outlines a destiny and direction for their work in the struggle for authentic black empowerment. He avers,

> Negro churches are the only natural communities universal enough to command the loyalty and respect of the majority of Negro masses. They alone are so extensive as to form unity in political power. . . . Despite weaknesses of the churches by any objective criteria, the affinity of the Negro masses provides them with the greatest potential for strength. To mold this potential into reality the Negro churches would be emphasizing and reaffirming the Negro folk religion of freedom and equality, the original purposes of their creation.[48]

Moreover, Washington's change in perspective was signaled by his participation as a key presenter at a conference whose stated objective was to move beyond debating the desirability of a black theology, choosing instead to discuss its content. Washington's presentation was titled "How Black Is Black Religion?" In a rather interesting and poetic spin on the Johannine text, he says,

> In the beginning was the black church, and the black church was with the black community and the black church was the black community.

> The black church was in the beginning with the black people; all things were made through the black church, and without the black church was not anything made that was made. In the black church was life, and the life was the light of the black people. The black church still shines in the darkness, and the darkness has not overcome it.[49]

But not only does he affirm the existence of black churches, in contra-distinction to his earlier arguments; he actually sees their emphasis on freedom as essential to their peculiar meaning and mission among American churches. "Given the American pattern of churchianity, *black churches have every right to exist*. But with rights come responsibilities. The particular responsibility of black churches is to contribute to the needs of black people and therefore to the society as a whole. In fact, *black churches have no other responsibility than to contribute to the freedom of black people*" (emphasis mine).[50] Moreover, when one considers the main thesis of *Black Religion*, it is quite significant for Washington to later say, "Black theology breaks from white theology in the affirmation that what is good for black people is good for all people, that to work for the best interest of black people is to work for the best interest of all people. The experience of being at the bottom in this society and being rejected throughout the world because of sharing an African heritage *brings something new to the faith*" (emphasis mine).[51]

While this represents a remarkable shift from Washington's earlier position, he was not the only person whose perspective and work changed as a direct result of the birth of black theology. J. Deotis Roberts, who had previously focused his scholarly work on Christian Platonism and other areas of classical Western philosophy and theology,[52] became one of the outstanding proponents of black theology. Emphasizing the theological theme of *reconciliation* in relation to *liberation*, he and Cone have had some rather spirited debates over the years, and he is perhaps most often discussed by students of black theology in the context of their differences.[53] Even so, Roberts deserves attention in his own right, both for his academic work and his continual efforts to do it, in various jobs, in direct relationship to the ministry of black congregations.[54]

Henry Mitchell, who became the dean of the newly formed Black Church Studies Program at Colgate Rochester Divinity School, authored important works on black preaching and black belief.[55] Moreover, Gayraud Wilmore, a Presbyterian Church executive who had earlier expressed concern regarding "the secular relevance of the church,"[56] namely, its ability to speak effectively in the modern world through political and social action, grew to apply his incisive writing, historical imagination, and theological acumen more explicitly to the problem of race. He says, regarding his earlier 1962 text, "I had not yet gone through my second conversion experience."[57]

As one born and raised in the AME Church, Cone avers that, for him, "the turn to blackness was an even deeper conversion-experience than the turn to Jesus": "It was spiritual, transforming radically my way of seeing the world and theology."[58] Similar to Martin King, Cone's "turn to Jesus," his first conversion experience, was less dramatic because it had more to do with the native religious ethos of his childhood and was thus basic and formative for his self-understanding. It is what King describes, in his "Autobiography of Religious Development," as "the gradual intaking of the noble (ideals?) set forth in [his] family and environment."[59] While that experience was formative for King's sense of self-awareness, it is markedly different from the dramatic "kitchen conversion"[60] that he later experienced in the heat of battle in Montgomery and to which he refers as an existential anchor throughout his career. It is in that sense that, for Cone, "the turn to blackness" was deeper. Informed by the liberationist theological claims of Martin Luther King, Jr., and elevated into black consciousness through Malcolm X's sharp analysis of whiteness, recapitulated after his death in the black power movement, Cone says that he *"was born again into thinking black"* (emphasis mine).[61]

In a real sense, with the unfolding of the civil rights and black power movements, the entire nation went through a social *metanoia*, a dramatic shift in consciousness. And within that larger context, a new black ecclesial consciousness emerged among a radicalized remnant of black theologians and pastors in independent black churches and in black churches and caucuses in white denominations. As an intellectual discipline, black theology set out to clarify the meaning of the gospel as a divine word about salvation in history and about the church's mission if it would be a faithful instrument. Many, including Joseph Washington and a host of others, were converted in the process. The question is, to what extent had the institutional black church itself been converted?

3

BLACK THEOLOGIANS ON THE MISSION OF THE BLACK CHURCH

BLACK THEOLOGY EMERGED as the last of four critical moments in the black church's apprehension of a holistically salvific faith, one providing principled Christian resistance to racism. It represented a new and self-conscious form of God-talk, a sophisticated apologia for a faith formed in slavery and in defense of a black liberationist trajectory that continues to bear witness against the sins of a nation that is at once putatively Christian and profoundly racist. Black theology is best understood in relationship to the liberationist God-talk shaped in the brush arbors of the invisible institution; lived out in the varied aggregations of black Christians that constitute the social reality of the black church, resident in both black and white denominations; and activated by various liberationist efforts that culminate with the civil rights movement.

That part of nascent black theology's very raison d'être was to offer a reasoned exposition of the true gospel of liberation and consequently a defense of the liberationist faith lived out in black churches is a fact often overlooked in the debate about the problematic relationship between black theology and the black church.[1] It is a very significant fact nonetheless. First, it provides the historical background for carefully examining the nuances of abiding theological tensions between black theologians and black pastors, as well as within the divided mind of the black church itself regarding the church's essential mission. We shall examine those tensions as they emerge in the methodological approaches of selective first- and second-generation black theologians in this chapter and among varying pastoral perspectives to be discussed in the next.

Second, this historical acknowledgment of the abiding kinship and incorrigible connection between black theology and the black church provides the necessary basis for a much-needed discussion between black theologians and black pastors. Third, it is quite significant that an academic theology actually emerged in defense of the liberating legacy of the black church when one simply observes that the black church, then and now, represents the most misunderstood and caricatured religious institution both in American popular culture and in the world of intellectual discourse.[2] Not unlike the people who constitute its membership, the black church is quite often the object of a culture that gazes on it with what Du Bois called "amused contempt and pity."[3] It is too seldom taken seriously by academics and too often caricatured and stereotyped within popular culture. Yet, aroused by Joseph Washington's tough questions regarding the Christian identity of the black church, inspired by the Christian activism of the civil rights movement, and challenged by the militancy and moral claims of the black power movement, black theologians defended the black church's liberationist heritage and lifted it up as both antecedent and natural ally to black power.

Yet, even as black theologians have defended the black church, they have also been its most consistent and principled critics. At the heart of their concern has been the issue of the depth of the black church's commitment to a liberationist understanding of the gospel and the extent to which that understanding is (under)represented in the organizational structure and agenda of its institutional life. It is to this concern and its influence on the development of black theology that we now turn our attention.

The sense that the institutional life of the black church reflects a weak and wavering commitment to the project of liberation and to the true gospel as a gospel of liberation manifests itself in key texts written by black theologians. I argue that it is indicative of differences in theological emphases between the pietistic and liberationist dimensions of black salvific understanding. In this way, the debates among black theologians themselves and between black theologians and black pastors have often been manifestations of themes dialectically related, shifting at different historical moments, in the saga of black faith.

Moreover, the emergence of black theology, with its strident critique of the black church, represents a self-conscious, *theological* development within a larger and much-longer discussion within the black community and among black intellectuals in particular, of various ideological persuasions, regarding the effectiveness, even the usefulness, of the black church in the continuing project of racial uplift. For black people, inside and outside the churches, have long held a deep communal expectation and a general assumption that the work of racial uplift is integral to the responsibility and vocation of the black church.

It is an abiding assumption recorded, among other places, by St. Clair Drake and Horace Cayton, in their engagement of the people of Bronzeville. They observe that "both members and non-members expect the church to play a prominent part in 'advancing The Race,' and they often judge the institution from this angle alone."[4] Benjamin E. Mays and Joseph W. Nicholson confirm this communal sentiment when they state that, among blacks in rural and urban areas, "it is taken for granted that Negro ministers will courageously oppose lynching, Jim Crow law, and discrimination."[5] Charles Hamilton and Charles Shelby Rooks observe the same general expectation.[6] Because white churches have not had the burden of being the most prominent, stable, and autonomous institution in an oppressed community, because white culture has generally observed a sharper dichotomy between the secular and sacred realms of human experience, and because white Christianity has not posited a biblical view of divine salvation that places black liberation and racial justice at its center, this tacit assumption about the social and political nature of pastoral work in the black community is foreign to most white churches and their pastors.

Nonetheless, that the church will address itself to the work of social transformation and political involvement for the express purpose of racial uplift has long been an abiding expectation within the African American community. The expectation has been largely *nontheological*, and among intellectuals, it is manifested in a history of black church interpretation that recalls, among others, such names as

W. E. B. Du Bois,[7] Booker T. Washington,[8] Carter G. Woodson,[9] St. Clair Drake and the black researcher who worked under his direction, Horace Cayton,[10] the Swedish researcher Gunnar Myrdal,[11] Benjamin E. Mays,[12] and E. Franklin Frazier.[13]

It has always been the case that few issues are more hotly debated in black life, even among those outside the church, than the putative and, if one accepts the prevalence of the claim in the literature from the turn of the twentieth century to the present, *perpetual* decline of the black church. Moreover, for good and obvious reasons, African American scholars and scholars of African American life are not exempt from this deep investment and sharp focus on that which sits at the center of the community's life. Consequently, they have been active participants in the debate and have brought to the conversation their scholarship and their concerns, their disciplined critical insight and their impassioned political agendas, their scientific research and their class bias.

To be sure, much of this scholarship, beginning with Du Bois's work at the turn of the twentieth century, has yielded important insights into the historical development and sociological character of the black church, without which black and womanist theologians could hardly conduct their work. The secular scholarship of earlier interpreters provided an important and necessary angle of analysis. Yet the black church is first and foremost a faith community. Thus, a comprehensive analysis of its condition would require some sustained engagement on the terms of the faith itself and the faith claims, explicit and implicit, found therein. Or else, absent a critical *theological* principle for evaluating the work of black churches, one is forced to uncritically accept as a theological plumb line the faith claims of white Christianity (Joseph Washington) or to posit a purely functionalist approach to the study of black religion that ignores theology altogether (e.g., Myrdal, Frazier). In either scenario, the analysis is, at best, incomplete and, at worst, distorted. Consequently, the black church is inherently and unavoidably viewed as a problem.

Thus, an examination of key texts by black theologians reveals that black theology's important contribution to this ongoing conversation was the addition of something very fundamental—a critical *theological* principle, based on the experience of black people, the witness of scripture, *and* a distinctive understanding of the meaning of Jesus Christ, for testing the faithfulness of the church to its essential mission. In this way, the social and historical concerns of black identity, appropriately investigated within the secular disciplinary parameters of earlier investigators *and* the theological concerns of black Christian identity, raised by an emerging generation of black theologians, could be connected in a systematic way and collated in a new theological analysis of the vocation of the black church in a revolutionary age.

The significance of black theology, as a scholarly development in the apprehension of the black church's mission, is best understood in the light of this conversation that had been so central for so long in the black community, at large, and among black intellectuals, in particular, regarding the appropriate role of the black church. Therein one sees both the continuities and discontinuities of black theology's liberationist agenda with the concerns of previous generations of scholars to "uplift the race," and one is given a larger historical context for understanding the dialogue between black theologians and black pastors regarding the essential mission of the black church.

Black Intellectuals, the Negro Church, and Racial Uplift

INDEED, IT WAS the primacy of an agenda to uplift the race and W. E. B. Du Bois's lifelong commitment to the social and political advancement of African Americans that spurred his concern for the church and his critical examination of "the faith of the fathers."[14] From the early days of his involvement with the Niagara Movement and the NAACP to the day of his death in Ghana on the eve of the March on Washington, Du Bois was a trained historian with an interdisciplinary methodology and an intense social agenda.[15] He was never disinterested or dispassionate when it came to the well-being of African Americans, and the conclusions he draws in his classic work *The Negro Church* are best understood when read through the lens of his larger ideological presuppositions and political agenda. It is from a functionalist

perspective of racial uplift that he avers, "The church is probably losing its influence on the young people because of the scarcity of ministers able to meet the intellectual needs of the times and the emphasis
which the church is compelled to place on eternal things."[16]

What is conveyed is an abiding suspicion among intellectuals, of
various political persuasions, that the Negro church of the early twentieth century, that is, the folk church of the black masses and the religion found therein, is a problem. In the case of Du Bois and others,
the issue is the extent to which it furthers or hinders the agenda to
advance the race.

Armed with this sense that the church is too otherworldly and
suspicious of its emotionalism, Du Bois records "the opinions of sev-
enty-five intelligent colored laymen" in the state of Illinois regarding
the state of the Negro church in 1903. Du Bois does not indicate his
criteria for determining that the laymen whom he interviewed were
intelligent, nor does he clarify the basis on which he arrives at "intelligence" as an essential control category for his scientific sample. Ever
concerned about uplifting the race and desirous of the emergence of
a distinct class, a "Talented Tenth" who would accomplish that end,
Du Bois records the following regarding the state of black Christian ministry:

> The majority think that the present condition of the churches is bad.
> The churches' influence is, on the whole, toward better and more
> upright life, but there is great room for improvement. The ministers
> are said not usually to be the right sort of men, their faults being igno-
> rance and immorality, and in some cases, drunkenness. Opinions are
> divided as to the efficiency of Sunday-schools. Not much charitable
> work is done and the church is not attracting young people.[17]

In that regard, it is interesting to note that Booker T. Washington,
who was himself a thoroughgoing political accommodationist, representing, in juxtaposition to Du Bois, a countervailing view of racial
uplift, agreed nonetheless with Du Bois concerning the accommo-
dating otherworldliness of the Negro church.[18] Booker T. Washington opines,

From the nature of things, all through slavery it was life in the future world that was emphasized in religious teaching rather than life in this world. In his religious meetings in *ante-bellum* days the Negro was prevented from discussing many points of practical religion which related to this world; and the white minister, who was his spiritual guide, found it more convenient to talk about heaven than earth, so very naturally that today in his religious meeting it is the Negro's feelings which are worked upon mostly, and it is description of the glories of heaven that occupy most of the time of his sermon.[19]

Evincing a similar assumption regarding the peculiar mission of the black church as that of racial uplift and cultural refinement, the liberal pan-African scholar Orishatukeh Faduma, writing during the same period, laments "the defects of the Negro church."[20] To be sure, he concedes that "the defects of the Negro church are found more or less in churches of other races. They are the same in kind but differ in degree, on account of difference in environment."[21] Inasmuch as Du Bois, Booker T. Washington, and others saw the black church as largely otherworldly, it is interesting that Faduma argues just the opposite. Among many defects, he observes "the tendency to lay stress on outwardness rather than inwardness, . . . [and] its organization lacks an organ with a spiritual life deep enough to suppress worldliness." Presumably, it is this emphasis on the "outward" that evinces itself in an "excessive emotionalism" and "a revival of the latent paganism in the Negro." "The weird songs, the wild excitement of the people followed by the unchaste exposures and hysteria of women, the physical agony and wallowing on the floor, and the violent physical gymnastics among both sexes is a species of voodooism imported from the religion of heathen Africa. It is deplorable because its after effects are demoralizing."[22]

Du Bois, intrigued and awed by the same phenomenon, described it as "a suppressed terror . . .—a pythian madness, a demoniac possession, that lent terrible reality to song and word. The people moaned and fluttered, and then the gaunt-cheeked brown woman beside me suddenly leaped straight in the air and shrieked like a lost soul, while round about came wail and groan and outcry, and a scene of human

passion such as I had never conceived before."[23] Observing the emotive quality of the spirituality and revivalistic piety among the masses
in black churches in rural Tennessee, William Wells Brown, regarded
by many as America's first black man of letters, echoes Faduma's clear
disapproval. He laments, "The only remedy for this *great evil* lies in
an educated ministry, which is being supplied to a limited extent. It is
very difficult, however, to induce the uneducated, superstitious masses
to receive and support an intelligent Christian clergyman" (emphasis mine).[24] Indeed, the perspective expressed by Joseph Washington
in *Black Religion*, half a century later, is consistent with the views of
Faduma and Brown. Writing toward the end of the period of the great
migration of black southerners to the urban North, Washington credits the emergence of folk churches in urban centers with "giving birth
to the most degenerate form of Negro religion—gospel music."[25]

E. Franklin Frazier's *Negro Church in America*, with its less-than-
favorable view of the future of the Negro church and its decidedly
assimilationist thesis, was posthumously published in 1964, the same
year of publication as Washington's *Black Religion*. Like Washington,
Frazier saw the Negro church as having outlived its usefulness in an
increasingly open and pluralistic society. He welcomed its demise
because in his view, "the Negro church and Negro religion have cast
a shadow over the entire intellectual life of Negroes and have been
responsible for the so-called backwardness of American Negroes."[26]

Surveying this history of interpretation, one can see how countervailing political visions of racial uplift, the rationalistic framework of
black intellectuals, and the intimate world of black folk spirituality
with its exuberant, emotive physicality and strange interior freedom
present a real conundrum in any honest and nuanced discussion about
the black church's essential mission and its faithfulness to the same. On
the one hand, it can clearly be said that there is a prominent pietistic
impulse within the black church that has and does evince an escapist
and otherworldly quality, eschewing political engagement in exchange
for a freedom emphasized in worship but not in worldly struggle.
Martin King criticized this church that "burns with emotionalism, . . .
reducing worship to entertainment, places more emphasis on volume
than on content and confuses spirituality with muscularity." In his

famous sermon "A Knock at Midnight," he avers that over against the midnight of social injustice, war, poverty, and spiritual despair, "this type of church has neither the vitality nor the relevant gospel to feed hungry souls."[27]

Yet Martin King clearly understood that there is no necessary correlation between emotive spirituality and escapism. The former could manifest itself in a liberationist impulse, an eschatological counterworldliness expressed in worship and evinced in worldly confrontation with "powers and principalities," even in the face of overwhelming odds and the severe limits of history. King, who had initially rejected the "backward" emotional spirituality of the mass black church, was reclaimed, as Stewart Burns so eloquently and powerfully argues, by this "elevated world of spirit" in the first mass meeting of the Holt Street Baptist Church and in the revivalistic mass meetings that followed, as he "stood face-to-face with the fierce raw emotionality of black church culture."[28] Emboldened by his own divine encounter in his kitchen at midnight, he would effectively channel the radical side of this spirituality into a massive social movement. Creating freedom songs out of revival hymns, the mass meetings that characterized the movement tapped into an internal freedom, a holy boldness that made it possible for one to fight for external freedom, even to the point of risking death.[29]

Yet, in a study titled "Religion: Opiate or Inspiration of Civil Rights Militancy?," Gary Marx, a scholar who operates from within the theoretical framework of his famous namesake, fallaciously concludes that there is an inverse relationship between the depth of pietistic faith and the intensity of civil rights militancy among African Americans. He draws this conclusion even while acknowledging the activist ecclesiology and radical social ministry of Martin Luther King, Jr. Operating from a classic Marxist view of history and of religion as false consciousness, Gary Marx holds out for a time when "religion loosens its hold over these people, or comes to embody to a greater extent the belief that man as well as God can bring about secular change."[30]

To be sure, the Marxist critique has much to teach the black church. Indeed, it has played an important role in the maturation of black theology as an intellectual discipline, deepened black theology's apprehension of the interconnectivity of racial and class oppression, and provided critical tools for a black church that has yet to awaken to a substantive Third World consciousness.[31] Yet Gary Marx's analysis is flawed by a paternalistic bias with respect to *faith, culture,* and *experience* that trivializes black struggle against the obduracy of white capitalistic forces and lumps all forms of black denominational and sectarian identity together in an undifferentiated way that hardly makes it possible for those who are its subjects to see themselves in the discussion.[32]

What Marx's and other analyses show is that what was needed in the history of black church interpretation, in addition to the foregoing methodological approaches, was a *critical theological principle* that inquires into the church's mission with respect to the gospel's meaning, endeavoring to hold at bay the class-biased politics of respectability, the religious homogenization of a nontheistic framework, and certain ideological sensibilities that may impair the interpreter's ability to fully appreciate the dialectical complexities of internal and external freedom in the folk religion of the masses. In that regard, the rise of black theology is important because it afforded a radical theistic framework, a christological lens, and a critical form of analysis capable of speaking *about, for,* and *to* the black church, its pastors, and its people.

Because secular scholars such as Du Bois, Frazier, and Marx, limited by the parameters of their disciplines, could not be expected to engage the black church from the standpoint of Christian faith itself and because religious intellectuals such as Faduma and Joseph Washington accepted uncritically the theological claims and cultural biases of white Christianity, the emergence of a *critical, systematic,* and *self-conscious* black theology represented a critical turning point in the history of black church interpretation. For black theology offers an analysis of the black church that takes into account the distinctive theological norms, sources, biblical hermeneutics, and culture that constitute the complex development of the black church as a historical community of faith. Unlike any discipline before it, black theology is able to challenge the black church from the standpoint of Christian faith itself and on the terms of the black church's best self-understanding—from the formation of African American Christian faith to the founding of independent black churches to the fomenting of revolutionary moments that culminate with the civil rights movement.

Yet, as I engage the theological perspective of selective black theologians, part of what I ask is the extent to which their theological assertions, their methodological approaches, and their omissions *re-present*, in a later era, biases or methodological challenges similar to those focused on the mere functionality of the black church with respect to the agenda of "racial uplift" or "civil rights militancy," as black theologians address their liberationist concerns to the complex pietistic dimension of black faith and the spirituality lodged within black churches. In other words, to what extent has the "Negro church," that church of a pre-black-consciousness era that, according to Frazier, "cast a shadow over the entire intellectual life of Negroes," been a source of consternation and challenge for the liberationist agenda of black and womanist theologians after the civil rights movement? What are their class biases? How have they addressed anti-intellectualism in the black church? And how have they accounted for the difference and disconnect between their understanding of the black church's mission and liberating heritage and the complex, political reality of black churches? Put another way, to what extent have black theologians had to negotiate, like intellectuals before them, the scandal of the Negro church?[33]

The Scandal of the Negro Church

SOME TWENTY YEARS after E. Franklin Frazier's work was presented as the Frazer Lecture in Social Anthropology in Liverpool and ten years after it was published as a book, C. Eric Lincoln, a sociologist and an important voice in the black theology movement, did not deny Frazier's sense and suspicion that "the Negro church" about which Frazier wrote was a problem. Scandalized by the difference in consciousness between that church and the new and bold black church he desired, Lincoln argues, in his companion volume titled *The Black Church since Frazier*, that

> the "Negro church" that Frazier wrote about no longer exists. It died an
> agonized death in the harsh turmoil which tried the faith so rigorously

in the decade of the "Savage Sixties," for there it had to confront under the most trying circumstances the possibility that "Negro" and "Christian" were irreconcilable categories. The call to full manhood, to *personhood*, and the call to Christian responsibility left no room for the implications of being a "Negro" in contemporary America. With sadness and reluctance, trepidation and confidence, the Negro Church accepted death in order to be reborn. Out of the ashes of its funeral pyre there sprang the bold, strident, self-conscious phoenix that is the contemporary Black Church.[34]

Although Lincoln was a first-rate sociologist of religion, he was writing, in a very real sense, on behalf of the black theology movement. Hence, his pronouncement about the death of the Negro church said as much about the black ecclesial consciousness and liberationist sensibilities of the movement that he represented as it did about any pervasive and unambiguous reality within the black church. The death certificate is actually a *death wish*.

It is interesting to note that Lincoln's claim about the "death of the Negro church" comes on the heels of the famous controversy stirred by the "death of God" theologians, Thomas Altizer, William Hamilton, and others.[35] Clearly, the issues and sensibilities are very different. The theological claim that "God is dead" is alien to the culture of the black church and foreign to the black theology agenda. Even so, the hermeneutical moves are similar. The shocking claim that "God is dead" came as a radical theological response to a change in consciousness in an emerging postmodern age—an age in which traditional claims about God suffered a crisis in credibility. In the "secular city" (Harvey Cox), the traditional God must die in order to enter more fully into human history (Altizer). Similarly, Lincoln is saying that with the rise of black consciousness, the old Negro church, and the fundamentalistic religion therein, had to die so that black people could claim their personhood in a revolutionary historical moment. If "death of God" theologians were asking, what does authentic faith look like in an emerging postmodern age and in the secular city? black theologians were asking, what does the true church look like in the wake of black power and black consciousness? But in each case, a cultural contradiction emerged and a radical hermeneutical move is made in response.

In that regard, Lincoln's bold pronouncement is quite instructive. For it helps one to understand the way in which the representatives of black theology have offered their version of the meaning of the gospel and, by extension, the mission of the black church while also endeavoring to account for the significant differences between their own theological sensibilities and sociopolitical agenda and the ambiguous theological and political reality of the black church. Like Lincoln, other voices within black theology have made similar hermeneutical moves. Their varying theoretical frameworks and methodological responses to the identity of the black church underscore significant tensions between black theology and the church that gave it its life. Indeed, those tensions emerge within the discussions between black theologians and black pastors regarding the church's essential mission. Moreover, part of what the varying theoretical frameworks of black theologians regarding the identity of the black church reveal is the extent to which the black church of a new era, not unlike the Negro church of a previous era, has been a problem for the black theology agenda.

First-Generation Black Theologians

THESES PUT FORTH by several key texts within black theology might well be read as varying methodological responses to negotiating the same problem—tensions between the black-consciousness and liberationist sensibilities of the black theology movement and the institutional reality of the church from which it emerged. While it is most clearly seen in Lincoln's thesis regarding "the death of the Negro church," similar hermeneutical efforts are evident in James Cone's distinction between the antebellum and postbellum black church, Gayraud Wilmore's thesis regarding "the deradicalization of the black church," J. Deotis Roberts's outline of "a black ecclesiology of involvement," and Albert Cleage's positing a "black Christian nationalism" as the most authentic expression of the black church. On the other hand, Cecil Cone's thesis regarding the "identity crisis in black theology" represents the earliest sustained treatment of the divide between black theology and the black church and deserves to be examined for both its insights and its limitations. Yet voices from the second generation of black theologians can also be heard articulating new methodological questions, as both black theologians and black pastors navigate the pietistic and protest dimensions of black faith while negotiating in theory and through praxis differences that sometimes erupt into a divide.

THE ANTEBELLUM AND POSTBELLUM BLACK CHURCH

Because James Cone is internationally recognized as the father of black theology and has been the most prolific contributor to the shaping of its content and meaning, we shall give primary attention to his work. The prominent voices of other first- and second-generation black theologians will be placed in conversation with his, as a way of teasing out the differences among them and showing how each represents a methodological approach to negotiating the tensions between the pietistic and liberationist dimensions of black faith and the dialogue between black theology and the black church.

Cone identifies liberation as the central message of the gospel and the most distinctive mark of the historic black churches and denominations. His work accounts for the difference between his theological assertions regarding the centrality of liberation in the heart of black faith and the more ambiguous institutional reality of contemporary black churches by making a distinction between the antebellum black church and the postbellum black church. The former, he argues, was revolutionary, while the latter, with few exceptions, has been largely counterrevolutionary.[36] Indeed, it is a severe critique and a rather sweeping historical interpretation. But it is best understood as a working historical referent, a heuristic framework for concerns that are primarily theological, namely, the extent to which the institutional churches serve as "a visible manifestation that the gospel is a reality."[37] For whether one believes that the churches are indeed a credible representation of Christ in history depends on one's interpretation of the gospel. Cone has always insisted that the central theme of the gospel is liberation. On this point, he has been quite consistent and very clear.

Thus, if he posits a bold and bipartite historical reading of the black church that judges the pre–Civil War black church to be revolutionary and the post–Civil War black church to be counterrevolutionary, it is only because his understanding of the essential message of the gospel has been unequivocal. The gospel *is* liberation.

From the very outset of his career, Cone has consistently argued that the message of the gospel, in both the Old and New Testament witness, is that the salvific work of God in history is about the liberation of the poor from bondage and that God sides with them in their struggle against oppression. His distinctive voice as a theologian emerges with the 1968 publication of his first essay, titled "Christianity and Black Power."[38] Although the poignant and powerful voice that will explode on the scene with the publication of his first two books, *Black Theology and Black Power* (1969) and *A Black Theology of Liberation* (1970), is just beginning to emerge, both the content of this first article and the subject matter already represent a decisive departure from the pristine discussion and dispassionate theoretical analysis of the theological anthropology of Karl Barth in his dissertation.[39]

He had suggested in his dissertation that if Luther's impact in the sixteenth century might be referred to as a "Copernican Revolution," "we may similarly refer to Karl Barth's achievement in twentieth century Protestant Christianity."[40] But three years out of graduate school and in the heat of urban riots in the summer following Martin Luther King, Jr.'s death, Cone (like Luther, Barth, and King) undergoes his own crisis experience, a *metanoia*, incited by the pain of the black poor exploding in riot-torn cities and the search for a theological word that would ring true for his own people in this moment. By the time of his second book, *A Black Theology of Liberation*, he would make bold to say that "Black Theology seeks to do in American theology what Copernicus did to thinking about the physical universe." If Copernicus offered a heliocentric corrective to the error of a geocentric worldview and if Luther and Barth each, in his own way and in his own context, addressed his theology to the problem of an anthropocentric Christianity, "the black Copernican revolution" set out to turn the christological distortion of the white American Christ on its head.[41]

But Cone's systematic contribution to this work begins in 1968.

Ironically, it is also the year of Karl Barth's death. So too begins the death of a black neo-orthodox theologian and the birth of a black theologian. Cone avers, "What World War I did for Barth, the Detroit Riots and the Civil Rights Movement did for me."[42] Coming to voice amid the rubble and cries of black power and the "gross distortions of truth" about which the NCNC had spoken so eloquently two years earlier but against which they had yet to develop a full-orbed systematic language, Cone, "born again into thinking black,"[43] was beginning to develop such a language.

Cone audaciously argues that black power "is not an antithesis of Christianity nor is it a heretical idea to be tolerated with painful forbearance. It is rather Christ's central message to twentieth-century America."[44] A careful reading clearly shows that it is a message that Cone directs primarily to the church and not the academy in this earliest piece. He argues that "unless the empirical denominational Church makes a determined effort to recapture the Man Jesus through a total identification with the suffering poor as expressed in Black Power, *that Church will become exactly what Christ is not.* . . . If the Church is to remain faithful to its Lord, it must make a decisive break with the structure of this society by launching a vehement attack on the evils of racism in all forms" (emphasis mine).[45] In this way, it must champion unequivocally the cause and principle of black power. For black power is *not* "the work of the Antichrist," he sets out to prove in this first essay.[46] It is the message of Christ. But he will go one step further with the publication of his first book, arguing there, for the first time, that it is the white church, given its support of slavery and segregation, and not black power that *is* the Antichrist.[47]

Thus begins Cone's decisive break with white Christianity and the commencement of his constructive work as a theologian of black liberation. Yet, true to his roots in the black church and consistent with his Barthian training, it is a decisive break, guided conceptually by a sharp emphasis on christology, his understanding that the nature of the revelation of Jesus Christ is the starting point for all God-talk that is truly Christian and all talk about the human condition that is faithful to the gospel. While the black experience is his focus and clearly the most definitive source in the development of his theology, the Barthian framework, particularly with its christological focus, served Cone's theoretical efforts to speak as a systematic theologian similarly to the way in which liberalism and Boston personalism served Martin King.

In fact, Cone, unbeknownst to himself, had already cogently stated, within the dissertation, the christological foundations on which his radical God-talk and analysis of racism would later be built. Interpreting Barth, he says, "To know the divine attitude toward man is to know the particular man Jesus Christ, and to know man is to know the human nature of Jesus." Anthropology can only be done in the light of christology. Moreover, "if the task of theology is conceived as being that of analyzing the proclamation of the Church, and if the essence of the church is Jesus Christ, then all Christian doctrines must be interpreted in the light of Jesus Christ."[48]

Thus, it is only in the light of a theological methodology that takes seriously christology as theology's only appropriate point of departure that one can understand Cone's claim that the white church is the Antichrist. In view of its historical sacralization and active support of slavery and segregation in the society and its creation and maintenance of the conditions under which an independent black church had to emerge, he reasoned that the white church is precisely what Christ is not. Aligning itself with that which is opposed to God's intentions for humanity, "it is the enemy of Christ."[49]

Yet God intends the liberation of the oppressed. This is clearly expressed in Luke 4:18, a key text for Cone's interpretation of the ministry of Jesus:

> *The Spirit of the Lord is upon me,*
> *Because he has anointed me to preach the good news to the poor,*
> *He has sent me to proclaim release to the captives and recovering*
>   *of sight to the blind,*
> *To set at liberty those who are oppressed,*
> *To proclaim the acceptable year of the Lord.*
> (Luke 4:18, 19)[50]

Hence, it is not in spite of Christ but precisely because of Christ, "the man for others," that the poor are given the freedom necessary to rebel against that which is inimical to their humanity. To say that black power represents the work of the gospel is not, Cone argued, to reduce the gospel to ideology or to ignore what Barth, quoting Kierkegaard, called "the infinite qualitative distinction between God and man."[51] Rather, it is to take the resurrection seriously. For if the resurrection has any meaning at all, then it must mean that Christ is alive and active among the struggles of the poor, as they seek empowerment in the context of the twentieth century. Christ has taken on their struggle as his own. "Christianity, therefore, is not alien to Black Power; it is Black Power."[52]

In this regard, the black church, born for the cause of freedom, is the antecedent to black power and its most natural ally. In fact, the liberationist impulse was not simply one among many items on the faith agenda of the invisible institution but was the antebellum black church's very raison d'être.

> The black church was born in protest. In this sense, it is the precursor to black power. Unlike the white church, its reality stemmed from the eschatological recognition that freedom and equality are at the essence of humanity, and thus segregation and slavery are diametrically opposed to Christianity. Freedom and equality made up the central theme of the black church; the protest and action were the early marks of its uniqueness, as the black man fought for freedom.[53]

This is not disinterested or dispassionate historiography. Nor does it claim to be so. Cone employs historical imagination with a sense of urgency and on behalf of a movement. The theology and the historiography go hand in hand as he and other black theologians sought to ground an emerging theological discourse in the memory of a revolutionary past. Rediscovering, like Josiah of ancient Israel,[54] the ancestral canon, he reconnects it to a contemporary program of revolutionary change. Invoked for their blessings are heroic names in black church history, such as Richard Allen, Henry Highland Garnett, Henry McNeil Turner, Gabriel Prosser, Daniel A. Payne, and Nat Turner.[55]

The methodological import is clear. Locating black theology along the historical trajectory of revolutionary black Christian thought, Cone and other black theologians then argued that their embrace of black power, as the clearest manifestation of the gospel in their times, was not only consistent with the witness of the early pre-Constantinian church but also the very essence of black religion.

Moreover, Cone argues that the antebellum black church's emphasis on freedom and equality was not simply a historical characteristic. Rather, it was a theological mark of the true church and the criterion by which the faithfulness of American churches was to be measured in all times. Arguing against Joseph Washington, who, in his earlier work, had named the peculiar sensibilities of a faith created in struggle "folk religion," placing it outside the realm of "historic Christianity," Cone insists that

> it was, rather, white Christianity in America that was born in heresy. Its very coming to be was an attempt to reconcile the impossible—slavery and Christianity. And the existence of the black churches is a visible reminder of its apostasy. The black church is the only church in America which remained recognizably Christian during pre–Civil War days. Its stand on freedom and equality through word and action is true to the spirit of Christ.[56]

But if the antebellum black church is to be praised for its courage, tenacity, and passion for justice, the postbellum black church, Cone suggests, must be criticized for its apostasy and failure to remain true to the revolutionary implications of the gospel. He posits that following Reconstruction and the birth of Jim Crow laws in the South and the North, "the black church lost its zeal for freedom in the midst of the new structures of white power. The rise of segregation and discrimination in the post–Civil War period softened its drive for equality. . . . Black churches adopted, for the most part, the theology of the white missionaries and taught blacks to forget the present and look to the future."[57] Quoting Joseph Washington, Cone opines that while the black minister remained, during this period, the spokesperson for the community, "faced by insurmountable obstacles, he succumbed to the cajolery and bribery of the white power structure and became its foil."[58] Agreeing with Washington again, he asserts that black churches became "amusement centers," "arenas for power politics," providing an "organ for recognition, leadership and worship."[59]

Cone's interpretation of the historical development of the black church advances the project of black theology in at least three ways. First, it is a thesis that offers a historical accounting of the difference between his liberationist perspective on the meaning of the black church and the more ambiguous political reality of the black church's institutional life. Second, by summoning the heroic witness of the ancestors, Cone offers to the black church a view of its own salvation history, an understanding of itself that is theologically self-conscious and historically grounded in the story of black faith and resistance. Third, Cone's historical reading posits a revolutionary ecclesiological norm that serves a priori as the standard bearer by which the faithfulness of the black church is to be judged in all times. The theological implications that are drawn out here can be clearly seen in a 1970 article titled "Black Consciousness and the Black Church: An Historical-Theological Interpretation." In it, Cone posits the following,

> The Christian Gospel is a gospel of liberation. The pre–Civil War black churches recognized this, and that was why they refused to accept an interpretation of Christianity that was unrelated to civil freedom. Unfortunately, the post–Civil War black churches forgot about this emphasis and began to identify religion with piety. But the rise of Black Theology in the black churches is a renewal of the pre–Civil War emphasis. It is not certain whether the major black denominations will respond positively by re-ordering their structures in the light of Black Power. What is certain is the black community's awareness of its blackness as a tool for liberation. And unless the black churches redefine their existence in the light of the fathers who fought, risking death, to end slavery, the judgment of God will descend upon it.[60]

Disavowing this overemphasis on piety and the marginalization of protest, Cone continues to trace the trajectory of black Christian revolutionary thought, seeing it reemerge in important moments and

personalities in black church history. Figures such as Adam Clayton
Powell, Jr., Martin Luther King, Jr., Jesse Jackson, and Albert Cleage
are seen as rare and exceptional churchmen who operate almost
in spite of the church.[61] For, as he sees it, "except in rare instances,
the black churches in the post–Civil War period have been no more
Christian than their white counterparts," causing many in the black
community to regard the black church as "nothing but a second-rate
oppressor."[62] It has been, in this sense, a barrier to black liberation.

Yet Cone has never lost hope in the promise of the black church,
seeking always to challenge it as a critical theologian. The tensions
between the pietistic and liberationist dimensions of Christian faith
in general and black Christian faith in particular have been a concern
that he endeavors to address in his theology. In a 1976 essay titled
"What Does It Mean to Be Saved?," Cone observes the false dichotomy that Christian faith has historically made "between the spiritual
and the physical, as if political freedom is either unrelated or second-
ary to God's work of salvation in Jesus Christ."[63] He rightly points out
that this is a "radical error" and seeks to unmask it by explicating his
understanding of the biblical view of salvation. Salvation, in the Old
Testament, he observes, is always rooted in history, and its root word
has literally to do with the broadening of space for living and "victory
in battle."[64] The God-talk and rhetoric of praise that ushers from the
Exodus narrative is central to his discussion:

> *"I will sing to the Lord, for he has triumphed gloriously*
> *The horse and his rider he has thrown into the sea.*
> *The Lord is my strength and my song,*
> *And he has become my salvation;*
> *This is my God, and I will praise him. . . .*
> *The Lord is a man of war;*
> *The Lord is his name."*
> (Exodus 15:1–3)

As this ancient salvation poem suggests and Cone argues, the salvific activity of God, announced in varying Hebrew terms to include
deliverance, redemption, and healing, has to do with God's concern

for the victims of history. Elsewhere he shows the way in which this fundamental understanding of God's salvific activity on behalf of the oppressed comes as a word of judgment by the prophets against the liberated and exploitative classes of ancient Hebrew society. "Sin," he concludes, "is not primarily a religious impurity, but rather social, political, and the economic oppression of the poor."[65] The New Testament, Cone argues, does not negate this fundamental understanding of salvation but reinforces it in the life, ministry, death, and resurrection of Jesus Christ. "That is why it is reported that Jesus was born in a stable at Bethlehem. . . . He came to and for the poor; he ate with the outcasts, the 'bad characters' of his day, the ones whom the Pharisees called 'sinners.'"[66] Inasmuch as Jesus died while engaged in struggle on behalf of the oppressed, the resurrection signifies a future for those who struggle beyond the limitations of history. In this way, the New Testament extends the narrative of salvation history in the Old Testament into eschatological dimensions. Because death has already been defeated, the oppressed have every reason, in spite of historical and empirical evidence to the contrary, to fight for their freedom.[67]

As a theologian, Cone sees his critical work as that of explicating for the church and its ministry a biblical view of salvation that overcomes the Greek dichotomy between bodies and souls,[68] situating the work of the black church as an instrument of salvation within the memory of its revolutionary past. The black church has been a central area of concern because Cone sees himself as "first and foremost a black theologian and preacher whose primary commitment is to the black church and community."[69] Hence, while there are continuities between the concerns of black theologians such as Cone for the church and those raised by intellectuals prior to black theology, the emergence of black theology represented a new phenomenon, the emergence of a *critical theological principle* capable of speaking about the church on the terms of a radical reinterpretation of Christian faith. Moreover, it has been the conscientious task of black theologians, given the kerygmatic nature of theological speech, not only to speak *about* the black church but to speak directly *to* the black church, proffering for its consideration a liberationist view of its essential identity.[70]

Yet it is important to see that similarly to Lincoln and interpreters of the black church prior to the rise of black theology, Cone is also negotiating the scandal of the Negro church, that is, the considerable disconnect between the politics of an emerging black ecclesial consciousness and the institutional life of the church from which it emerged. If Lincoln engages it by boldly pronouncing the death of the Negro church, Cone employs the historical imagination in order to ground the black theology movement in the sacred past of the true black church, most clearly embodied within the historical antebellum black church, measuring the faithfulness of the contemporary black church by its essential marks.

THE DERADICALIZATION OF THE BLACK CHURCH

For black theologians, those essential ecclesiological marks of the contemporary black church were blackness and political radicalism. And no one has done more to provide a sustained historical explication of both than Gayraud Wilmore. In his classic work *Black Religion and Black Radicalism*, Wilmore argues that, given the deracination and death of millions of Africans during the Middle Passage and the dehumanizing experience of chattel slavery and oppression in the United States and the Caribbean, black religion has always been, at its core, a radical religion. In this regard, Wilmore would argue, the true black church is a radical church. The centrality of this motif of radicalism, as Wilmore defines it, is cogently stated in the introduction to the first edition:

> Black religion has always concerned itself with the fascination of an incorrigibly religious people with the mystery of God, but it has been equally concerned with the yearning of a despised and subjugated people for freedom—freedom from the religious, economic, social and political domination that whites have exercised over blacks since the beginning of the African slave trade. It is this radical thrust of blacks for human liberation expressed in theological terms and religious institutions that is the defining characteristic of black Christianity and black religion in the United States.[71]

A product of the black theology movement, *Black Religion and Black Radicalism*, like all histories, is as much reflective of the tenor of its time, the political agenda, and historical imagination of the interpreter as of the history it seeks to interpret. In the way that the Deuteronomistic historian's redaction of ancient literary traditions in Israel was informed largely by the questions of a later generation[72] regarding the meaning of faithfulness and covenantal fidelity in their own time, Wilmore's treatment of the historical development of black religion is, in large measure, an effort by a black theologian and historian to apprehend the "God of our weary years" and that God's position in the raging debate about what it means to be black and Christian after the civil rights movement and in the era of the black power movement. Thus, it is not surprising that Wilmore's historiography presupposes, like Cone's, a definition of "radicalism" on the terms of the movement he represents.

While Wilmore, not unlike most black theologians of this era, remained a part of a predominantly white denomination,[73] his aim and agenda were to provide a historical interpretation of black religion and to proffer a black theological perspective that would challenge those who were the heirs to the Independent Black Church Movement. According to Wilmore, this was the first freedom movement among African Americans, and those who were its heirs ought to be more responsive to the urgent cry of young black nationalists. That which falls outside the pale of a revolutionary Christianity, as he and other black theologians defined it, is labeled, in chapter 6 of his book, "The Deradicalization of the Black Church."

Like Cone's sharp distinction between the antebellum black church and the postbellum black church and similar to Lincoln's pronouncement of death, Wilmore's deradicalization thesis also represents an effort to come to terms with the scandal of the Negro church. The scandal which black theologians had to negotiate was the glaring disconnect between the radicalism and black ecclesial consciousness which they claimed as the religious corollary to the secular activism of black power and the more conservative perspective of many pastors within the black churches. Wilmore's thesis accounts for the disconnect on historical terms, grounding contemporary black theology in the sacred memory of earlier forms of black religious resistance to racism and setting the bar for determining the faithfulness of the black church's witness as an instrument of political salvation in the era of black power.

A BLACK ECCLESIOLOGY OF INVOLVEMENT

Although there are sharp differences and debates among J. Deotis Roberts, Cone, and Wilmore regarding the appropriate content of a black theology, Roberts evinces a similar political commitment in his theology[74] and to that extent has also sharply critiqued the black church regarding the depth of its commitment to the gospel of liberation. Echoing a common complaint, he observes that "black churches are often burning up with piety and emotionalism while those who are concerned about social change operate outside the church, believing it is not in the nature of the black church to be where the action is." Reflecting, like Cone and Wilmore, on the historical development of the black church, he argues that it "should have become a revolutionary power for liberation, but with few exceptions it has become a dispenser of spiritual aspirins."[75]

Yet he insists that it is in the very nature of the black church to act as an instrument of liberation from oppression. Thus, he outlines "a black ecclesiology of involvement." It is a methodological response which seeks to engage both the prophetic and priestly dimensions of the black church's radical witness, seeing it as "a chosen people," "a family," and "a body." For Roberts, the biblical import of all of these ecclesiological categories must come into play as the black church, "a pilgrim church," acts as "a socializing agent" on behalf of an oppressed community. As a pilgrim church, marginalized from the American mainstream, its unique vocation is to stand over against the civic religion of white churches, challenging their tendency to conflate patriotism and piety while also extending to them a word of reconciliation. As socializing agent, it must act and provide support for other institutions to act on behalf of the black community in the areas of health, political economy, and the preservation of black culture. For "if the black church is not busy making life more human for black people, it denies its right to be."[76]

Indeed, Cone, Wilmore, Roberts, and Washington would all agree on this point. While there are important debates among them, black theologians have all emphasized a black ecclesiology of involvement which accentuates blackness as the true revelation of Jesus Christ in a racist culture and political liberation as essential to the church's work as an instrument of salvation. In that sense, they recapitulate and recast in theological terms the concerns of an earlier generation of scholars regarding the extent to which the black church was living up to its vocation as an instrument of racial uplift.

Gayraud Wilmore argues, in his landmark text, that during the entire interwar period, black mainline churches retreated into a kind of safe, moralistic piety that offered little in the way of resistance to forces inimical to black humanity.[77] It was in this context that black messiahs such as Father Divine, Daddy Grace, and W. D. Fard emerged, capturing the imagination of the masses. Wilmore argues elsewhere, "It is certain that the ghost of the politically irrelevant, culturally obtuse, and religiously fundamentalistic 'Negro' church of the early twentieth century still haunts the leadership of the black church today."[78]

When one considers the broad spectrum of black Christian witness in North America, before and after the Civil War, manifested in both mainline black churches and among the masses in small sects and large movements from the Azusa Street revival to the civil rights movement, it is indeed this "stormy admixture of diverse responses to oppression and heartfelt yearning for both spiritual and material salvation"[79] that sits at the very heart of the discussion among black theologians and the contested dialogue between black theologians and black pastors over the mission of the black church. Inherent tensions within the dialectical relationship between their respective emphases on individual conversion and social transformation, the liberationist and evangelical dimensions of black faith, have been the crux of the problem. Cecil Cone, the older brother of James Cone, identified this problem as early as 1975 and was the first to treat it in a sustained way. However, in his book *The Identity Crisis in Black Theology*, he places the blame and the onus for addressing the tensions and closing the gap squarely on the shoulders of black theologians.

THE IDENTITY CRISIS IN BLACK THEOLOGY

The Identity Crisis in Black Theology is an important text in which Cecil Cone critiques the work of James Cone, Joseph Washington, and J. Deotis Roberts. His critique of black theologians emerges from his presupposition that black religion (for him, the black church), and nothing else, must serve as the proper point of departure for a black theology. In fact, "there can be no black theology which does not see as its primary focus or starting point the black religion it purports to represent."[80] Thus, owing to black theology's apparent commitment to the ideology of the black power movement, its sharp political emphasis, and its inordinate dependence on norms, sources, and heuristic categories foreign to black religion, Cecil Cone argued that it suffered from an acute crisis in identity.

Cecil Cone, along with Gayraud Wilmore and historian of religion Charles Long,[81] placed more emphasis than James Cone on the role of engaging traditional African religions, as a way of getting at the content and meaning of black faith in America. In contradistinction to James Cone, who was closer to the Frazier side of the Frazier-Herskovits debate,[82] raising doubts about the possibilities of apprehending the content and import of Africanisms in the sacred cosmos of blacks in North America, and who has thus tended to emphasize the American situation (not fully European or African) as the interpretive context for a unique African American faith, Cecil Cone argued that black theology could, indeed it must, engage the content of its African influences.[83]

Moreover, it is a religious worldview centered around an encounter with an almighty and sovereign God, a pervasive idea essential to traditional African societies, reconfigured and reinforced in the slaves' experience of individual conversion. Informed by the coupling of a liberationist and evangelical hermeneutic, the piety and religious experience of the black church, though inextricably connected to the quest for political liberation, cannot be reduced to this single concern.

The latter issues from the former, and both are grounded in the "living reality" of Jesus, "a close companion" and "a fellow sufferer who understands the trials and tribulations of oppressed people."[84] Probing the content of this African-derived worldview, institutionally embodied in the black church and unified as "a continuous tradition of celebration and struggle from slave days to the present time," is, according to Cecil Cone, the unique task of the black theologian.[85]

The Identity Crisis in Black Theology is the first text to raise, in a sustained way, the failure of black theologians to adequately engage the issue of personal salvation and wholeness, the distinctive evangelical piety at the very heart of the black church's faith, in a more serious and integrated way. Cecil Cone describes it as an encounter with and an abiding faith in an almighty and sovereign God. This encounter is initiated in the experience of conversion, celebrated and reaffirmed in worship each week. An essay by James Cone titled "Sanctification and Liberation in the Black Religious Tradition, with Special Reference to Black Worship" endeavors to engage this identity crisis as explicated by Cecil Cone. In that essay, James Cone concedes, "in our effort to show that the gospel is political, we black theologians have sometimes been in danger of reducing black religion to politics and black worship to a political strategy session, thereby distorting the essence of black religion." Observing the critical relationship between sanctification and liberation in black religion and the black church, James Cone identifies six components through which both are ritually celebrated and affirmed within the context of worship. They are preaching, singing, shouting, conversion, prayer, and testimony.[86]

This essay is clearly indicative of James Cone's dialogue with his brother and other black theologians, and it bespeaks the way in which black theologians have continually endeavored to clarify the precise character and mission of the black church. For while maintaining the quest for political freedom as absolutely essential to a proper understanding of the gospel, James Cone acknowledges here the profound way in which *"in the act of worship itself, the experience of liberation becomes a constituent of the community's being. . . . Liberation is not exclusively a political event but also an eschatological happening. It is the power of God's Spirit invading the lives of the people, 'buildin' them* up where they are torn down and proppin' them up on every leanin' side'" (emphasis mine).[87]

James Cone's second two books, *The Spirituals and the Blues* (1972) and *God of the Oppressed* (1975), also represent the evolution of his theological program, as he sought to more firmly situate black theology within the context of the black religious experience he encountered as a youth in the black church.[88] In that regard, it is significant enough to quote the dedication of the latter text: "To Macedonia A.M.E. Church where I first heard shouts of praise to the God of whom I speak and to my brothers, Charles and Cecil, who struggled with me to figure out what all the shouting was about."[89]

With James Cone having been initiated into the privileged world of academic theological reflection and baptized in the hermeneutics of black power, *God of the Oppressed* represents his reimmersion into the formative waters of the black church experience. To his reading publics, the theologian now internationally known confides,

> As a child I could not really understand the meaning and depths of my parent's faith. It was only recently that the profundity of their religious affirmation broke through to me. I realized that they and the others of Macedonia possessed something essential to the very survival of black humanity, and it ought not be dismissed or belittled. *They were in fact providing me with my only possible theological point of departure.* (Emphasis mine)[90]

Thus, recognizing the faith and culture that emerges from the black church as his *only possible theological point of departure*, Cone endeavors to engage its content as expressed in black music, folklore, humor, preaching, and prayer. These raw materials of the black faith and culture are placed in conversation with social theory, Christian theology, Christian ethics, and biblical criticism, as Cone endeavors to speak both rationally and passionately about the God who is always on the side of the oppressed.

He observes that black Christian thought, like its white counterpart, has been shaped by its social context.[91] But unlike whites, the faith of black people was informed by the experience of racial oppression.

This, more than anything else, accounts for the difference between white Christianity and the God of the oppressed. Given these different experiences, Cone argues that "while white preachers and theologians often defined Jesus Christ as a spiritual Savior, the deliverer of people from sin and guilt, black preachers were unquestionably historical. They view God as the Liberator in history. That was why black preachers were involved in the abolitionist movement in the nineteenth century and the civil rights movement in the twentieth."[92]

BLACK CHRISTIAN NATIONALISM

None of the pioneers in black theology was more suspicious and more deeply alienated from the piety and proclamation of black churches than Albert Cleage (Jaramogi Abebe Agyeman). A Detroit pastor in the United Church of Christ at the height of that city's urban uprisings, the more Cleage became involved with the urban poor and with young black power activists, the more he became disconcerted with the black church. Frustrated, as a black pastor involved in the black theology movement, by the extent to which the black church was still, in his estimation, a "Negro church," he too had to respond to the disconnect between his own politics of blackness and the politics of the churches located in the heart of the urban ghetto and at the center of black life. For him, the churches were very much a part of the problem. Accordingly, he observes, "In Harlem half a million Black people crowd into thousands of little churches every Sunday and nothing is done to change the Black man's condition in New York City. The ineffectiveness of the Black church is reflected in the condition of Harlem. The black church could change Harlem any day it offered Black people leadership here on earth by bringing black people together."[93]

No doubt, it was Cleage's faith in the leadership potential of a new and radical black church for "bringing black people together" that caused him to found the Shrine of the Black Madonna, positing black Christian nationalism as the antidote to the individualistic soteriology of "black preachers . . . standing up on Sunday morning taking people to heaven one by one."[94] If the interpretive work of Cone, Wilmore, and Lincoln can be characterized as varying *methodological* responses to the scandal of the Negro church, Albert Cleage's black Christian nationalism represents a response in *radical pastoral praxis*.

But unlike Cone, Wilmore, and others, Cleage makes no distinction between the black church of the nineteenth century and the church which became "deradicalized," as it were, some time after Reconstruction. For this black Christian nationalist, the black church, during and after slavery, was primarily a barrier to black liberation. In this regard, he makes no significant distinction between the faith perspective of the slaves and that of the slaveholders. Because Cleage's critique of Christian orthodoxy was more severe, he saw "Slave Christianity" as the tragic participant in a religion that had been utterly distorted by Paul and the Christian West. In Cleage's view, Slave Christianity was essentially a "survival instrument" which kept black people sane but precluded the possibility of organizing a united front for liberation.[95] Completely absent from his perspective is any sense of the clandestine power and counterworldly consciousness of the invisible institution or the revolutionary spirit of the independent black church movement.

Yet he saw in the black church the locus of black people's best hope for liberation. To young black militants who were completely alienated from Christianity and had given up on the church, Cleage rejoined, "Christianity belongs to us. We are not going to give it up just because white people have messed it up."[96] Instead what was needed was a total restructuring of everything in the church, including its historical analysis, biblical interpretation, worship, rituals, preaching, and praxis. The chief aim of this complete overhaul of the church's perspective was to completely undermine the evangelical side of black Christianity which emphasizes individual conversion and, in Cleage's view, "a petty morality too trivial for God's concern."[97] All of this was a kind of escapism which undermined the revolutionary potential of black churches, with very few exceptions,[98] throughout their entire history. Thus, attempting to chart new directions for the black church, Cleage posits a revolutionary exegesis of the biblical witness, organically connecting it to a program of black Christian nationalism.

Cleage sees Jesus as the revolutionary leader of the Zealot movement,[99] following the death of John the Baptist, and understands the mission of the black church as that of calling together the "Black Nation Israel" for collective struggle against oppression.[100] Accordingly, he totally rejects the Pauline portions of the New Testament. For Paul, in his day, was analogous to an "uncle Tom" who was more concerned about his Roman citizenship than the liberation of the black Nation Israel.[101] Because of this, Paul distorted the revolutionary message of Jesus, and from him comes the basis of the antirevolutionary message of Christian faith.[102]

Thus, in order for the black church to truly understand its mission, it must focus on the "tribal ethic" of Jesus. In this way, the teachings of Jesus regarding love were intended to articulate a form of self-love among members of the black Nation Israel falsely universalized by the Apostle Paul.[103] Cleage seems to be responding, at this juncture, to the theology of the black church as embodied in King. Rather than King's emphasis on loving the enemy, black people must learn instead to love themselves, as Malcolm X had taught and Stokely Carmichael and others were presently teaching. Moreover, they must discover the power of their collective struggle and destiny as a nation. The roots of this new black Christian nationalism are old. They are to be found amid the myths of the Old Testament, in the revolutionary teachings of Jesus, and in the contemporary movement for freedom.

What is important for our purposes here is to see the way in which Cleage's program of black Christian nationalism comes from yet another black theologian and pastor who had high expectations for the black church, endeavoring to provide a radical corrective to its evangelical theology and a refocusing of its institutional commitments. Clearly, at issue for him was both the black church's understanding of its mission, focused on individual conversion and its understanding of its meaning inasmuch it is a separatist institution that has not typically emphasized black nationalism as the cornerstone of its justice-seeking tradition. In this way, black Christian nationalism is Cleage's effort to challenge the church which Lincoln claimed had already "died an agonized death in the harsh turmoil that tried the faith so rigorously in the decade of the 'Savage Sixties.'" Operating primarily in the arena of the academy, Cone and other black theologians posit radical methodological responses to this problem. On the other hand, Cleage, working from within the institutional life of his own nationalistic black church movement, offers a response in radical pastoral praxis.

It is ironic that although Cleage operates from within the church rather than the academy, his perspective represents the most radical perspective among the black theologians, with perhaps the exception of William R. Jones.[104] In fact, Cleage ruefully refers to his "very good friend" James Cone as "our apostle to the Gentiles" who "drags white Christians as far as they are able to go (and then some)."[105] Cleage's colleagues shared his core convictions regarding the liberationist intent of the gospel. But they disagreed with his conclusions. Indeed, his theological conclusions coupled with the sectarian ecclesiology of the Shrine of the Black Madonna, centered exclusively around his leadership, undermined prospects for his having a widespread impact on ecumenical black Christianity. Yet his work is very significant inasmuch as it represents a creative and sustained effort to develop a means through which black theology could live, move, and have its being within the institutional life of black congregations. That is an ongoing struggle addressed also by black theologians of the second generation.

Second-Generation Black Theologians

SECOND-GENERATION BLACK theologian Dwight Hopkins outlines, in the third chapter of his survey of black theology titled *Introducing Black Theology of Liberation*, what he sees as the major challenges to be met by black theologians at the turn of the twenty-first century. Hopkins suggests that, building on the groundwork laid by the first generation, the new generation of black and womanist theologians must (1) maintain a clear focus on the poor as the crucial link which ties all academic and disciplinary concerns together, (2) "assure that intellectual work remains in service to the church and the community," (3) develop sophisticated theoretical frameworks capable of grounding black theology in historical black experience while creatively exploring its contemporary meaning and connection to the struggles of the world's poor, (4) identify the "passions of resistance" among poor people today and the places where they most acutely experience the

brokenness of human relationships, (5) conduct prolonged and organized conversation and praxis between womanists and black male
theologians, and (6) "build and evaluate models of basic Christian
communities in local areas."[106] Furthermore, he suggests that the conversation regarding the meaning of black liberation theology must
take place at three different levels. Academics at the graduate and
undergraduate levels constitute one audience. The second audience is
black clergy engaged in pastoral ministry. The third audience is made
up of the masses of ordinary, poor and working-class black people.
"The challenge," Hopkins suggests, "is to speak on three levels with
an emphasis on the third audience."[107]

An examination of the field of second-generation black theologians and womanist theologians suggests widespread agreement
among them regarding the need to speak on all three levels with an
emphasis on addressing the prophetic concerns of black theology to
the churches and the larger community. However, the methods for
doing so, as well as the theological content and thematic emphases,
vary among second-generation black theologians, just as was the case
among first-generation black theologians. All generally agree regarding the continuing cultural primacy of the black church as the oldest
and most indigenous institution within the African American community. Yet the manner in which it figures in the theological imagination
of black theologians as interpreters of black religious experience var-
ies from theologian to theologian.

Hopkins, for his part, along with George Cummings, has emphasized a hermeneutic that focuses on the wisdom of slave religion
and the cultural insights and lessons of the poor black masses in the
development of a self-conscious, constructive theological statement
regarding black liberation.[108] Hopkins's methodological approach to
addressing himself as a black theologian to the church and the community stems from the conviction that "if black theology remains
accountable to the Good News for oppressed people and recognizable to the African American folk, then it must be indigenous to the
folk's faith." As a systematic theology, its task is to provide the critical
means for holding a faith community accountable to its commitment
to divine freedom "in new situations and for new generations." As a

theology sourced by the "cultural strands found in the fabric of black North American life," black theology equips the faith of black people with "shoes that fit" in their trek toward liberation.[109]

Hopkins's *Down, Up, and Over: Slave Religion and Black Theology* provides the most elaborate development of this basic thesis put forth in his earlier work. In it he argues that "essentially, African and African Americans sowed the seeds for a systematic black theology by synthesizing a reinterpreted Christianity, everyday common sense wisdom, and remnants from West African indigenous religions."[110] Proceeding from that premise, his work, like that of first-generation black theologians James Cone and Gayraud Wilmore, situates the radical thesis of black theology within the larger narrative of black religious resistance, both inside and outside the black church. Moreover, by underscoring the folk wisdom of the masses as a primary source, he too offers a methodological response to the charge of an identity crisis in the discipline first raised in a sustained way by Cecil Cone. Calling on the black church to struggle more diligently and intentionally for liberation, he endeavors to incorporate the masses' unsystematic coconstitution of the black self, particularly as evinced in the religion of black slaves, into a systematic theology of liberation, focusing on the doctrines of God, Jesus, and human purpose.

In an interesting shift, some newer voices in the discipline of black theology are advising a second look at some of the classical, premodern figures in Christian theology as a means of disentangling Christian orthodoxy from the ideology and heresy of whiteness, "the core theological problem of our times," calling on the likes of Irenaeus, Gregory of Nyssa, and Maximus the Confessor as unlikely cohorts in the apprehension of an antiracist appropriation of Christian faith.[111] A primary interlocutor among these new voices is J. Kameron Carter, who identifies the racial imagination of modernity as a product, in large measure, of Christian theology.

Carter argues that the depth of the problem is to be seen in the wrongheadedness of Western Christianity's effort to dissociate itself from the Jewish body of Jesus. Crafting a "rational" discourse that envisages the embodied particularity of Jewishness as inherently problematical and whiteness as somehow transcendent of difference itself, white supremacy emerged, in effect, as "a replacement doctrine of creation," justifying colonial conquest from the fifteenth century onward.[112] In this way, Carter situates the problem of racism along a continuum of other heresies such as Gnosticism, raising in the conversation the volume of these marginalized Christian voices, such as that of Irenaeus, the "anti-Gnostic intellectual," and Gregory of Nyssa, who, though he could not have imagined in the fourth century the distinctive character and brutal nuances of American chattel slavery, was in fact an "abolitionist intellectual" who vociferously opposed slavery as he knew it.

Yet Anthony Pinn—whose work extends, in some sense, the sharp theodical emphasis of William R. Jones[113] and Charles Long's non-Christocentric approach to black religious experience[114]—in his book *Varieties of African American Religious Experience*[115] cautions against what he perceives as black theology's unwarranted and unwise relegation of itself to the normative gaze of Christian faith, its doctrinal categories, and its churches. To be sure, he observes that Christian faith and its churches are clearly a major sector within the complex matrix of black religious experience. But he objects to the methodological tendency to marginalize or co-opt other traditions, theistic and nontheistic, before and after the Second Great Awakening, for the sake of a master narrative whose sharp Christian focus and church-centered bias assumes the path of least resistance. Pinn notes that "prior to the aggressive introduction of slaves to Christianity during the Great Awakening revivals, there was a roughly one-hundred-year period during which complex African traditions could have taken root." In his continuing project of providing a corrective to a discipline that he suggests "has considered the church its sole conversation partner,"[116] Pinn endeavors to extend the canon of black theological reflection into a deeper theological engagement of such traditions as Yoruba, Vodou, Santeria, Islam, and black humanism, on the terms of the traditions themselves.

But while Dennis Wiley and James H. Harris, in all likelihood, would not take issue with Pinn's focus on the varieties of black religious experience, as it helps to complete the picture of the sundry, subtle, and secret ways in which black people have had to struggle against systemic evil arrayed against their humanity, they would not agree at all that the discipline of black theology "has considered the church its sole conversation partner." Neither would I. Like Wiley and Harris, respectively trained by black theologians James Cone and J. Deotis Roberts and actively serving in pastoral ministry, I would argue that black theology's most consistent conversation partner has not been the black church or the black mosque but the white academy.

Dennis Wiley, who received the doctor of philosophy degree in systematic theology under the tutelage of James Cone and now serves as copastor of Washington, D.C.'s Covenant Baptist Church, says, "My primary concern is not so much the survival of black theology, or even the survival of the black church, as it is the survival and liberation of black people."[117] However, he is committed both to black theology and the black church because, as he says,

> the black church is the key to the salvation and liberation of the African-American community, and black theology is the key to the survival and power of the black church. Whereas the black church is "the spiritual face of the black community," black theology is that which seeks to guarantee the integrity of the black church's vertical relationship with God as well as the integrity of its horizontal relationship with the African-American community. . . . Without black theology, the black church will crumble, and without the black church, the African-American community will be destroyed, from within as well as from without.[118]

In this regard, Wiley questions James Cone's suggestion that during the 1970s black theology, as part of its third stage of development, returned to the black church. He asks, "In what sense did it return? Just how complete was its return, and where is the evidence? Upon its return, did it remain, or did it leave once again? In essence, was black theology graciously welcomed home to the black church like the prodigal son, or was it left standing outside, knocking at the door?"[119] Wiley encourages black theology to complete its return to the black church, affirming the church's historical mission and identity but refusing to withhold its critique. Such is the key to an "internal propheticism"[120]

that would challenge the powers of domination and oppression outside and inside the black church and the black community.

But three years prior to Wiley, James Harris had already urged black
theologians to consider more seriously the need to bridge the gap
between the reflections of academic theologians and the work of the
black church. Harris serves as professor of pastoral theology at Virginia Union University and senior minister of Second Baptist Church
in Richmond, Virginia.[121] Thus, moving daily between Jerusalem
and Athens, he has been rather strident in his critique of black theology's alienation from the church. He and Gayraud Wilmore have had
some interesting exchanges and lively debates on this issue.[122] Also, he
writes in his book *Pastoral Theology: A Black-Church Perspective*,

> James Cone's statement that black theology is not academic theology
> is more myth than reality because outside the halls of academia, black
> liberation theology seems to be more foreign to the black community
> than evangelical theology. How can it be anything other than academic
> if only the academicians are discussing it and writing about it? . . . Black
> theology will have meaning and power when the masses of blacks
> begin to accept and practice it. This is not going to happen unless there
> is a conscious and systematic approach developed to gradually infuse
> the church with the concepts of liberation.[123]

Harris is particularly concerned that if the theological method of
black and womanist theologians does not provide a bridge between
liberationist God-talk and the practice of ministry, increasing numbers of black churches will become little more than poor facsimiles
of white evangelicalism.[124] In addressing this problem, he proffers,
in another work, the concept of "liberation preaching." "Liberation
preaching is preaching that is transformational. This means that it
is intended to effect change in the nature and structure of persons
and society."[125]

Forrest E. Harris, director of the Kelly Miller Smith Institute on
the Black Church at the Divinity School of Vanderbilt University and
president of American Baptist College of Nashville, Tennessee, has
also recognized this enduring problem. Thus, under the auspices of

the Kelly Miller Smith Institute, named in memory of the NCBC's last president, Harris brought together theologians and pastors for dialogue between pulpit, pew, and academy on the question which black theologians raised decades ago: "What does it mean to be black and Christian?"[126]

Indeed, it is the relationship between one's understanding of the meaning of blackness and the meaning of the gospel, as well as the tensions between Christian proclamation that focuses on individual salvation and that which engages social transformation, that sits at the heart of the rub between black theologians and black pastors regarding the church's essential work as salvation's instrument. We will see this even more clearly as we engage, in the next chapter, the reflections of black pastors who have provided some written record of their perspective on black theology and its challenge to black churches.

Some black pastors, particularly during the era of the NCBC, have been among black theology's staunchest advocates. One can say that they have been conscientized by the liberationist vision of the civil rights movement and have embraced the systematic project of black theology as the third and fourth steps in a developmental process of black Christian resistance to racism. Following the era of the NCBC, Dennis Wiley and James H. Harris, who have been very intentional about organically incorporating the liberationist and self-critical principles of black theology into their respective pastoral ministries, are just two examples of pastors who would fall into that category.[127] So if they are concerned to address what they perceive as a considerable divide between the academic work of black and womanist theologians and the pastoral praxis of black pastors, it is clearly because, as students of the black theologians, they know firsthand that the discipline has a great deal to offer the churches.

A Critical and Self-Conscious Theological Principle

BLACK THEOLOGY PROVIDED, for the first time in black church history, something that was definitely needed: *a critical and self-conscious theological principle* for speaking about black faith on its own terms. Such a principle aims to hold the churches to the radical demands of the gospel while reminding them of their own liberationist heritage. Black theology is, in that sense, both continuous and discontinuous with the work of earlier generations of black scholars who endeavored to address their critical work to the institutional life of the churches in relation to the goals of racial uplift and civil rights militancy. It is continuous with their work inasmuch as it too has inherited a generalized communal sensibility that assumes that any institution so central to black life is obliged to address itself to the liberation and holistic redemption of black lives. Moreover, as an intellectual discipline, black theology carries with it what Gayraud Wilmore has aptly identified, in retrospect, as "a basic distrust of folk religion [and] the institutional black church."[128]

Yet black theology is discontinuous with the work of earlier generations of black interpreters of the black church because it is, as theology should be, a critical church discipline. As a servant of the community of faith, its critical task is to examine the faith, but from within the circle of faith itself. In the case of black theology, such a disciplinary stance served a distinctive and unprecedented role in the history of black church interpretation. It provided an answer to the previous conundrum of either accepting uncritically the racialized theological norms of white Christianity or being limited in one's investigation to a materialist and functionalist approach to black church interpretation that diminishes or dismisses theology and, by extension, the internal tension between the pietistic/spiritual dimensions of faith, its dogmatic assumptions, and its social manifestations.

Given the history of slavery and segregation in America and the white churches' complicity and participation therein, the problem with the former alternative is obvious. But the latter approach, in isolation, is also problematic. For the relationship between the theological infrastructure of a faith community and its social manifestations is circular, each influencing the other. Sociology influences theology, and theology influences sociology. Thus, the sociological studies that dominated black church interpretation for much of the twentieth century only got at part of the equation as one tries to evaluate the why and the how of the black church's participation in and response to social phenomena. Owing to the investigative parameters of the secular disciplines, the question of the true meaning of Christian faith could never be central to the sociological analysis of a Gunnar Myrdal or a St. Clair Drake or to the social agenda of racial uplift represented by black scholars such as Du Bois and Frazier. That is a concern to be addressed by theology.

Thus, following the conscientizing work of King's ministry and the activism of the civil rights movement, what the black church needed, in addition to this earlier scholarship, was a critical theological principle by which it could judge its faithfulness to its own best self-understanding in the light of the biblical witness and as seen through the prism of its own history. Black theology, sourced by the hermeneutical insights of slaves who rejected a truncated understanding of the meaning of divine salvation and conscientized by the radical ecclesiological implications of a church-led civil rights movement, provided that.

Yet what black theologians and pastors such as Wiley, Harris, and I have agonized over is the question of how best to incorporate into the institutional practices of black churches this critical theological principle, a fourth step that represents a self-conscious break with an uncritical white Christianity, extending the liberationist legacy of black churches to its logical conclusion as witness against the unconscious missionary zeal and unrepentant apostasy of the Christian West. Some black theologians situated within the academy have been asking the same question. In *We Have Been Believers: An African American Systematic Theology*, James H. Evans states the matter plainly:

> It would not be an exaggeration to say that the leadership of many black congregations, large and small, and the ranks of professional black theologians have looked on one another with caution and, at times, suspicion. This has resulted in a chasm in the black religious community between the theology and practice of Christian faith, leaving the churches with a religion that appears to be no more than a cultural performance, and the theologians with a theology that seems to consist only of abstract concepts. The question, then, is "How can the dialogue between professional black theologians and other members of the African American churches be strengthened so that it becomes

clear that black theology is rooted in the faith of the church and that
the faith of the church is given intellectual clarity and expression in
black theology?"[129]

"How indeed?" is a question central to this much-needed discussion.
For as we shall see, some black pastors have incorporated what I am
calling the third moment inasmuch as they embrace in principle and
praxis the liberationist tendency in black faith most clearly embodied
in the ministry of Martin King. Yet, like King, they struggle with the
notion of blackness as defined by the black power movement and, notwithstanding James Cone's principled theological reflections on the
Black Christ, have not necessarily embraced blackness as a *theological*
symbol. Moreover, they have not given much thought to what might
be *theologically distinctive* about a faith that resisted slavery and segregation in a putatively Christian nation, ultimately giving rise to the
civil rights movement, and the meaning of that faith for the doctrine
of all churches, black and white.

Sadly, some other pastors and denominational leaders, steeped in
the most conservative expressions of evangelical faith, have embraced
neither the liberationist impulse of the third moment nor its more
radical and self-conscious implications as carried out in the fourth
moment, the systematic project of black theology. If pastors such as
Dennis Wiley and James Harris are representative of those on the radical side of this four-step continuum, pastors and denominational leaders such as the renowned Joseph H. Jackson, for nearly three decades
the leader of the largest black denomination, have been on its most
conservative and reactionary side. Still, both of these sharply divergent perspectives and those in between not only explain the difficult
dialogue and disconnect that often exists between black theology and
the black church but underscore the continuing tensions between the
evangelical pietistic and political liberationist dimensions within black
church culture.

4

BLACK PASTORS ON THE MISSION
OF THE BLACK CHURCH

The Need for Dialogue

IN THE COMPLEX historical narrative of black religion in America, the emergence of black theology represented a new moment—a fourth moment—in the development of an antiracist and holistically salvific appropriation of Christian faith. Drawing insight from both the strengths and limitations of the preceding three, this new moment was an important turning point, characterized by the formation of *a critical and self-conscious theological principle.* Informed by it, the black church could evaluate, in view of its own distinctive history and witness, its continuing faithfulness to the work of divine liberation. We have shown that notwithstanding important differences between the distinctive steps that each moment represents, they are formed by an essential subterranean unity, as African American Christians have wrestled through the complex dilemma and double-consciousness of a faith that is both unmistakably evangelical and profoundly radical.

To be sure, this dilemma sits at the heart of Christian faith itself, particularly within the American context.[1] Moreover, it animates the debate among black theologians and black pastors regarding the essential mission of the church. A brief repartee between black theologian Gayraud Wilmore and Emmanuel McCall, who represents the conservative wing of black evangelical thought, throws into bold relief theological tensions that sometimes rupture into a divide. Relative to the true meaning of black faith, it is clear that each side thinks that the other suffers from an identity crisis. This is why McCall opines that by no means does black theology "represent the thinking and attitudes of the 'rank and file.'"[2] Wilmore rejoins that if McCall is correct, it is not because black theology is

> obscure, unbiblical, or has no doctrine of the Church, but because the majority of Black preachers confuse themselves with Billy Graham and the most unenlightened versions of White evangelicalism. *Because they do not know the rock from which they were hewn*, they and their people do not know who they are and the inheritance that was passed on to them by men like Benjamin Tucker Tanner, William W. Colley, and Alexander Walters. Because *their sense of sin is personal and individualistic they have an understanding of redemption that cannot admit the sanctification of secular conflict and struggle*. Because they are willing to accept what [C. Eric] Lincoln calls "Americanity" as normative Christianity, they are unable to see how their own ethnic experience in the United States authenticates the truth of God's revelation in Scripture and how the gospel then illuminates and gives meaning to *the most profound symbol of that experience—the symbol of Blackness*. (Emphases mine)[3]

Indeed, as Wilmore references the determinative power of one's view of sin and understanding of redemption in a postmodern world characterized by conflict and struggle as the interpretive key, he places his finger squarely on the rub that often divides black theologians and black pastors regarding the work of the church as an instrument of salvation. If it is the case, as Wilmore suggests, that "the majority of black pastors confuse themselves with Billy Graham . . . and cannot admit the sanctification of secular conflict," it is because they have not fully integrated the *theological* implications of the third moment, the civil rights movement, into their doctrine of the church. Indeed, it is quite possible to evince an appreciation for the political significance of the civil rights movement as an *extraordinary historical moment*, in which the black church acted as an instrument of social transformation, without reflecting deeply or embracing fully the radical implications of that moment for the churches' self-understanding and sense of mission *at all times*. This is why many in the black church have celebrated the liberationist vocation and political effectiveness of Martin

Luther King, Jr., but do not necessarily see liberation, as did King, as the church's primary vocation, indeed its very raison d'être.

On the other hand, there are pastors who have indeed embraced a Kingian liberationist understanding of the gospel but have not responded in the same way to black theology. In that sense, they have embraced the third moment but not the fourth. Or they have not been clear about how one relates to the other. In each case, it seems to me that what is still most urgently needed is sustained theological dialogue between theologians and pastors regarding the nature of the church's mission and its public role as an instrument of salvation in a world of sin, brokenness, and injustice.

Herbert Edwards, who lent his expertise as a social ethicist in the early development of black theology,[4] identified this as a critical issue as early as 1975. In an article titled "Black Theology: Retrospect and Prospect," he avers, "Black Theology finds itself today in the rather unenviable position of having gained the somewhat positive attention of some European theologians, remaining a frightening enigma to most white American Protestant theologians, and still being largely ignored by the Black churches of the masses."[5] But reflecting on that same period (1970–1976), even Gayraud Wilmore, who often warned his academic colleagues of the need for black theology to remain in dialogue with the black church and accountable primarily to its people, had this to say:

> Today I see more clearly than I did ten years ago that an elitist guild was premature and a strategic error on our part. While it was inevitable that black scholars would want to "credentialize" a theological perspective that was misunderstood if not maligned in the predominantly white seminaries, it was both unnecessary and contrary to the best interests of black theology to turn the movement over to professional theologians who had one eye on their latest books and the other on the tenure track. We were back into the academic gamesmanship of the Joseph Washington days when it was deemed important that white colleagues understood that we were sufficiently knowledgeable of Western philosophy and theology for our black God-talk to be taken seriously. . . . This is not to deny the significance of the work of the

Society for the Study of Black Religion, but by its very nature it could not supply the critical mass of grassroots participation without which the movement would dissolve into a circle of elite theoreticians.[6]

The clergy who were involved with the early development of black theology as a *public* theology[7] tended, like Wilmore, to be well-educated;[8] most were members of white denominations, and most were active in the NCBC. But with the decline of the black power movement, as the institutional embodiment of black theology shifted from the activist National Conference of Black Churchmen (founded 1966) to the academic Society for the Study of Black Religion (founded 1970), and with the short life span of the Black Theology Project, active clerical leadership ceased to be a significant part of the black theology movement, pastors became marginal to the dialogue, and over several years the paucity of sustained conversation between black theologians and black pastors regarding the future of the black church's ministry has been a continuing problem.[9]

Opposing Pastoral Views on Blackness

THUS, AS A way of contributing to the renewal of what I see as an urgent and critical conversation between pastors and academic theologians, I want to discuss, in view of the emergence and development of black theology, the varying perspectives of black pastors who have explicitly addressed the subject of black theology in their writings. As they address themselves in varying ways to black theology's theme of liberation *and* its symbol of blackness, their views underscore the complex relationship between the civil rights movement and the black theology movement—moments within the history of the black church that are integrally related yet distinctive in their contribution to the continuing conversation regarding an appropriate Christian response to racism, America's original sin. Our discussion of the historical development of black faith, along four distinctive moments, provides a heuristic framework for understanding the inextricable relationship and similarities. But it also underscores the differences.

Indeed, the differences between these last two moments are important because they help to account for the respective differences in the way in which some black pastors have responded to them. The writings of the clergy show that some black clergy have accepted, in their thinking and praxis, the basic tenets of the civil rights movement but reject or are ambivalent toward black theology. In large measure, the difference in response can be accounted for through some combination of the following issues: (1) the latter movement's sharp emphasis on the theological significance of *blackness*, (2) its sophisticated ethic and biblical hermeneutics on violence (self-defense), given the pervasive presence of violence (e.g., as state-sanctioned force) for maintaining the social structure,[10] and (3) the extent to which clergy may view the civil rights movement as an extraordinary moment in American history and black church history but have not considered its larger implications for the development and pursuit of a self-conscious theology of liberation or its radical character as a key to their doctrine of the church.

Yet the voices of other black pastors, both during the period of nascent black theology and during its second generation, show the way in which they have either accepted or abandoned both moments wholesale. If the former represent the radical spirit of the black church, I submit that the latter embody what Gayraud Wilmore calls "the ghost of the culturally irrelevant, fundamentalistic 'negro church.'"[11] Yet their respective voices show how piety and protest both complement and compete with each other in the faith of the black church and its pastoral leadership. A comparison between the opposing pastoral views of Joseph A. Johnson and Joseph H. Jackson on the claims of black theology is instructive on this point.

Contemporaries during the civil rights movement and the nascence period of black theology, both were accomplished churchmen and leaders at the highest ecclesiastical level within their respective denominations. Joseph A. Johnson, presiding bishop in the Christian Methodist Episcopal Church who, as a pastor, had previously served as vice president of the Nashville affiliate of King's Southern Christian Leadership Conference, became one of black theology's staunchest advocates.[12] Relatively early in its development, he articulated for clergy "the need for a black Christian theology."[13] Black theology's critical task, as he saw it, was the "detheologization" of black minds, a systematic process of supplanting the Jesus of Western imperialism, slavery, colonialism, and neocolonialism with a "quest for the black Jesus."[14] On the other hand, Joseph H. Jackson, the president of the National Baptist Convention, then the largest black denomination, rejected black theology just as he had rejected the activist ministry of Martin Luther King, Jr., disavowing Kingian principles of civil disobedience as an appropriate Christian response *and* Cone's focus on blackness as an appropriate theological response to the problem of racism within the American context.[15] If Johnson saw black theology's emphasis on blackness as part of a necessary process of "detheologization," Jackson decried it as "a theology of polarization."[16] Johnson and Jackson are helpful points of departure for apprehending how the leadership of the black church has responded to black theology. Indeed, like them, the varying perspectives of other pastors regarding the true mission of the church can be best understood in relationship to the civil rights movement and the black theology movement, and their positions can be located somewhere along the continuum between the opposing views of these two towering black denominational figures.

BLACKNESS AS "DETHEOLOGIZATION"

When elected on January 15, 1958, to serve as vice president of NCLC, an affiliate of SCLC under the presidency of Kelly Miller Smith,[17] Joseph Johnson was serving as pastor of the Capers Memorial CME Church. At the time, he was completing his second doctorate degree, a Ph.D. in New Testament at the Divinity School of Vanderbilt University, having been admitted as its first African American student in 1955.[18] James Lawson, who was to play a pivotal role in the Nashville movement, joined Johnson as his Vanderbilt classmate in the fall of 1958, and Nashville became a cauldron for student activism.[19]

But Johnson, who moved to Atlanta in 1960 to teach at the Interdenominational Theological Center (ITC), came to see himself less as an activist and more as a theologian of the movement, endeavoring to use his considerable training as an interpreter of the liberationist gospel of African American experience. In 1977, Johnson relayed to his colleagues in the College of Bishops a revelation experience that had come to him on February 24, 1976, in which he was reminded by Jesus Christ of his "special commission and assignment" to (1) "preach the gospel," (2) "devote [his] talents to a writing ministry," (3) "care for the churches," and (4) "write about Him."[20]

Indeed, Johnson's influential essay "Jesus, the Liberator" represents his effort to dismantle a distorted "Jesus [who] has been too identified with the oppressive structures and forces of the prevailing society"[21] and to "write about Him" who is actively engaged in the struggles of the black poor. At the time of the writing of this essay, Johnson was serving, along with Preston Williams, as cochair of the Theological Commission of the NCBC. The essay (originally a sermon) appears in *Quest for a Black Theology*, a collection of lectures given at a conference at Georgetown University, the aim of which was to determine the character and content of a black theology that all of the participants agreed was already aborning.[22]

Observing that "white theology is severely limited in its interpretation of the Christian faith insofar as the non-white peoples of the world are concerned," Johnson argues for a new christology that engages the black experience. White theologians, blinded by their own cultural narcissism and racist assumptions about God, had never imagined "Jesus walking the dark streets of the ghettos of the North and the sharecropper's farm in the Deep South without a job, busted and emasculated. These white theologians could never hear the voice of Jesus speaking in the dialect of Blacks of the ghetto."[23] The bishop's christological assertions are reminiscent of Cone's in his landmark text *Black Theology and Black Power*: speaking of the Black Christ, Cone says,

> He meets the blacks where they are and becomes one of them. We see him there with his black face and big black hands lounging on a street corner. . . . For whites to find him with big lips and kinky hair is as offensive as it was for the Pharisees to find him partying with tax-collectors. But whether whites want to hear it or not, Christ is black, baby, with all of the features which are so detestable to white society.[24]

Reflecting on "the white Christ of the white church establishment," whose teachings are "used to justify wars, exploitation, segregation, discrimination, prejudice, and racism," and identifying this Christ as "the enemy of the black man," Johnson, a trained academic theologian and scholar of the New Testament, commends a conscientious "Quest for the Black Jesus."[25] If Rudolf Bultmann set out to demythologize the New Testament, Johnson suggests that the black theologian and preacher must detheologize black minds of racist interpretations of the meaning of the revelation of Jesus Christ in history. Accordingly, Johnson commends a conscientious project of christological deconstruction aimed at "a recovery of the humanity of Jesus."[26]

But unlike earlier Euro-American quests for the historical Jesus, this one was embarked on not in response to modernity and modern historical criticism but in response to a Western theological tradition that aided and abetted the co-optation of an oppressed, Palestinian Jew for the purposes of political domination. It is in this very different sense that a new form of demythologization was under way, so as to disentangle the *historical Jesus* from the *white Christ* of a distorted faith. A liberationist faith and mission demanded that the black church be reintroduced to the historical Jesus, who like "most of the world's babies are not born in the palaces of kings or the government houses of prime ministers, or the manses of bishops . . . [but] in the ghettos of corrupt cities, in mud houses, in disintegrated cottages with cracked floors and stuffed walls where the muffled cries of unattended mothers mingle with the screams of newborn infants."[27]

Having been fully immersed in the evangelical, liberal, and neoorthodox traditions of white theology but then baptized within the ethos of civil rights militancy and black consciousness, Johnson, the churchman and denominational leader, could no longer imagine how black churches could think that the God-talk of white theologians could adequately address the condition of black people or the transformative mission of the black church. But if Johnson could see and explicate "the need for a black Christian theology" as a necessary form of "detheologization," Joseph H. Jackson, the president of the National Baptist Convention USA, who was writing during the same period, saw it as "a theology of polarization."[28]

BLACKNESS AS "A THEOLOGY OF POLARIZATION"

Responding to James Cone's second book, Jackson, the autocratic leader of the denomination, placed into the record of its ninety-first annual session what he designated "The Basic Theological Position of the National Baptist Convention, U.S.A., Inc." While Jackson identifies his statement as the official position of the denomination, one might caution against taking that assertion at face value. For the history of the National Baptist Convention, characterized by intense infighting and Jackson's own autocratic leadership style, would mitigate against the simplistic assumption that he is simply echoing the sentiments of all the pastors in the convention. Yet his perspective is important inasmuch as he was the president of the largest black denomination and he does echo a perspective and theological sensibility held by many black pastors other than himself.

The heart of Jackson's rejoinder to black theology is his interpretation of a New Testament text cited at the beginning of the document and used consistently in his response to black theology in other places. "God is a spirit; and they that worship Him must worship Him in spirit and in truth" (John 4:24). The hermeneutical inference is that while black churches and black denominations, including his own, have been, because of history, black-separatist institutions in a white-supremacist context, their mission and meaning point beyond race to a race-neutral understanding of the gospel.

This is why he can call Cone's work "brilliant" while insisting that its "outstanding weakness" is the effort "to reduce all of the great historic theological truths of the Christian religion, to the historic conflict between blacks and whites."[29] In this way, it is the theological scandal of particularity and the ethical question of how black churches ought to respond to the thorny contradictions of ecclesial identity in a race-conscious society that is the source of the rub. In that regard, Jackson echoes a common theme in the black church when he says that "there is no revealed truth that teaches us that God is white or black. God is a spirit. National Baptists was founded and organized by Negro Christian leaders, and they themselves refused to restrict their message to their own race and their own nationality." Misreading black theology,

Jackson argues that National Baptists "have not written a creed of exclusiveness against other races or nationalities. What we say against white segregationists by the gospel of Christ we must also say against members of our own race who insist on interpreting the gospel of Christ on a strictly anti-white and pro-black foundation."[30]

In this way, Jackson clearly reads black theology as a narrow and negative reaction against the racist ecclesiology of white churches and the patronizing assumptions of white interpreters of black religion in America. For him, black theology is therefore inconsistent with the meaning and mission of the black church. In his book-length treatment of the history of the largest of the black denominations, *A Story of Christian Activism: The History of the National Baptist Convention, U.S.A., Inc.*, he addresses the matter in this way:

> Just as we have often been victimized by the white historian who refuses to acknowledge our existence so also we have been misunderstood by those among our own people who attempt to reduce all of theology to the matter of color. In the materialistic conception of life, men have been tempted to write about a theology of color without Christ, of pigmentation without inculcating divine principles. When we call to the bar of religious thought and opinion these so-called supporters of "Black Theology," they bring some beautiful theories and philosophies that may encourage sincere minds devoted to civil rights and to the struggle of the race, but this has nothing to do with the theological notion of God as Spirit. None of this squares with the facts of a sound philosophy of religion or with a Christ-centered theology.[31]

As the leader of the largest black denomination, a national organization of black Baptist churches, born in resistance to racism, it is quite interesting and instructive, for understanding the perspective of some other pastors, that Jackson can so easily separate spirituality from civil rights struggle. In any case, Jackson felt strongly enough about the matter of black theology to address an entire chapter to it in his retrospection of the Fifth Assembly of the World Council of Churches, held in Nairobi, Kenya, in 1975. His perspective came as the result of his involvement as a member of the powerful Central Committee, the controlling body of the Council. Jackson observed that while black theology held no prominent place on the official agenda, much to his chagrin, there were enough quotations and references to it by conference participants to suggest its growing influence. In a chapter titled "A Theology of Polarization," Jackson remarks that "of all of the divisions apparent at the World Council of Churches, perhaps no one presented a potentially more dangerous polarity than that presented by Black Theology."[32]

Disagreeing with black theologians' christological conclusions regarding the partiality of a black Christ in the struggle against oppressors and using the Johannine verse which he consistently cites as the biblical basis for his argument against black theology, he emphasizes that "God is a Spirit" (4.24*a*). Accordingly, he found "the logic difficult to follow which indicates that Jesus is black because He identifies Himself with the suffering, with the troubled, and with the dispossessed. These problems are not restricted to any race or nationality. They are found among all nations, in all levels of culture."[33]

Notwithstanding Jackson's obvious lack of critical, historical reflection on the issue of race, it is important to observe that part of what informs his argument is his sense of himself as an ecumenist. This is why he had written an earlier text on Christian ecumenism titled *Many, but One: The Ecumenics of Charity*, following his attendance at the Second Vatican Council at the invitation of Pope John XXIII. Reflecting on the problem of sectarianism within the Church Universal, Jackson states in this 1964 text that "we now await a new school of theologians who will help us to rise above the landscape of divisions. We await theologians . . . who will tell us a new story of our togetherness, fellowship, and oneness in Christ."[34] In this sense, he sees the emergence of black theology and its emphasis on the Black Christ not as a statement regarding the theological meaning of Christ's incarnation in a world divided by race and defined by whiteness but as a form of racialized sectarianism further dividing the Body of Christ. This is the theological side of his assertion that "black theology is too restricted and too bound by the particularity of race or color to meet the demands for universality of a world religious fellowship like the World Council of Churches."[35] Taken on its own terms, the essay asks whether black theology supports or undermines the catholicity and unity of the church, essential marks readily recognizable and debated by those who operated within the ecumenical movement.

Varying Pastoral Views on Blackness, Ecumenism, and Universalism

THE ISSUES BROUGHT up by Joseph Jackson were issues to which other black pastors who were advocates of black theology were already responding. Leon Watts, for example, a minister in the African Methodist Episcopal Zion Church, was asking serious questions about the ecumenical movement, as controlled by whites, and its failure to seriously engage racism and the church's deep complicity and participation in it for centuries. Alluding to the Consultation on Church Union (COCU), a historic attempt by six predominantly white mainline denominations to overcome denominationalism and to work toward the unity of the church, Watts responds, "The Black Church, Yes! COCU, No!" Inasmuch as white churches were not willing to divest themselves of privilege and a sense of entitlement, within the structures of the respective churches and the ecumenical movement itself, Watts concluded that the language and gestures toward reconciliation "looks like a game of co-optation."[36]

The NCBC of which Watts was a member was, in fact, an ecumenical organization, with members from both black and white denominations.[37] Most of its members, however, were pastors within the white denominations. Joseph H. Jackson, on the other hand, was president of the largest black denomination. Yet Watts's statement and the overall position of the NCBC, in contrast to Jackson, demonstrate that while the historical reality of the black church is rooted in the independent black church movement, its contemporary manifestations cannot be limited to the historical black denominations.[38] Rather, its reality has more to do with the varying and sundry ways in which black Christians engage in the conscientious formation of Christian community —whether in denominations, congregations, or caucuses—informed by a history of shared struggle against oppression and in memory of the radical witness of Jesus Christ.

In that sense, Watts and the NCBC, more than Jackson and the National Baptist Convention, represented the independent spirit of the nineteenth-century black church. In a way akin to its nineteenth-century antecedent, the NCBC rejected ecclesial integration without shared power and the appearance of Christian ecumenism without a commitment to justice. Manifesting its own radical form of black ecumenism, the organization marshaled the language of Malcolm X, a Muslim cleric, in a statement of its commitment to the empowerment of "the black community, economically, socially, and politically *by whatever means necessary* and consistent with the spirit of the Christian gospel."[39]

Yet there is also a political side to Joseph H. Jackson's rejoinder to black theology and its emphasis on blackness. If theologically Jackson's position is informed by his view of the universal implications of the gospel and his understanding of himself as an ecumenist, politically it is his accommodationist orientation that explains his approach. For among the competing visions of racial uplift proffered by black leadership, Jackson represents that line of thought embodied most clearly in the life work of Booker T. Washington.[40] Jackson emphasized racial advancement through racial self-development and self-reliance rather than through the politics of civil disobedience, which he saw as unnecessarily divisive and disruptive to national unity, and he urged African Americans to move "from protest to production." In his 1962 annual address to his denomination, he argued, "We must go from protest to production. That is, we must seize every opportunity new and old, in order to become creators as well as consumers of goods. We must become inventors as well as users of the tools of production and also the investors of capital as well as the spenders of it."[41]

A fierce patriot who clung to the principles of law and order and a belief in the fundamental goodness of America, its charter documents, and its channels for legal forms of redress, Jackson saw the tactics employed by King as something of a nuisance and suggested that they helped to create the environment for the urban riots. In a 1966 statement that sets in bold relief the differences between him and the Martin Luther King whose vision of the transformational role of the church in America required that he speak out against Vietnam,

Jackson has this to say: "We are in a national crisis and at this moment are engaged in a bloody conflict with international communism in Vietnam, and are potentially in conflict with the same forces through-out the world as well as at home. Americans can no longer afford the luxury and the negative weights of past prejudices, hatred, envy, dis-crimination, disrespect for law and order and for one another, race riots and bloodshed. All of us must unite and work together as one for the nation's life and cause or eventually perish."[42] Seeing King's politics of confrontation as counterproductive to racial advancement and divisive to a putative national unity and viewing black power as its violent expression, it is not at all surprising that Jackson would also reject black theology.

Joseph H. Jackson represents the black church's most conservative side, the "Negro church" that Lincoln claimed was already dead. Oust-ing King from the convention and changing the address of his Olivet Baptist Church in 1968, in an apparent move to avoid having the new street name of Martin Luther King, Jr., on his stationary,[43] it is clear that Jackson resisted, in principle, both the third and fourth moments in the development of black Christian resistance to racism. By con-trast, Gardner Taylor, president of the Progressive National Baptist Convention, a split from Jackson's group, had this to say regarding "the power of blackness":

> I find it illuminating that Jesus called his disciples apart, as it is recorded in the ninth chapter of Luke. Jesus must have seen that every group must at some time or the other get with itself, find itself. . . . The same applies to a race such as ours. Not in isolation but in retreat and com-munion among ourselves we must find our true selves in terms of those shaping events which have formed our peculiar and singular his-torical experience in this land. The scriptures suggest that the apart-ness into which Jesus led his disciples was redemptive, cleansing, cre-ative, restoring, preparatory. He called them apart that they might be empowered. "He gave them power and authority" (Luke 9.1). Is this the valid word in the pained shrieks and the angry screams of the young black power men?[44]

Yet it is important to note that the reflections of other pastors on black theology reveal that while they reject the accommodationist politics of a Joseph H. Jackson, they would sound a similar emphasis on the universality of the gospel, expressing in varying ways ambivalence toward black theology's emphasis on *blackness*. But, as we shall see, what is not always clear is whether all the pastors who have rejected black theology's emphasis on the symbol of blackness fully appreciate the universal implications of black theology's claims regarding the God who sides with the poor *within* history. Blackness has been, for black theologians, a universal invitation to solidarity with the God who saved the Hebrews and drowned the Egyptians and the Jesus who directed the preaching of Good News to the poor in a world defined by the powers of domination. Yet, while Jackson's rejoinder represents an outright rejection of black theology in principle by an ultraconservative cleric, other pastors have struggled with the rhetoric of partiality and blackness while sometimes missing its theological implications.

A. Roger Williams is a good example. Pastor of the Union Baptist Church of Hartford, Connecticut, he provided one of the earliest written responses by a black pastor to James Cone's work. His response to Cone's first two books is quite instructive for understanding the discussion and the differences between black theologians and black pastors over the essential meaning of the black church. For while he embraces the liberationist theological perspective of Cone and rejects the accommodationism of Jackson, he struggles with black theology's "scandal of particularity."[45] All of these sentiments are simultaneously present in his response to black theology.

As one committed to a social and political understanding of the gospel and of the church's role as an instrument of liberation, Williams applauds Cone's theological imagination and commends his impatience. He says, in fact, "I wish that more were!" Moreover, in an obvious critique of Jackson and others, he laments that "judging from pronouncements of older black convention presidents and black Methodist bishops, many have not caught up with Martin L. King, Jr., much less the black Revolution." Yet, regarding Cone's perspective, he says,

I must disagree with his concept of God. To be sure God is the God of the oppressed. This indeed is comforting knowledge. But Abraham asks, "Will not the judge of all the earth do right?" We learn from the exalted teaching of the prophets that God cares for all the peoples of the earth. *His sun shines "on the just and the unjust." While the oppressor is always under the judgment of God, the Eternal still hovers over him with yearning love.* This element is absent from Cone.[46]

Part of what Williams does not acknowledge is the way in which Cone does insist that the judgment and love of God hovers over the oppressed *and* the oppressor. And the appropriate response, Cone would say, is for the oppressor to repent by becoming completely identified with the suffering and struggles of the oppressed. If the white church would become the true church of Jesus Christ, it too must become ontologically black. For by so doing, it will have identified itself fully with that which represents shame in the world but the revelation of God in human history.[47]

Yet Williams does represent the perspective of many black pastors who see clearly the sociopolitical mandates of the gospel, standing well within the liberationist legacy of the black church, Martin Luther King, Jr., and black theology. But because of the universalistic orientation of the black church, embodied in a love ethic that emphasizes the God who "lets [the] sun shine on the just and the unjust,"[48] many of the same pastors express varying levels of apprehension regarding black theology's sharp focus on the particularity of blackness.

Samuel DeWitt Proctor, for example, who served as senior pastor of the Abyssinian Baptist Church, one of the most politically active black churches in the twentieth century, recognizes the conditions that gave rise to black theology and its important contribution to theological understanding. Yet he suggests that "there should be an acknowledged tentativeness about Black theology."[49] While black theologians see their work both as an indictment of white theologians' failure to address racism *and* as an honest acknowledgment of the fact that indeed all God-talk is partial, Proctor would seem to understand black theology solely as evidence of the former. For in his view, to make "black" the adjectival modifier of "theology" can only mean a failure to create "genuine community" and nothing else. Suggesting that it is embarrassing to admit that the "scandalous separations in America" evince themselves even in our God-talk, he wonders, "Will we have to live with this hyphenated theological expression indefinitely?" Proctor concedes that as long as the legacy of colonialism, Third World poverty, and economic disparity exist, marginalizing and stigmatizing people of color all over the world, the "metes and bounds" of black theology will extend all over the globe. Still "black theologians should be the first to rejoice to see their witness become irrelevant and the 'metes and bounds' of black theology get lost and erased in a new emergence of strong and convincing movement toward a genuine community in the world."[50]

Indeed, the search for genuine Christian community in a world marred by the contradictions of race is part of the bedrock of black Christian faith. And while Proctor and Cone differ in their respective sensibilities about the character of God-talk, their assertions emerge from a common justice-making tradition that challenges white churches and white Christians to demonstrate the authenticity of their Christian witness through the denial of white privilege and meaningful solidarity with the oppressed. Cone would say that, given God's partiality toward the poor, genuine community means that whites must become ontologically black, that is, demonstrate an unqualified commitment with God to the poor with whom God stands.

Yet Proctor, who discusses in an autobiographical text his own moral formation toward a conscience that responds "equally as sharply in matters of social failure and injustice" as "matters of personal behavior," expresses the gospel mandate of genuine solidarity with the oppressed in anecdotal form. Riding with two white pastors, in 1947, to a conference sponsored by the American Baptists on Christian social concern, they stopped late at night in search of lodging at the a YMCA.

When we appeared to register, a crippled night attendant, hobbling on a cane, shouted at me that no "colored" could stay at the YMCA. My companions, John Zuber and Artemis Goodwin, were two wonderful white pastors. They and I left in quiet resignation and went to the "colored" Young Men's Christian Association to spend the night. We represented genuine community traveling together, and we confronted denial of community at the Young Men's Christian Association.[51]

In this way, both Williams and Proctor are pastors who have a liberationist understanding of the gospel but have some misgivings about black theology's sharp emphasis on blackness as a theological point of departure.

However, pastors such as J. Alfred Smith, Sr., have expressed no discomfort with this emphasis at all. For Smith, pastor emeritus of Oakland, California's Allen Temple Baptist Church, and many others have a view of the incarnation that emphasizes the meaning of particularity in the cosmic struggle against "powers and principalities," and they understand the ways in which the distinctive concerns of the oppressed are easily dismissed as the powerful wax eloquently about universality while refusing to divest themselves of enormous privilege. An urban pastor at the height of the black power movement, Smith has written about the impact of the black consciousness of black theology on his own ministry.

As a part of a group of clergy influenced by black power, called the Alamo Black Clergy, Smith is representative of many clergy who, in the 1960s, were trying to find a way to translate the meaning of the gospel of liberation to young black men and women who were committed to the salvation of their community but alienated from the church.[52] Illustrative of the way in which the emergence of a new radical black church had much to do with pressure exerted from the community itself, Smith observes in his autobiography, On the Jericho Road: A Memoir of Racial Justice, Social Action, and Prophetic Ministry, that "the Black Muslims and other black power groups were calling preachers ecclesiastical pimps. They were saying that the black preacher and the black church were part of the dilemma that plagued black people rather than part of the solution."[53] The Alamo Black Clergy group emerged in response to the challenges of relevant ministry in a revolutionary context.

Smith says that the group "met on a regular basis to study black theology and black power."[54] Affirmed and theologically grounded in their ministerial efforts by black theology's claims, they organized the Urban Black Studies Center, an affiliate of the Graduate Theological Union in Berkeley, California, and annually they invited black theologians such as James Cone, Gayraud Wilmore, and J. Deotis Roberts to lecture and speak. Furthermore, Smith suggests that he and several other pastors, influenced by black theology, began to connect their work more deeply with the struggles of the poor in Africa and the Third World.

Insisting that the gospel required that the clergy define their ministry by an unqualified commitment to the black poor, Adam Clayton Powell, famed congressman and Proctor's predecessor as pastor of New York's Abyssinian Baptist Church, spoke of the need for "black power in the church." In a christological statement reminiscent of James Cone's defense of black power as "Christ's central message to twentieth-century America,"[55] Powell argues,

> All things are God's. And were Christ to return to earth today, he would be leading the boycotts. He would be signing the petitions. He would stand up and oppose the politicians who come to Harlem once every four years during an election year and then shut their eyes and their hearts to the pleas of desperately poor and deprived people. Christ would have walked in Selma. He would have marched in Washington, and He would have lived in Harlem.[56]

Also, Nathan Wright, an Episcopal priest who was a member of the NCBC, actually served as the chairperson of the first National Black Power Conference held in Newark, New Jersey, July 20–23, 1967.[57] In one of the earliest and most important texts written on the subject during that period, he too offers his own version of the theological significance of black power:

> In religious terms, a God of power, of majesty and of might, who has made man to be in His own image and likeness, must will that His creation reflect in the immediacies of life His power, His majesty and His might. Black Power raises, for the healing of humanity and for the renewal of a commitment to the creative religious purpose of growth,

the far too long overlooked need for power, if life is to become what in the mind of its Creator it is destined to be.[58]

But if the response to black theology's emphasis on blackness among black pastors in mainline denominations has been mixed, the response has tended to be negative, with few exceptions,[59] among self-identified black evangelicals in conservative white denominations. Anthony Evans, a very prominent preacher in the Southern Baptist Convention and a leader within the National Black Evangelical Association, makes this comment:

> Since the ecclesiology of Black theology is ethnically centered, it flirts with the danger of neglecting the universal nature of the body of Christ in favor of its ethnic concerns. This is no more permissible for the black church than it would be for the New Testament Jewish church to view ecclesiology apart from the inclusion of the Gentiles. The point is that ethnically oriented ecclesiology is not valid biblically unless its ethnicity includes the concept of the nature of the body of Christ.[60]

While Evans is a member of the staunchly conservative Southern Baptist Convention, his perspective is not much different from that of many pastors in the mainline black denominations. For in Lincoln and Mamiya's survey and summary of the impact of the black consciousness and black power era on the thinking of such black pastors, they observe that responses to their questionnaire had a great deal to do with age and education. Younger and better-educated clergy were more likely to have been influenced by the writings of key thinkers in the black theology movement. They were also more likely to respond positively when asked, "Do you think your ministry is essentially different because you are in a black denomination?" and when asked, "Does the black church have a different mission from the white church?" Yet it should be noted that nearly half of all black pastors responded negatively to the first question, and about two-thirds answered no to the second. Lincoln and Mamiya observe that "in interviews with the clergy, the negative answers of 'no difference' generally appealed to the universalism of the Christian ministry and its primary task as the saving of souls. As one Baptist minister said in his interview, 'The ministry of both black and white preachers is the same: the saving of souls . . . skin color is of no great significance in relating the message of Jesus.' "[61]

Martin Luther King, Jr., Black Pastors, and the Black Christ

THE VIEW, EXPRESSED in the earlier quotation by the anonymous Baptist minister, that privileges "the saving of souls" while ignoring or marginalizing the transformation of the social order as central to the soteriological message of the biblical witness and the essential mission of the church is clearly *inconsistent* with any doctrine of the church that can be derived from the radical side of the black church's witness. The liberationist thrust of black religion can be traced from slave religion to the freedom thrust of the independent black church movement to the ministry of Martin Luther King, Jr. The leader of a church-led movement for liberation, King and his SCLC challenged any narrow and individualistic understanding of the church's mission that focuses exclusively on "saving souls." Rather, King and those who served with him set out "To Redeem the Soul of America."

On the other hand, the anonymous Baptist minister's perspective is *consistent* with King's view with respect to the significance of the Black Christ. For when asked by a black person, "Why did God make Jesus white, when the majority of people in the world are nonwhite?" the Martin Luther King, Jr., of the pre-black-power era appeals to a christology that is race neutral. "The color of Jesus' skin is of little or no consequence. The whiteness or blackness of one's skin is a biological quality which has nothing to do with the intrinsic value of personality. The significance of Jesus lay, not in color, but in his unique God-consciousness and his willingness to surrender his will to God's will." Yet King's words reveal the dangerous side of his presumptions regarding Christian faith and race neutrality in a context of robust race consciousness and normative whiteness, as he continues: "[Jesus] would have been no more significant *if* his skin had been black. He is no less significant *because* his skin is white" (emphasis mine).[62]

That Martin Luther King, Jr., could tacitly presume the whiteness of a first-century, Palestinian Jew (or at the very least, not explicitly challenge the questioner's faulty premise) underscores the power of the white Christ in the theological imagination of the black church. It also demonstrates the difference that black power and black consciousness have made in the development of black people's understanding of the Christian faith and of their messianic mission as the critical consciousness of American Christianity. For while King remained an integrationist until the day of his death, the tough-mindedness of an emerging black consciousness would later come to ground his universalism more deeply in the particularity of his own cultural heritage and the theological significance of that heritage for all churches in America and for ecumenical Christianity throughout the world.

As James Cone has pointed out, after the emergence of black power, King later said to a group of Miami ministers, "Jesus was not a white man."[63] Furthermore, arguing that "Christianity is not just a western religion," he suggested that black ministers take more seriously the power and particularity of their own experience in the hope of achieving what he so often called "the beloved community." Reflecting on the suffering of black people and the liberationist legacy of the black church, he said, "We have the power to change America, and give a kind of new vitality to the religion of Jesus Christ."[64] Indeed, as Cone has observed, King was too much of an integrationist to argue, on theological grounds, that "Jesus is black."[65] Yet there can be no gainsaying the fact that he had been impacted by the consciousness of young black power activists. In the same way, black theology seeks to impact, even transform, the consciousness of the black church, grounding its universalistic impulse within the particularity of black experience. This is what Cone means when he says,

> To say that Christ is black means that black people are God's poor people whom Christ has come to liberate. And thus no gospel of Jesus Christ is possible in America without coming to terms with the history

and culture of that people who struggle to bear witness to his name in extreme circumstances. To say that Christ is black means that God, in his infinite wisdom and mercy, not only takes color seriously, he takes it upon himself and discloses his will to make us whole—new creatures born in the spirit of divine blackness and redeemed through the blood of the Black Christ.[66]

Clearly, Cone's christology and ontology of blackness represent a creative theological option for the black church's own self-expression of the distinctive meaning of its messianic mission as the independent consciousness of the American church and of God's revelatory action through it as an instrument of divine salvation—for the oppressed and the oppressors. Furthermore, the Black Christ provides a transvaluative symbol for black churches in a culture in which "hidden primal myths" about the negativity, inferiority, and sinfulness of blacks and blackness are so deeply embedded in Christian Tradition[67] that even these churches and their denominations have been slow to address this problem in their hymnody, liturgy, iconography, and theology.

Yet ontological blackness, as a theological symbol, has always been a contested option, not only among pastors but also among black religious intellectuals. Victor Anderson, for example, regards ontological blackness as a limited methodological option "that requires for its legitimacy the opposition of white racism," relegating all transcendent possibilities to "the blackness that whiteness created."[68] Moreover, in the post-black-power era, some in the churches and some black religious intellectuals, including first-generation black theologian J. Deotis Roberts, have explored the school and worldview of *Africentrism* (sometimes spelled "Afrocentrism") as yet another hermeneutical possibility for the apprehension of an internal and external freedom and the fulfillment of a holistic black humanity.[69] In this way, the thorny issue of identity is part of a continuing dialogue in the African American community, contested terrain that plays itself out in the theological discussions among black theologians and between black theologians and black pastors regarding the meaning of a self-conscious theology of the black experience and the mission of the black church.

The Problem of Biblical Fundamentalism

AS BLACK THEOLOGIANS and black pastors discuss competing and complementary options for the apprehension and development of a holistically salvific theology of black experience (e.g., blackness, Afri-centrism, womanism) in this postmodern moment, the issue is further complicated and made all the more urgent by the problem of biblical fundamentalism, its invasion and its rising influence within the culture of the black church.[70] To be sure, African Americans were not signifi-cantly represented in the earliest manifestations of Christian funda-mentalism and its response to the crisis of modernity.[71] However, this began to change in the decades following World War II and accelerated roughly during the same period as the rise and development of black theology.[72] One consequence of this historical shift, characterized by larger numbers of African Americans who are self-conscious and self-identified "Bible-believing" evangelicals, is the appeal to authoritative truth claims and a biblical worldview that transcends history, race, and culture.[73] It is the fundamentalist perspective, or a putatively unmedi-ated biblical faith, that is universal.[74]

What is significant is that under such a theological scenario, even classic cultural and liberationist readings of biblical self-understanding, employed by African Americans and their churches negotiating, for generations, the "Egypt land" of American experience, are relativ-ized, held in suspicion, or held at bay altogether. For "the Protestant-defined Bible is considered the deracialized, depoliticized, and univer-sal guide to truth and salvation."[75] To be sure, there are important nuances of understanding and debate among black evangelicals on this issue as some, such as William H. Bentley, have cautioned against "negating blackness as the price of racial harmony within the Chris-tian context."[76] Again, this uncritical universalizing tendency among growing segments of black evangelical culture, inside and outside the Black Evangelical Association, is expressed in the sentiment of Anthony T. Evans. He avers that the witness of African American Christians "must rest on the Word, be unified in theology, not culture, color or history."[77]

The problem with the kind of reasoning that Evans represents is that not only does it displace questions of black Christian identity and heritage with a presumed position of pure doctrine and biblicistic transcendence, but it also undermines the black church's distinctive legacy and peculiar vocation as the conscience of the American churches, speaking to their failure to address clearly and prophetically the nation's original sin and its most intractable social problem—racism. Moreover, the easy and ahistorical rhetoric of universal claims in a deeply divided world also short-circuits the black church's ability to critically probe the radical implications of its own distinctive liberationist heritage and contrarian voice for clues on how to think about the deep contradictions of sexism and homophobia within its own ranks. The work of womanist New Testament scholar Clarice J. Martin makes the point exceedingly clear. In discussing the contradiction between the black church's hermeneutics of inclusion with respect to racial justice and its biblical fundamentalism with respect to issues of gender justice, she rightfully asks,

> Why is the African American interpretive tradition marked by a forceful critique and rejection of a literalist interpretation of the slave regulations in the *Haustafeln*, but not marked by an equally passionate critique and rejection of a literalist interpretation regarding the subordination of women to men in the *Haustafeln*? . . . If liberating biblical traditions regarding the kinship of humankind under God have comprised a treasury of antislavery *apologia* in the struggle for African American emancipation in the eighteenth and nineteenth centuries, why have we not witnessed the creation of a treasury of pro-women *apologia* to insure the full empowerment of African American women in the religious and socio-political spheres of African American culture and American national history?[78]

Martin concludes that "a true understanding of the mission of the church requires that African Americans embrace a resocialized vision of the liberating character of the new creation of God for humanity in the most comprehensive and inclusive sense." Moreover, she suggests that an examination of the divergent hermeneutical strategies through which the black church has responded to "slaves obey your masters" versus "wives be obedient to your husbands" compels an examination of our understanding of the Christian gospel itself.[79]

My point is that with the encroachment of conservative biblical fundamentalism and its authoritative claims to absolute biblical truth, the black church needs, now more than ever, a *critical theological principle* for probing the meaning of black Christian identity. It especially needs such a principle as a critical lens in a so-called postracial era in which previous forms of black marginalization morph into new, complex, and intractable systems of social death that are in many ways worse than anything a previous generation of civil rights warriors could have imagined.[80] Moreover, internally the black church needs a *sophisticated ethic of accountability* that calls the church to examine the contemporary implications of its highest theological and moral claims about itself for those who are marginalized within its own family. Indeed, black and womanist theologies, unlike any other forms of academic discourse, are uniquely apt to this task.

Yet decades after black theology's birth, black pastors and black theologians, caught up in the institutional silos of professional expectations and trapped by the comfort of their respective enclaves of academic and ecclesial privilege, have yet to have a serious and sustained conversation with one another about the mission of the black church. I submit that the concerns of the poor and the most marginalized members of the black community, and nothing else, must be at the center at that much-needed conversation. Absent that serious and sustained conversation, black theology has been left without a robust public witness within the very institution that gave birth to its prophetic voice, and the black church has been left without the critical tools necessary for probing the theological meaning of its black identity and what that might mean, in this moment, for a nation in crisis. Moreover, absent a critical hermeneutics of collective historical memory for engaging biblical texts, the church that has provided America's most radical witness with respect to racial justice and the ethics of inclusion is left appealing to the most conservative tenets of evangelical Christian culture and reactionary, hermeneutical modes of biblical interpretation when it comes to addressing the concerns and questions being raised by the poor, women, and gays and lesbians within its own ranks.[81]

I submit that the critical tools for responding to questions regarding the meaning of authentic and just Christian community within the black church are found within the hermeneutical logic of its own liberationist and pietistic heritage. As the black church wrestles through questions of inclusion around gender and sexual orientation, it ought at least to remember that it was not simplistic appeals to biblical quotations (i.e., "the Bible says . . .") without regard for actual experience that led to the abolitionist position of black Christians in the first and second moments of African American Christianity or even their resistance to segregation during the third moment. In fact, proslavery apologists had at least as many individual scriptural quotations on their side of the polemic as those who enlisted scripture in support of slavery's abolition.[82] Notwithstanding the revolutionary character and profound democratic implications of that classic Protestant assertion, *sola scriptura* never solved a political problem or negated the need to wrestle and work through the communal and continuing dance of hermeneutical assessment, theological engagement, and ethical discernment.

Clearly, it was the peculiar experience of African American Christians *in faithful conversation with scripture* that both sourced a countercultural piety and provided a critical understanding of the liberationist intent and meaning of the gospel. If the black church is to strengthen and maintain its prophetic voice, it must ask itself, "What does that basic liberationist trajectory mean today for both the American churches and the American nation?"

The Message of the Black Church in the Age of Obama

IRONICALLY, THE URGENT need for the black church to engage in serious and sustained self-examination, so as to clarify the theological content of its own message, was brought into sharp focus during Barack Obama's run for the presidency in 2008 and in the wake of his public statements in support of gay marriage while running for reelection in 2012. A new age had emerged. To be sure, this was no postracial America, as some had claimed.[83] Indeed, the existential reality of the masses of black people, including high unemployment, high incarceration rates, and disproportionately high mortgage interest rates, even in black neighborhoods with exceptionally high-income households, belies any easy claim to a postracial America. But forty years after Fannie Lou Hamer, the Mississippi sharecropper turned civil rights activist, challenged the racism of the National Democratic Party and twenty years after Jesse Jackson's second symbolic run for the presidency, a black man, informed by the spirituality and activism of the black church, was making a formidable run for the presidency.

The black church, so central to black life yet barely understood by mainstream America, was thrust to the center of the national dialogue —both during the Jeremiah Wright debacle of 2008 and the controversy over gay marriage in 2012. One had to do with race and the other had to do with sexual orientation, but both had to do with the meaning of justice for marginalized persons in a nation that claims "justice for all."

If during the former, the black church was scrutinized and attacked for the liberationist content of its message, during the latter, that same community was forced to wrestle with the implications of its liberationist message for gays, lesbians, and transgendered persons sitting in its own pews and already active in its ministries. Both require deep soul searching and honest dialogue among black pastors and theologians and between black pastors and theologians. However, let us examine first what might be instructive about 2008, as black theologians and black pastors are urged to take more seriously the inescapable interconnectedness of their respective vocations as they each seek to give voice to an oppressed community and bear witness to the God of love and justice in a world where the forces of lovelessness and injustice win many proximate victories. Indeed, the high stakes and the high costs of an extended disconnect between black theology and the black church were played out on television screens in the spring of 2008, with critical implications for black theology, the black church, and the black community.

It happened when owing to the pervasive reach of electronic media and the political machinations of powerful, partisan interests caught up in a colossal contest for control of the most powerful nation on earth, millions of Americans, indeed people around the globe, were exposed to a thirty-second clip of a fiery black pastor preaching to his own congregation on a Sunday morning. Extracted from its theological and rhetorical context and looped to the point of ad nauseam was the most provocative phrase: *"God damn America!"* The clip drew attention because that pastor, the Reverend Jeremiah Wright of the Trinity United Church of Christ, happened to be the pastor of Barack Obama, then the nation's *only* black senator, engaged in a formidable contest to become the first black president. The burning question within mainstream America was, what kind of church was this? What was the meaning of this kind of "hate-filled" preaching? Furthermore, what was the impact of this kind of preaching and this activist black church on the worldview and politics of this black man who would be president? Suddenly, journalists, politicians, political pundits, and laypersons in churches, white and black, were asking, "What is black theology?"

Meanwhile, as an academic discipline and discourse, black theology was already entering its fourth decade as a key influencer on the theological thinking and ministry of scores of pastors who had read black theologians among other emergent liberationist voices coming from Latin America and throughout the Third World. Yet, having become largely an academic discourse, confined largely to seminaries and meetings of the American Academy of Religion and the Society for the Study of Black Religion, never before had black theology been thrust on the national stage as a primary interlocutor in a national conversation about the true meaning of Christian faith and the message and meaning of the Christian Church.

Moreover, as white Americans mused over doing the unthinkable —making a black man president of the United States and leader of the free world—the very notion of a decidedly *black theology* was not only strange and new but frightening. Furthermore, for those who were beginning to open themselves up to the idea of a President Obama, this strange, black theology was most unwelcome in the new postracial America that some believed had suddenly emerged. What is the meaning of this *black* theology? And how had it shaped then Senator Obama's worldview? What did a man who spent twenty years in a church led by this guy named Jeremiah Wright really think about white people and about America? Is this Barack Obama the twenty-first-century version of the safer and more domesticated Martin Luther King, Jr., created after the real Martin Luther King, Jr., was killed, or is he really Malcolm X in Martin Luther King's clothing? If not, why does he attend a church that teaches a decidedly race-conscious "Black Values System" and whose mantra is "Unapologetically Christian, Unashamedly Black"? What does being black have to do with being Christian? For if Christian faith posits God's universal claim on all of humanity, why qualify and thus pigeonhole that universal claim with the cultural particularity of blackness?

These are all important questions. Yet, because truth is always the first casualty not only of war but of politics, there was simply no way there was going to be an honest and informed discussion about a little-known black theology and a still largely misunderstood black church while powerful people and powerful interests were fighting feverishly for control of the country. Moreover, because there had been a disconnect and very little dialogue, across several decades, between black theology and the black church, the church born fighting for freedom found itself in the position of having to simply react to the anxieties of those for whom the black church is still an "invisible institution," rather than laying out a clear public-policy agenda rooted in a justice-centered theology.

The latter could not happen because while the public debate around the meaning and mission of the Trinity United Church of Christ revealed how little people in the white community and the white church understood about the black church, it also underscored how unfamiliar many in the black church were with black theology. Like long-lost siblings separated shortly after birth, black theology and the black church were awkwardly reintroduced to each other by outsiders, who could hardly know the subtle and intimate nuances of their familial relationship, under the hot glare of unceasing cable-television coverage, partisan political posturing, and media hype.

Additionally, part of the disconnect in the national dialogue was cultural, as those who were unexposed to the worship and preaching of the black church sought to interpret the "bombastic" character of black prophetic preaching, as it is buoyed and heightened in the "whooping" moment by the emotive spirituality and exuberant response of those who are in the pews. In this way, there was a disconnect between black and white Americans, as the latter were televisually translated to a black church on any given Sunday where preachers are expected, indeed encouraged, to speak the truth, "tell Pharaoh," and "tell it like it is," with clarity, creativity, and passion. In that sense, Jeremiah Wright was right when he proffered that the vicious caricature and political attack on him was, in a real sense, an attack on the black church.[84]

To be sure, in some of Wright's public pronouncements and manner, following the initial controversy, he himself contributed to the caricature in ways that drew more attention to himself than to the issues he had so effectively raised, his entire career, both in speech and in praxis, as a preacher in the African American prophetic tradition. This was unfortunate. Aside from the difficulty and distraction that Wright's subsequent public performance created for his most famous parishioner and his historic candidacy, it, along with the media's own caricature and distortion, made it virtually impossible for the general public to know that his actual sermon, heard in its entirety, was a very thoughtful and compelling discussion on how a Christian should view government.

Titled "Confusing God and Government," the sermon presented the critical reflections of a serious theologue on this fundamental question with which Augustine wrestled in *City of God*, Martin Luther in "Temporal Authority: To What Extent It Should Be Obeyed," Dietrich Bonhoeffer as he discusses "State and Church" in *Ethics*, and Martin Luther King, Jr., in his "Letter from Birmingham Jail."[85] Preaching the Lukan narrative (19:37–44) in which Jesus weeps over the city of Jerusalem, Wright told his congregation that Palm Sunday of 2003 that the church was inept in its response to the Iraq War and to poverty and racism at home and abroad because "we confuse God and government." In the best tradition of the Christian Church and Christian theology, he counseled against this dangerous yet pervasive heresy.

The sermon embodied the radical spirit of both the third and fourth moments in African American Christian faith, and in it one can clearly hear how Wright is shaped by both. Like many preachers, he laid out a basic three-point sermonic outline. Etched against the backdrop of the Iraq War, an immoral war of choice, he argued that people of faith should not confuse governments, even the American government, with God because (1) governments lie, (2) governments change, and (3) governments fail.

In the sermon, Wright argued that the United States of America, not unlike ancient Rome and all other governments, will have to answer for its treatment of the most marginalized members of the human family. Contrary to the platitudinous pronouncements of politicians, America's moral and spiritual failure to seriously address itself to what Martin King called "the triplet evils of racism, poverty and war" could not be answered or assuaged by simply saying or singing "God Bless America." Like his ancient Hebrew namesake and the other Old Testament prophets, Jeremiah Wright told his congregation that Palm Sunday morning, five years prior to Obama's 2008 candidacy, that in God's moral universe, public policies and foreign policies that crush the poor are not without moral consequences. That is what he meant when, after listing a litany of wrongs including the mistreatment of Native Americans, Japanese Americans, and African Americans, he cautioned that while our songs and political pronouncements may say "God bless America," our actions may say "God damn America."

When it came to treating her citizens of African descent fairly, America failed. She put them in chains. The government put them in slave quarters, put them on auction blocks, put them in cotton fields, put them in inferior schools, put them in substandard housing, put them in scientific experiments, put them in the lowest paying jobs, put them outside the equal protection of the law, kept them out of their racist bastions of higher education and locked them into positions of hopelessness and helplessness. The government gives them drugs, builds bigger prisons, passes a three-strikes law, and then wants us to sing, "God Bless America." NO, no, no. Not "God Bless America"; God damn America! That's in the Bible, for killing innocent people. God damn America for treating her citizens as less than human. God damn America as long as she keeps trying to act like she is God and she is supreme![86]

It is provocatively put, but the thrust of the argument is consistent with prophetic speech. As Wright later puts it in the same sermon, "Blessings and cursings is in the Bible."[87] It is a sermonic argument akin to that of Martin Luther King, Jr., when he wrote the outline of the sermon he was scheduled to preach the Sunday following his assassination, titled "Why America May Go to Hell." Jeremiah Wright was as disillusioned in 2003 as King was in 1968 by the intractable character of America's original sin: racism. Yet, for all the discussion in 2008 about Wright's hatred for white people, he posits a sophisticated understanding of racism and other forms of oppression as he was careful in the same sermon to say, "All colonizers ain't white. . . . Oppressors come in all colors." In this way, Wright's sermon was consistent in style and substance with the peculiar witness of a church that has had to be the conscience of America. Influenced both by the civil rights movement and black theology, his ministry represents the ecclesial embodiment of the third and fourth moments in African American's appropriation of Christian faith.

Wright himself has written about the impact of black and womanist theologies on his ministerial vision and practice.[88] Wright was intentional about doing black theology,[89] and by the time his Trinity Church had become fodder for presidential politics, it had been known and respected for years in Chicago and nationally in the black church community and among people in the predominantly white denomination of which it is a member as a very vibrant, culturally self-conscious, and politically active congregation in the heart of urban Chicago. While the theological sensibilities of the church were informed by black theology, its cultural self-consciousness was largely informed by nationalistic movements in the African American community, including Afrocentrism.

Accordingly, the congregation adopted in 1971, under the leadership of Wright's predecessor, Reuben Sheares, the motto, "Unashamedly Black and Unapologetically Christian." In 1981, the lay leadership actually developed a document whose purpose was to provide content and meaning to the motto by responding to the question, "What Does It Mean to Be Black and Christian?" Wright is careful to cite specific examples of what he calls "'the word' of black theology becoming flesh" in the ministries of the Trinity Church.[90] Prominent among them is a prison ministry, inspired by the work of Gayraud Wilmore,[91] in which parishioners are working in prisons and with the families of prisoners every week. The church also has African-centered Rites of Passage Programs for boys and girls, has a Sojourner Truth Cultural Institute, and conducts a Black Liberation Workshop once a month. These and other efforts, including workshops on HIV/AIDS, sexuality, and other issues affecting the survival and well-being of African American people, are reflective of a liberationist understanding of ministry and emerge, in part, from Trinity's engagement of black and womanist theologians.

Yet, even among politically active black churches, Trinity's intentional engagement of academic black theology, as a part of its Christian education ministry, make it part of a radical remnant, an exception rather than the rule among black churches. Moreover, the theological vacuum that attends this long absenteeism of a critical, self-conscious theology in the masses of black churches has been increasingly filled by an ethos of biblical fundamentalism, a relatively late development among African American Christians—one with troubling implications for the future of the black church, black theology, and their liberating potential as partners in the struggle for humanity.

Indeed, both of these issues, namely, the disconnect between black theology and the black church and the rise of biblical fundamentalism, help to account for the ways in which the black church community was again divided and exploited as a political tool during the 2012 presidential election and the debate about same-sex marriage. To be sure, these issues are thorny and complicated for all involved. In fact, reflecting years earlier on the challenges of womanist God-talk with respect to sexism in the black church and black and womanist theologians' stance against heterosexism and homophobia in the black church, Jeremiah Wright confided, regarding his own congregation, "We are supposed to be an advanced, progressive church, yet many of the members have negative reactions to the developments of black theology."[92]

That negative reaction is magnified all the more in the majority of black congregations and among black pastors who are more influenced by white evangelicalism than by black theology. Devoid of a self-conscious, theological principle for thinking about the history of their own hermeneutical engagement of scripture with respect to their own experience, black churches have too often been radical on race and conservative on almost every other issue.

Black women pioneers in ministry, such as Prathia Hall-Wynn, who prior to her death in 2002 served as Associate Dean of Spiritual and Community Life and Director of the Harriet L. Miller Women's Center at United Theological Seminary in Dayton, Ohio, and pastor of Mt. Sharon Baptist Church in Philadelphia, Pennsylvania, have long challenged this contradiction in the black church. A participant in an important 1992 dialogue between black theologians and pastors, sponsored by Vanderbilt Divinity School's Kelly Miller Smith Institute on the Black Church, Hall-Wynn issued this cogent challenge to the black church and to black male preachers and theologians: "You cannot be a disciple of Jesus and harbor sexism in your heart, accommodate it with your mind, and give it life in your practice."[93]

Karen Mosby-Avery, pastor of the Good News Community Church of Chicago, Illinois, goes one step further. She posits that authentic Christian identity requires not only that one refuses to accommodate injustice but that one is actively engaged in fighting it. This is why she says, "We cannot continue to bear the name Christian, if we will not join God in eliminating marginalized people's suffering, if we will not join Christ in rebelling against injustice."[94]

Yet the black church needs the critical insights of its theologians to help keep it honest about its faithfulness to its vocation and raison d'être as a church born rebelling against injustice. In that regard, it is quite ironic that in recent years, the black church's public voice has not been heard on the government's treatment of the poor or the devastating impact of America's growing prison-industrial complex on its own community, but it was heard loud and clear in opposition to gay marriage, as if that has been the threat to black people's survival. Moreover, too many preachers and their churches have embraced a distorted theology of personal prosperity that is disengaged from the needs of the poor who are often surrounding the church and is discon-nected from any theological vision of communal liberation.

Such a church lacks what Dennis Wiley, a black theologian and pastor of the Covenant Baptist Church in Washington, D.C., calls an *"internal propheticism* that would empower the Black Church to chal-lenge not only the *outer* but also the *inner* systems of domination and oppression."[95] This has to be corrected, or else the message of the black church, which in many ways gave birth to the hope and promise of a Barack Obama, will lack clarity, credibility, and spiritual power in the Age of Obama and in the age to come.

5

Womanist Theologians on the
Mission of the Black Church

Black Theology, Womanist Theology, and the Black Church

THE ANALYSIS PUT forth thus far has consisted of an examination of black theology's unique contribution to a long and ongoing discussion regarding the mission of the black church. As we have endeavored to build on a historical interpretation and heuristic framework, outlined in chapter 1, the preceding chapter examined varying pastoral responses to the ecclesiological implications of Martin Luther King's ministry (the third moment) and the truth claims of black theology (the fourth moment) regarding the essential mission of the black church. Nuances in the varying responses of pastors are indicative of similarities and differences between the pastors themselves and between the civil rights movement and the black theology movement. Yet much of the discussion is animated, in each moment of the black church's history, by age-old tensions between the liberationist and pietistic dimensions of its historical self-understanding and vocational identity. Still, the issue is further complicated, on all fronts, by the distinctive challenge of womanist God-talk.

Womanist theology, which gives primacy to black women's experience, has sought to ensure that its God-talk is *multidimensional* in scope, raising new challenges regarding the doctrinal assertions of orthodox Christian speech and its implications for black women, men, and children, inside and outside the churches. Indeed, womanist theological reflections about the nature and scope of *divine liberation* are essential to the discussion both because of womanism's principled challenge to the patriarchal structure of the black church, a church born fighting for *freedom*, and its challenge to the androcentric assumptions of black theology, a theology of *liberation*.

Yet womanist engagement of *personal piety* is just as critical because, unlike any other discipline, womanist theology raises the voices of ordinary churchwomen, the black church's marginalized majority, and pushes pastors and theologians alike to reconsider the complex intersectionality between black women's piety and black people's liberation, internal and external freedom—before, during, and after the civil rights era. In this way, the exuberant and emotive black folk spirituality to which Martin King was reintroduced during the mass meetings of the Montgomery Bus Boycott and the "elevated world of spirit,"[1] about which intellectuals, white and black, are often bemused, may require a new hearing with regard to its role in black people's survival and its usefulness in their *worldly* struggle for liberation from social structures of evil and injustice.[2]

Perhaps this is why womanist theologians were brought together to discuss the folk spirituality of ordinary women in Emilie Townes's edited work *Embracing the Spirit: Womanist Perspectives on Hope, Salvation and Transformation*.[3] In that work, Karen Baker-Fletcher affirms that in black churches, "the Spirit is a healing, reviving source of positive power that gives new insight, courage, endurance, and meaning." Yet in the best of the black church tradition, she suggests that the need to "'discern the spirits' is advice well given" so as to avoid the physical, sexual, and emotional abuse that women too often suffer both in the church and at home. For "sometimes the pastor or deacon who is so deeply moved by the Spirit during church service returns home to beat his wife."[4]

Thus, among the questions that womanists such as Baker-Fletcher are putting to the pietistic practice and spiritual pronouncements of black folk and black churches are, "How do we discern when a religious experience is truly an experience of the Spirit and a revelation of God? Who is God? What is the Spirit? How do we know when revelation has truly occurred? How do we know when we have read God's message to us correctly? How clear is our vision? Do we have a darkened eye that needs to be restored?"[5] It is in this and other ways that womanists are critically yet respectfully engaging the complex intersectionality between piety and radical public witness, otherworldly sensibilities and this-worldly concerns, as they challenge the church to develop a vision of salvation that is truly holistic and a mission for liberation that embraces all people, bearing prophetic witness against the violence perpetrated against them and the earth. In fact, Delores Williams argues in the same volume that principled opposition "to all forms of violence against humans, nature, the environment and the land" should be regarded, along with the classic marks of apostolicity, catholicity, unity, and holiness, as a distinguishing mark of the true church.[6]

Yet the black church has been slow, even resistant, to incorporating the insights of womanist theologians into its institutional life. This is so because of the black church's conservatism around issues of gender, the profound investment of pastors and lay members alike, both male and female, in sinful, human structures of patriarchy, and the organizational and logistical disconnection between the critical work of academic theologians and the ministry of black churches. I shall offer some suggestions for addressing this problem in the conclusion.

By contrast, black theologians have been much more responsive to the truth claims of womanist theology. In fact, while womanist theology is theology in its own right, its emergence cannot be fully understood apart from both feminist theology and black theology and the creative space that the black theology movement has sustained for principled self-criticism regarding its theological blind spots and for rigorous inquiry into the nature and scope of the gospel of liberation.[7]

James Cone, who trained several of the leading womanist scholars, was the first black male theologian to address the issue of sexism directly in his writing. In 1976, at the request of black women at Garret Evangelical Seminary in Evanston, Illinois, he addressed a conference which they had convened on the topic "New Roles in the Ministry: A Theological Appraisal." At a time when most black male pastors and many black male theologians dismissed the issue of sexism as a joke or as a part of a white feminist agenda that had nothing to do with black experience, Cone had this to say:

It is a contradiction for black men to protest against racism in the white church and society at large and then fail to apply the same critique to themselves in their relation to black women. . . . We cannot support a subordinate ministry for women and also claim to be for the liberation of the oppressed. How is black men's insistence on the subordination of black women in the church and society any different from white people's enforcement of black subordination? No matter how much we wish the similarity to be nonexistent, it is unmistakably present.[8]

Cone was right. Yet there is a truth about black women's experience that only black women could speak.[9] In fact, reflecting on that first attempt to speak about the issue, Cone comments, "When I now read that October 1976 paper, I am embarrassed by how mildly and carefully I approached the theme of women's equality in the church. It was anything but radical, somewhat analogous to a southern white liberal reflecting on racism."[10] The truth of the matter is that the black theology movement, a male-dominated space with deep gender contradictions, needed to be evangelized by the critical insights of black women.

To the extent that black male theologians have been open to the lessons that only their sisters can teach, black theology has matured in its vocation as a theology of *liberation*. And to the degree that the black church, in most instances, has been recalcitrant in its studied maintenance of patriarchal privilege and power and has not been an active and integral part of what ought to be a pedagogical circle of critical, communal dialogue, it has not kept pace with the prophetic insights of its theologians or fully lived up to the promise of an egalitarian church. Born protesting discrimination on racial terms, black churches have been shamefully slow in applying the theo-ethical principles of their own liberating heritage to the issue of gender within their own ranks. While increasing numbers of black women are being ordained for professional ministry in the second decade of the twenty-first century, few black male pastors see active participation in the work of eradicating sexism and uprooting patriarchal structures in the churches and the society as fundamental to the work of witnessing to God's justice in the world or inextricably linked to the liberationist mission of the black church. If racism is for them a sin, sexism is, *at worst*, an inconvenience.

The Importance of Womanist Theology

THESE ARE AMONG the reasons why womanist theology, as a distinctive theological discourse articulated by and for black women, is important. It emerged as a necessary and distinctive movement within the black theology movement because, as black feminist Frances Beale put it back in 1970, the black woman has been a "slave of a slave."[11] Yet womanist theology is not simply an amalgam of the critical insights of white feminists on the one hand and black male theologians on the other. Emerging during the 1980s, womanist theology is theology in its own right.[12] As a distinctive theological discourse, it is sourced by the raw materials of black oral tradition, sacred and secular, and is informed by the intersectionality of the concerns raised by white feminists, black theologians, and other marginalized peoples. Thus, it has posited a *multidimensional* approach to its principled criticism and constructive God-talk.

An essay by Pauli Murray, an Episcopal priest who was also a legal scholar, holding a master of divinity degree from General Theological Seminary and a juris doctor from Yale Law School, represents one of the earliest articulations by a black religious intellectual of the need for *multidimensional* analyses of interlocking structures of oppression, a critical methodology which is now a hallmark of womanist ethics and God-talk. The insight emerges as she compares black theology and feminist theology. She observes that liberation theologies are careful to own their contextuality and the particularity of their concerns. "Black theology focuses upon the black experience under white racism; feminist theology is concerned with the revolt of woman against male-chauvinist structures of society; Third World theologies develop out of the struggle for national liberation." Moreover, she observes that "perhaps the greatest danger to the effectiveness of specific theologies is a tendency to compete with one another in defining a particular form of oppression as the 'source of all evil,' and thus losing sight of the goal of universal liberation and salvation." She concludes that "women, through coalitions on issues of common concern, can begin to transcend barriers of race, class, and nationality. They can provide a basis for intercommunication and interpenetration of all social structures and act as leaven within all groups."[13]

One place where womanist theologians have endeavored to serve as leaven, addressing the complex and multidimensional character of sacralized human oppression, is within the context of the black church. But this work is met with at least two obstacles. First, there is the issue of sexism, which both marginalizes and silences female voices within the context of many churches, irrespective of their academic theological credentials. Second, black theology emerged from among the ranks of radical black pastors and thus has had deep roots within the black church, even as it has challenged the black church. On the other hand, although womanist theology is sourced by the pain, experiences, and wisdom of ordinary black women, it was born in the academy. In that sense, it embodies even more deeply than black theology the class tensions and institutional barriers that have made it difficult for black theology, as a movement, to fully ignite the fires of radical discontent latent in the religion of the black mass church. While many womanists, including those discussed here, have been active in their respective denominations and some have addressed their work directly to the church,[14] *womanist God-talk is even more unfamiliar to pastors and ordinary black women in the churches than is black theology.*

This is why some womanists, such as Kelly Brown Douglas, have challenged their colleagues to conduct less of their dialogue at the American Academy of Religion and more of it inside black churches and other spaces in the black community where black women can hear it. "Black church and community-based women should be our primary audience. They should be our most significant interlocutors. This necessitates that womanist theologians create opportunities to debate and discuss their ideas where black women in struggle are the main audience. Such opportunities provide another means to be accountable to the very women whom womanist theology claims to represent."[15]

Traci West has made a similar point and has also been quite intentional in her own efforts to engage the women about whom she writes

directly in the church and elsewhere as she pursues her work on intimate violence as a Christian ethicist and United Methodist minister
who has served in both parish and campus ministries.[16] Daphne Wiggins, who is a womanist academic deeply engaged also in the work
of parish ministry, observes a few examples of Bible studies, weekly
meetings, and other gatherings of women in churches, informed by
a womanist thought. Observing still the deep disconnect between
the church and "a theology based in the academy" and seeing these
groups as, by far, the exception rather than the rule, she argues that
"the church could benefit from having more models at the congregational level that translate and embody womanist principles, empower
women, and encourage clergy to develop a critical ethical and biblical consciousness."[17] Raising similar concerns, Teresa L. Fry Brown
argues that "there needs to be an explanation of the womanist defi-
nitions in 'sisterspeak,' or the vernacular of the day-to-day, in the
trenches, ordinary sisters who provide supporting information and
who are potential procreators of womanist beliefs.[18]

As womanists, Brown Douglas, West, Wiggins, and Fry Brown all
acknowledge that those to whom theologians choose to speak, direct
their work, and share their insights is itself a theological issue. So, if
womanist and black theologians would give voice to the poor, they
must speak to the poor, earnestly engaging and challenging the poor
and the church structures in which the poor worship, including the
church's preaching, hymnody, polity, and pietistic speech. Yet Wiggins
is also correct as she cautions that "womanists should embark upon a
sustained analysis of the church's 'successes,' not just its limitations.
For womanism to have a decisive impact on the Black Church, it must
engage more thoroughly what the church does well for men, women,
families, and communities."[19] In that sense, what needs to emerge is
a sustained and serious conversation in which the church learns from
womanism, and womanism learns from the church. Indeed, the black
church is not one thing and womanism another. For good historical
and theological reasons, I would argue that the two are inextricably
connected. Moreover, black women who claim and are claimed by
both—churchwomen and womanists—are raising new questions that
should prompt the church to take an honest and self-critical look at

the broad ethical implications of its own liberationist mission (for women and gays and lesbians) while also reexamining the theological and practical import of its pietistic pronouncements for the most marginalized members of the human family.

Piety, Survival, and Liberation: Womanist Questions

SERVANTHOOD OR DISCIPLESHIP?

Jacquelyn Grant, for example, a leading womanist who has endeavored in some of her work to speak directly to the black church,[20] has asked about the pietistic language of servanthood that is commonplace in the church and its implications for black people in particular but especially for black women, who are "servants of the servants."[21] In an essay titled "The Sin of Servanthood and the Deliverance of Discipleship," Grant acknowledges the way in which the language of "service" and "servanthood" is seen to be a necessary corollary to the theological notion of the Lordship of Christ. In that sense, all are called to be servants. Yet the history of victimized peoples in the world discloses the contradiction between the sense that all are servants and the pain and perils of those who serve the privileged, without adequate remuneration, as part of a servant class. Succinctly put, "Some folk are more servants than others."[22] For black women, servanthood tends to mean servitude and all that accompanies it. Given the relationship between servanthood/service and suffering in black women's lives and the prominence of such language in the church, she asks, "Why do black women suffer so? Or even more pointedly, why does God permit the suffering of black women? Does God condone the fact that black women are systematically relegated to being 'servants of servants'?"[23]

What is at stake for Grant is the ways in which the pietistic language and God-talk of the church may advance patriarchal privilege, undermining the church's authentic mission as an instrument of justice and liberation. Thus, reflecting on the experience of black women, at least 70 percent of the black church, as a source for theologically evaluating

the faithfulness of the church's God-talk and witness, Grant's reflections are pointed when she asks and argues,

> How does one justify teaching a people that they are called to a life
> of service when they have been imprisoned by the most exploitative
> forms of service? Service and oppression of blacks went hand in hand.
> Therefore, to speak of service as empowerment, without concrete
> means or plans for economic, social, and political revolution that in
> fact leads to empowerment, is simply another form of "overspiritual-
> ization." It does not eliminate real pain and suffering, it merely spiritu-
> alizes the reality itself.[24]

Grant opines that the language of "discipleship" rather than "servanthood" is more appropriate to the distinctive mission of the black
church. The suggestion is that replacing such God-talk with meaningful language out of our theological heritage would do much to benefit black churchwomen, militating against sexism within the church.
Moreover, it would (1) prepare the church to be a better witness to
more just relationships between men and women in the society, (2)
address the enormous chasm between so-called public servants and
the powerful interests to which they are often beholden and the ordinary people they are actually elected to serve, and (3) sensitize public
policy to the service and plight of the working class in a global capitalistic economy. Grant argues that in a world characterized by injustice in human relationships, the church, called to stand over against the
world, does not need servants in order to fulfill its mission. It needs disciples. Moreover, it needs to invite women into the ranks of discipleship, a tight inner circle presumed to be the exclusive terrain of men.
Grant suggests that by inviting women to become disciples rather than
servants, black women and the church experience deliverance and are
empowered to bear witness to God's justice in the world.[25]

Frances E. Wood raises similar concerns as she addresses head-on
"the role of the church in the oppression of African-American women."
Just as Grant argues that "some folk are more servants than others,"
Wood suggests that, more often than not and more than to men, the

church's word to black women has been "take my yoke upon you."[26] For Wood, the yoke is not the one about which Jesus speaks in the New Testament.[27] Rather, it is "the yoke of oppression." Turning the language of a very familiar hymn in the black church, "Must Jesus Bear the Cross Alone," on its head, Wood pointedly asks, "Must women bear the yoke alone, and all the men go free?"[28]

THE CROSS, SURROGACY, AND SACRIFICE

Yet no one has pressed harder questions regarding the pietistic language of the church, especially notions of the cross, suffering, and redemption in relationship to black women's experience, than pioneering womanist theologian Delores Williams. Her questions and womanist reflections have struck right at the heart of the black church's self-understanding and mission, as she challenges traditional God-talk regarding the cross and the atonement.

In an article titled "Black Women's Surrogacy Experience and the Christian Notion of Redemption," Williams names the experience of *surrogacy* as perhaps the most distinguishing characteristic of black women's oppression in America.[29] Given the exploitation of black women's bodies for the purposes of sexual gratification and social control (before and after slavery), their common use as wet nurses for white babies, and the manipulation of their reproductive power as breeders for an enslaved labor force, surrogacy represents, in a system of white male patriarchy, the precise character of black women's oppression as compared to that of black men and white women.

Juxtaposing this distinctive history of violence and abuse against black women with the Christian understanding of Jesus as vicarious sacrifice or "the ultimate surrogate," Williams asks whether the view of one who saves through surrogacy has salvific power for black women or whether it actually reinforces their oppression by sacralizing it. Not unlike Jacquelyn Grant and Frances Wood, she is concerned about the theological reinforcement and reification of cultural and political notions of black women as servants for all others, even unto death. She insists, therefore, that true salvific power is present in black women's participation in the life and ministerial vision of Jesus.

The cross represents evil's desperate attempt to destroy that vision of life, and the resurrection is "the life of the ministerial vision gaining victory over the evil attempt to kill it." She avers,

> Black women are intelligent people living in a technological world where nuclear bombs, defilement of the earth, racism, sexism and economic injustice attest to the presence and power of evil in the world. Perhaps not many people today can believe that evil and sin were overcome by Jesus' death on the cross, that is, that Jesus took human sin upon himself and therefore saved humankind. Rather, it seems more intelligent to believe that redemption had to do with God, through Jesus, giving humankind new vision to see resources for positive, abundant relational life—a vision humankind did not have before.[30]

By raising poignant questions regarding the church's emphasis on the cross, as well as the salvific power of traditional language of atonement, Williams strikes right at the heart of black Christian faith, from slavery until the present postmodern moment. Born of the experience of slavery and suffering, the cross is a prominent theme in many of the spirituals.[31] It was a constant theme in the theological imagination and ministry of Martin Luther King, Jr., informing his understanding of suffering, nonviolence, and redemption. Moreover, it has been an important theme in the black church and black theology.[32]

This is why womanist theologian JoAnne Marie Terrell provides a sustained treatment of this issue in her important study titled *Power in the Blood: The Cross in the African American Experience.* She agrees with Williams that God did not condone the violence on the cross, nor does God condone black women's surrogacy or, for that matter, the violence perpetrated against the oppressed all over the world and sacralized by the powerful, even as they press their will on the powerless. Hence, this prominent trajectory of God's requiring the suffering of Jesus on the cross in Christian Tradition must be rejected. Yet Terrell argues for greater attentiveness to other Christian testimony within the synoptic gospels regarding the meaning of Jesus's death and resurrection. To that end, she argues that "Christians need to ponder the implications of Christ's death continuously, because the drama testifies to the exceedingly great lengths to which God goes to advise the extent of human estrangement." In contrast to Williams, she avers, "It is no slight on the intelligence of black women when they confess this; rather, it reflects on what they say they need and what they say Christ's real presence, mediated through the gospel, provides—redemption and release from the self-alienation and social alienation they experience in their workaday lives."[33]

In a work titled *What's Faith Got to Do with It? Black Bodies / Christian Souls*, Kelly Brown Douglas, like Williams and Terrell, raises concerns regarding the erroneous import and deleterious impact of classical Christian language regarding sacrifice. Addressing her work to the violence directed against black bodies in the name of Christian faith, she is careful to insist that redemption is never to be found in the sacrifice of the human body but only in the reclamation of it signified through the resurrection. Thus, she opines, "Those who opposed Jesus were the ones who crucified him. . . . I strongly contest any notion that God was party to or sanctioned in any way Jesus' crucifixion." Yet she concludes that the *crucifixion* itself does reveal at least two important theological truths: "the *revelatory privilege* of the 'least regarded'" and Jesus's *compassionate solidarity* with the poor within the very context of their dehumanization.[34]

I am in complete solidarity with womanists, as they raise critical and important questions about the significance of the church's pietistic language regarding the cross and sacrifice. Such language contains life-and-death implications for black women, men, and children negotiating the real world of suffering, surrogacy, and sacrifice. Yet I would argue that the concerns that womanists are raising regarding the import of Christian language of surrogacy and sacrifice are symptomatic of a more basic problem in the development of Western theology. It is a problem on which this discussion is largely focused and one central to the theological significance of the black church's historic oppositional witness to the white church, namely, the privatization of the meaning of all Christian doctrine such that the political meaning not only of the cross but of salvation, the ecclesial vocation of the church, and the reign of God itself are all lost to a truncated discussion limited to personal piety and interpersonal ethics (e.g., personal sacrifice in imitation of Christ). Meanwhile, the powers of domination are left unchallenged and intact.

I submit that it is the banishment of the faith into narrow and individualistic "enclaves of redemption,"[35] in the wake of Constantine's conversion and the emergence of the Christian empire, which gives rise to the sacralization of black women's surrogacy experience. Operating from within this cramped theological space, the church blesses the surrogacy experiences of black women as personal and pietistic responses in imitation of Christ rather than as signs of violence against those with whom Jesus stands in suffering solidarity. But in this instance, the cross is our best hope because it, more than anything else, actually signifies God's judgment against the empire and all its violent manifestations. The cross embodies the deep contradictions between the empire's claims about itself and the truth known only by the victims of the empire. It is Rome's premier instrument for political execution and thus represents, in the first instance, the powers of domination. Yet the pre-Constantinian Christian cultus, standing over against the empire, actually embraced this political instrument of death and domination as the power of God.

Clearly, Rome viewed the cross from the top down. But the church of the martyrs viewed the cross from the bottom up. The problem is that this view from the bottom up always presumes an oppositional witness, and in its absence, the church's own perspective on its most radical symbol of principled resistance is unavoidably distorted. In this way, the justification of black women's tragic historical experience of surrogacy (Williams), the oppressive manifestations of the "hermeneutics of sacrifice" (Terrell), and the sacralization of violence directed against black bodies (Brown Douglas) are symptomatic secretions of an apostate church co-opted by the powers of domination. Truthfully, a co-opted church knows *only* the cross of Rome, with its varying secretions of violence and victimization, and not the radical cross of Christ.

The church of the American Christian slavocracy, with its truncated theology of enslaved bodies and saved souls, was one representation of this problem. That was why black Christians rejected its Christ and embraced a Jesus who, like them, was crucified and who stood in solidarity with them as they suffered. His resurrection signified their victory over the powers of domination and death and emboldened them to *fight, even unto death*. But the church that Dietrich Bonhoeffer challenged in Hitler's Germany was another example of a co-opted church with a distorted view of the meaning of the cross. For the Third Reich had its own christology and vision of atonement, recited in one catechism for schoolchildren: "As Jesus set men free from sin and hell, so Hitler rescued the German people from destruction. . . . Jesus built for heaven; Hitler, for the German earth."[36] In opposition to this larger political reality, Bonhoeffer lifts up the cross of Jesus, whom he brilliantly refers to as the *Counter-Logos*. The empire and the empire's church cannot handle the dangerous cross of Christ.

> Man seeks to deny the one with whom he is confronted. Pilate asks, "who are you?," and Jesus is silent. Man cannot wait for the answer, because it is too dangerous. The logos cannot endure the Counter-Logos. It knows that one of them must die. . . . The incarnate Logos of God must be crucified by man's logos. . . . Christ goes through the ages, questioned anew, misunderstood anew, and again and again put to death.[37]

During Bonhoeffer's time at New York's Union Theological Seminary and while spending much time in Harlem, the German churchman had been exposed, prior to these christological reflections, to the deep spirituality and profound sorrow of the black spirituals.[38] Regarding the trial and execution of Jesus, one intones, "Dey whupped him all night long, . . . an' he never said a mumbling word." Bonhoeffer, like those who created the spirituals, had come to know the crucified Jesus, the Counter-Logos of God, the power and truth of whose cross can only be known *"from below"*[39] and *in resistance* to a determined evil.

Yet, in a real sense, womanists have always known that revolutionary change always occurs from the bottom up. This is why womanist ecclesiology has sought to address itself both to sexism in the pietistic language and practices of black churches and to what I call *the dewomanization of black radicalism* evident in the historical memory and theological imagination of black theologians.

The Dewomanization of Black Radicalism

BLACK THEOLOGY HAS sought to lift up the radical tradition[40] in black religious history as that which is most faithful to the liberationist intent of the gospel. Methodologically, this has been done in varying ways—by pointing out both a theological and a historical distinction between: the pre–Civil War black church and the post–Civil War black church (Cone); the Negro church and the black church (Lincoln); and the radical church of the nineteenth century and the deradicalized church that emerged sometime following Reconstruction (Wilmore). In the work of these and other black male theologians, prominent names in the radical black church tradition of the antebellum period have been Henry McNeal Turner, Gabriel Prosser, Alexander Crummell, Denmark Vesey, Nat Turner, and Henry Highland Garnett. On the other hand, prominent exceptions to the "deradicalized" black church of the postbellum period have been Adam Clayton Powell, Jr., Martin Luther King, Jr., Albert Cleage, and the Muslim cleric Malcolm X. Hence, on both sides of this theological and historical equation, the subtle, countercultural piety and political activism of ordinary black churchwomen, as they have fought against oppression in the society and the churches, have not been central to the analysis. I call this limitation in the interpretation of black religious history the dewomanization of black radicalism.

Sociologist of religion Cheryl Townsend Gilkes observes that "when describing, analyzing, and criticizing the black church, almost every eye tends to be turned toward the pulpits, pastors, and their convocations and conflicts." As a result, the "enterprising agency" manifested in the work of black women, inside and outside institutional church structures and in the worst and best of times, is not taken seriously, sometimes even by the women themselves.[41] Accordingly, she judges black male theologian Gayraud Wilmore's "deradicalization" thesis, not unlike those proffered by other male interpreters,[42] to be an "androcentric theory." Moreover, she points out that "the period of deradicalization that is often linked to the rise of the Sanctified Church (or black sects and cults) is also one of the most intense periods of activism of black church women" in the development of a distinctive black piety,

particularly in the Sanctified or Pentecostal-Holiness Church tradition, and the organizing of black women's political interests in organizations such as the National Association of Colored Women and the National Council of Negro Women.[43]

It shall be our task in this final section of our discussion on womanist ecclesiology to examine the Sanctified Church and the activism of black women within it and other black churches as well as in their women's conventions. What is recognized here is that "the tendency to view black churches only as agencies of sociopolitical change led by black male pastors . . . obscures the central and critical roles of black women."[44] Our aim, therefore, is to examine how womanist reflections on these neglected pietistic traditions, such as contemplative practices,[45] as well as alternative spaces of power and agency led by women inside and outside the institutional churches, might impact our appreciation for the diverse and complex character of black religious resistance to racism and our theological understanding of the mission of the black church, yesterday, today, and tomorrow.

THE SANCTIFIED CHURCH

Zora Neale Hurston has suggested that "the Sanctified Church is a protest against the high-brow tendency in Negro Protestant congregations as the Negroes gain more education and wealth."[46] In that sense, there is a distinct countercultural dimension to its rise and continued existence. As Cheryl Townsend Gilkes points out, the term "Sanctified Church" is itself an expression that came about in the black community to distinguish congregations of "the Saints" from those in other mainline black denominations. These congregations are a part of the intersecting Pentecostal and Holiness movements of the post-Reconstruction era, and the designations "the Saints" and the "Sanctified Church" relate a peculiar sense of ethnic and religio-cultural kinship while also serving as a kind of shorthand for a vast array of denominational histories and considerable diversity within the group itself.[47]

Emerging during the period of the black church's deradicalization, as black theologians have described it, the significance of the Sanctified

Church lies in its bold countercultural witness to the old-time religion of the slaves during a time when other black churches were uncritically imitating Euro-American styles of worship and polity; its positive redefinition of black womanhood in the face of racist stereotypes and stigma; the exercise of a "spiritual militancy" and piety that challenged racist assertions about black humanity; and greater and earlier access to pulpits for women than was the case for Baptist and Methodist women.[48]

This spiritual militancy manifested itself as a critical witness against racism within the traditions of the Sanctified Church.[49] Gilkes astutely observes that when white Americans were calling black people by their first names, irrespective of age, as a means of racial insult or by names intended to malign their character and diminish their personhood, members of the Sanctified Church were referring to each other as "Saints."[50] The majority of the Saints being protected from the onslaught of white supremacy were women, and the religious lingo was just one part of the church's resistance strategy to forces inimical to black humanity. Church members also resisted by refraining from the use of first names in any interracial setting, publishing only the initials and surnames of church officers on cornerstones and other public documents, and maintaining a studied and distinctive dress code. Encouraged to "dress as becometh holiness," one bishop opined that the sight of the women who followed the directions of the Women's Department would restrain the excesses of the most ardent racist.[51]

According to Gilkes's research, all of this was part of a kind of religious sensibility that was also intended to preserve a sense of dignity and personhood. This struggle for survival, dignity, and the maintenance of black personhood also manifested itself in a commitment to education, even within this church that has most often been stereotyped by interpreters as the domain of the illiterate and disengaged black masses. Over against these kinds of sweeping generalizations, women such as Arenia C. Mallory, of the Church of God in Christ, played an especial role in the work of racial uplift and through "a combination of male decisions and female enterprise" became educators of "the Race."[52]

The work of black women such as Arenia Mallory of the Church of God in Christ bespeaks parallel traditions of power and activism created within the patriarchal structures of black churches but largely ignored by interpretations that are focused on leadership as it emanates from the pulpit and male pastors. Described as a protégé of Mary McLeod Bethune, Mallory was hired first as a teacher at Saints Academy in Lexington, Mississippi. Following the death of the school's first principal, Mallory became the principal. Under her leadership, it expanded from a primary academy to a fully accredited junior college. For some time, Mallory was the only black woman serving as a college president in the nation.[53]

Emilie Townes has contributed much to our understanding of the moral agency exercised by black women, as they fought racism in the culture and patriarchy in the churches, by analyzing the life of Ida B. Wells-Barnett.[54] Wells-Barnett is an exceptional figure in black religious history who used her writing and speaking skills in a courageous campaign against lynching. She organized the first black woman's club in Illinois, and one of the club's first projects was to raise money in order to effectively prosecute a police officer in a case of police brutality which ended in the death of an innocent black man on the West Side of Chicago.[55] During the Springfield, Illinois, riot of 1908, Wells-Barnett organized the young men of a Bible class she taught at Grace Presbyterian Church into what became the Negro Fellowship League. With Wells-Barnett having raised their consciousness and organizational skills, the League established a Reading Room and a Social Center for men and boys.[56] Additionally, she was active in the women's suffrage movement and was present for the founding of the NAACP.

Finally, Townes observes that when ministers in her own AME Church debated, in 1894, whether to endorse Wells-Barnett's work, she audaciously responded by saying, "I cannot see why I need your endorsement. Under God I have done work without any assistance from my own people. And when I think that I have been able to do the work with his assistance that you could not do, if you would, and you would not do if you could, I think I have a right to a feeling of strong indignation."[57]

Womanist ecclesiology pushes our theological understanding of the mission of the black church and its relationship to black women's piety and culture as witness against racism. It insists that inasmuch as black women are, in fact, the majority of the black church, any methodological approach to interpreting its history and any theological assertion regarding its mission must ensure that black women's piety and culture are integral to the analysis. For to do so is to take seriously the status of women as members of the Body of Christ, disciples of the gospel of liberation who have been no weaker or less significant than the church's male members.

Yet part of the methodological challenge is that taking black women seriously requires a willingness to apply the tools of sustained inquiry to women's conventions, Christian education programs, and other parallel structures within the black church, where ordinary black women have organized their own resistance to racism while also negotiating and fighting the sexism and patriarchal structures of a church that most have not chosen to leave. The observation by Gilkes and others that the activism of black women in the Sanctified Church and other black churches has often heightened just at the time when bishops and other male leaders have been distracted by infighting for power and insignificant issues of institutional maintenance suggests the need for more nuanced and perhaps even gender-specific ways of evaluating what the church is doing at any given historical period.

In any case, the insights of womanist theologians and the womanist culture embedded within the black church and black culture suggest that the mission of the black church is both liberation and survival, the steady rekindling of a spiritual militancy and deep piety that manifests itself in political action. Womanist reflections on the piety of ordinary churchwomen show the extent to which faith confessions and sensibilities too easily overlooked by an intense revolutionary gaze or dubbed as "accommodationist" may in fact represent subtle but significant acts of resistance by the poor against forces arrayed against their humanity. In this regard, womanist theologian JoAnne Terrell has called for theologians to give greater attention to the exegesis of the "confessional utterances found in black hymnody" and in the folk sayings and testimony of black church culture beyond the spirituals and after slavery. Among these are pietistic affirmations and mantras such as "God is good—all the time," "watch, [*fight*], and pray," and "God is God all by Himself." Some of these "confessional utterances," she suggests, may, like the first, confirm the traditional meanings of biblical texts that the "steadfast love of God never ceases" (Lam. 3:22). But others, like the second and the third, amplify biblical texts, pushing them in distinctive ways, even as oppressed people affirm their own human agency to fight against the limits of history, giving voice to their obligation to resist the idolatrous overtures of other gods who would "usurp God's dominion over black peoples' lives."[58]

By probing the confessional language and critical insights of ordinary churchwomen, womanist ecclesiology is pushing the black theology movement to engage more deeply the pietistic dimension of black religion that has bemused intellectuals, black and white, for generations. Because women in the Sanctified Church and in mainline denominations have been the chief arbiters of the piety of the masses, greater emphasis on it will likely have the net effect of uprooting entrenched androcentric assumptions in black theological historiography about the character of the black struggle during the civil rights movement and in other moments in black religious resistance as well. Moreover, by positing a multidimensional methodology that unmasks the hidden demons of sexism in black church polity and orthodox Christian speech, womanist ecclesiology is providing critical markers for continuing dialogue between pastors and theologians about the future of liberation's mission outside and inside the church walls.

CONCLUSION

THE RELATIONSHIP BETWEEN black theology and the black church
—and concomitantly the state of their dialogue regarding the latter's
mission—has not improved since the issue was first raised in the mid
1970s.[1] Indeed, with the rising media presence and political influence
of an uncritical white evangelicalism, biblical fundamentalism, and
prosperity gospel preaching in black churches,[2] one might well argue
that the situation has gotten worse. That is why while many white
Americans were getting their first glimpse into the Sunday worship
and preaching of a black church during the Jeremiah Wright debacle
of 2008, most laypersons and far too many clergy in the black church
were for the very first time hearing the term "black theology." This
was true despite the fact that black theology was created in the black
church and is an extension of its radical and prophetic side.

Notwithstanding the distinctive roles of black theology and the
black church, I would still argue that the divide is unfortunate and
unnecessary. This becomes clear once one understands the nature and
nuances of the important historical relationship between the black
church and black theology and the ways in which the latter must be
regarded as the last of four critical moments in the centuries-long project of African American Christians' critical apprehension and development of an antiracist and holistically salvific faith.

Providing, for the first time in the intellectual history of black
church interpretation, a critical and self-conscious *theological* principle

for assessing the black church's faithfulness to its own best self-understanding, the etiology of black theology's meaning is inextricably connected to the black church's distinctive ecclesiological identity and liberationist mission. Moreover, the life of each occurs along an identifiable and distinctive liberationist trajectory of African American faith formed in the crucible of American chattel slavery. The first moment was *Christianization*, but in it, African Americans were not simply redeemed by the faith; they redeemed the faith itself, transforming it into an instrument of liberation. If the independent black church movement represented the *institutionalization* of that basic liberationist tenet of black faith, and if Martin Luther King, Jr.'s ministry of proclamation and activism, sourced by the dialectical tensions between black evangelical piety and black resistance, represented the developmental stage of *conscientization*, then the black theology movement provided, for the first time, its careful and self-critical *systematization*. Yet all four are *liberationist* moments tied together in the reality of an oppressed people's testimony to their spiritual encounter with the mystery of a sovereign and almighty God. In this way, it is not possible to identify an authentic black piety that is not connected to liberation, nor is it possible to fully account for the strengths and limitations of one of these four moments without reference to the others.

Moreover, subsequent developments within the fourth moment, culminating with the work of second-generation black theologians, newer voices within the movement, and the birth of womanist theology further clarify the difficult, complex, and multifaceted character of the liberationist project. Specifically, white supremacy has to be fought in varying ways, and the liberationist agenda of the church, as it aims toward the fulfillment of God's salvific purposes for humanity, must extend outward and inward in a truly multidimensional and radically improvisational approach that addresses the basic human need for personal fulfillment and existential meaning, even while challenging systemic structures of oppression in political economy, religious discourse (confessional and academic), and church polity.

Therefore, I argue that the continuation of this important but difficult work requires much greater intentionality and initiative toward the development of an organic institutional infrastructure, reminiscent of the NCBC or the black theology project but for a new era, that mediates honest, risk-taking dialogue between black and womanist theologians and black pastors. Such an infrastructure would provide the much-needed institutional foundation for the commencement of a fifth and necessary moment—an *integrative moment*, in the development of black people's apprehension of an antiracist and holistically salvific faith, that is, *the flowering of a self-critical liberationist community.*

Leadership for such a moment would come from black and womanist theologians and black pastors who conceive of their project as an organic movement between Athens and Jerusalem, Sanctified Churches and human rights marches, ivory towers and ebony trenches. In the age of new technologies, including the Internet and social media platforms which have the ability to facilitate the breadth, depth, and speed of democratic speech and participation in unprecedented ways, leadership in such a moment would seek to engage, empower, and energize the masses. Indeed, the only way to test whether our spiritual piety is authentic and our theological speech and proclamation is indeed *good news* is to see whether the poor will hear it and receive it as such (Luke 4:18).

Given the black church's current and acute crisis in identity and mission, signified by the rising influence of the most uncritical versions of white evangelicalism, biblical fundamentalism, and personal prosperity preaching, black academic theologians and black pastors who are committed to liberation need now, more than ever, to *create together* within the black church and black community spaces for serious, sustained, and regularly scheduled dialogue about the nature of black liberationist praxis in this postmodern moment. The analysis put forth here has demonstrated that central to that dialogue should be a discussion around the complex relationship between piety and protest, the evangelical and political dimensions of black faith that underscore differences in praxeological commitments among black pastors and animate tensions between black theologians and black pastors regarding the content of the church's mission as an instrument of divine salvation.

It is very clear that black churches cannot continue to marginalize (and in too many cases ignore) the work of political liberation without also undermining their own *liberationist* heritage and selling their own birthright as a distinctive and independent witness among the American churches. The black church was born fighting for freedom, and freedom is indeed its only reason for being. But neither can black theology afford to marginalize the importance of personal piety. Too often it has, and to that extent it disconnects itself from the *internal freedom* evinced in black evangelical piety and celebrated in worship. This piety, expressed as faith in the mystery and sovereignty of an almighty God, has helped to ignite the black church's quest for liberation and inspired the masses therein to fight and win improbable victories, against the tragic limits of history, from slavery on to the civil rights movement and beyond. Hence, a primary aim of this new institutional infrastructure that I am proposing would be to aid the church in the hard work of more fully integrating within its own self-understanding and self-consciousness the radical ecclesiological implications of the third moment. Only then can it begin to truly see itself and the theological meaning of its own continuing project of liberation as carried out by black theologians in the fourth moment and then prepare for the self-critical work that now demands the attention of both a radical remnant of black pastors and black theologians for the urgency of a fifth moment.

The Black Church and the Third Moment

IRONICALLY, THE BLACK church has celebrated Martin Luther King, Jr., while in large measure holding him at arms length, refusing to embrace the most radical ecclesiological implications of his ministry for the church's own self-understanding, mission, and institutional agenda. For Martin Luther King, Jr., was not simply a churchman who happened to be caught up in a revolutionary moment. Rather, he was one who, while caught up in a moment much larger than himself, came to see revolution as central to the church's *primary* reason for being. This is what he means when he says, "Any religion that professes to be concerned with the souls of men and is not concerned with the slums that damn them, the economic conditions that strangle them, and the social conditions that cripple them is a dry-as-dust religion."[3]

Yet the sociological evidence[4] suggests that the black church, even while continuing to focus on race and other issues of justice, has, in large measure, embraced a bifurcated understanding of salvation that privileges individual souls, not seeing the redemption of black bodies and the transformation of the whole of society as *central* to its vocation as an instrument of God's salvation. In this way, social action may be viewed as an important part of the church's outreach programs, but seldom is it reflected on theologically as an indispensable mark of the church's basic vocation. Consequently, social action focused around issues of justice is not prioritized along with worship, preaching, revivals, and other efforts seen as essential to God's saving work, mediated through the church and its witness.

This is to say that even in what has historically been America's most radical church, personal piety is given far more sustained and systematic attention than liberation. Black churches, largely unequipped with their own self-conscious theological principle (black theology) and a sophisticated biblical hermeneutics for fending off the unconscious assumptions of the American evangelical ethos, have embraced a bifurcated soteriology that privileges individual salvation and diminishes their role in the hard work of social transformation. Moreover, with the social upward mobility of a burgeoning black middle class and upper class and the concomitant immiseration of the poor, a bifurcated soteriology that clearly privileges "the slavery of sin" over "the sin of slavery" risks becoming a truncated soteriology that dismisses the concerns of the latter altogether. This is what makes the radical ecclesiological implications of Martin Luther King, Jr.'s ministry marginal, even to the church from which he emerged, particularly in this postmodern moment. What was always a radical remnant is quickly becoming a remnant of a remnant.

Thus, part of what the black church needs is a deeper understanding of the relationship between the ministry of social activism, embodied in the civil rights movement, and the reality of a liberationist faith rooted not only in the black church's history but in scripture. Because an enslaved people initially suspicious of "book religion" have become increasingly a people of the Book[5] and because a sustained engagement of the biblical witness is, in my view, indispensable to any authentically Christian theology, a theology that illuminates the biblical basis for freedom fighting, as the theological core of salvation's work, and thus more firmly situates the black church within the liberationist legacy of its own third moment is an important key to correcting this problem.

The doctrine of salvation is the place to begin when speaking of the church's mission because even if the Bible "does not always use a formally salvific terminology," it "introduces on practically every page the theme of salvation (or its absence)."[6] A sophisticated biblical hermeneutic shows that in contradistinction to the preaching of salvation in the American churches, salvation is not, in its ancient Hebraic context, a narrow idea.[7] Rather, it is a very broad and multifaceted concept, covering the full range of human concerns, including deliverance from dangers in battle (Psalm 18), from adversaries and wicked people (Psalms 7, 109, 12:1, 43:1, 86:16), and from death itself (Psalm 86:13). But it must be emphasized that "it is above all the whole people of Israel who receive salvation."[8] For ancient Hebrew slaves and for an enslaved black people whose faith was formed in the context of the "invisible institution," communal liberation was the focus of salvation talk, and its starting point is the Exodus story. There, the etymological root of salvation has first and foremost to do with the identity and mission of the God who has "come down to deliver them from the Egyptians, and to bring them up out of that land to a good and spacious land, a land flowing with milk and honey" (Exod. 3:8b). The God of Moses is known and worshiped as the God "who brought you out of the land of Egypt, out of the house of slavery" (Exod. 20:2b).

The theological import for the black church, as it reflects on its mission, is the recognition that ancient Israel's worship of Yahweh was never an apolitical, pietistic expression disconnected from the story of liberation. Salvation understood as liberation is the controlling category in God-talk and praise songs. "I will sing to the LORD, for he has triumphed gloriously; horse and rider he has thrown into the sea" (Exod. 12:1b). Moreover, Brevard Childs, a leading proponent of the canonical-critical approach to biblical studies, has argued that the story of the Exodus maintains its centrality and formative influence "throughout the entire Old Testament." The theme is present in Deuteronomy (5:6, 6:20ff., 26:5ff.) and in the redaction of the Deuteronomistic historian (3:1ff.). It is echoed in the hymnic and poetic reflections of the psalter (Psalms 78, 105, 14) and the oracles of the pre-exilic prophets (Amos 2:10, 9:7; Hosea 2:15).[9] Childs further observes that in the prophetic remembrances of Ezekiel and Deutero-Isaiah, it is expanded as they speak of an eschatological exodus (Ezek. 20:33–44; Isa. 52:11ff., 63:11ff.). While in exile, the memory of the exodus functioned as a paradigm of hope in the consciousness of an oppressed people, expressing itself in prayer and praise:

> *Awake, awake put on strength,*
> *O arm of the Lord!*
> *Awake, as in the days of old,*
> *the generations of long ago! . . .*
> *Was it not you who dried up the sea,*
> *the waters of the great deep;*
> *who made the depths of the sea a way*
> *for the redeemed to cross over?*
> *So the ransomed of the Lord shall return,*
> *and come to Zion with singing;*
> *everlasting joy shall be upon their heads;*
> *they shall obtain joy and gladness,*
> *and sorrow and sighing shall flee away.*
> (Isa. 51:9–11)

The formative influence of the exodus motif continues to hold sway in the late Old Testament period as well. Some examples are the prayer of Ezra (Neh. 9:6ff.), Daniel 9:15, 1 Chronicles 17:21, and 2 Chronicles 6:5, 7:22. In this way, the salvific moment of freedom from bondage is paradigmatic in the shaping of biblical faith and biblical expressions of piety.

Moreover, if the black church's mission is to be informed by the biblical witness, then it should know that the eighth-century prophets continued this salvific emphasis on social transformation. Yet such an understanding of the biblical witness, within the context of the American churches, does push against the grain. For as biblical scholar Marvin L. Chaney has observed, "Under the impress of the extreme individualism of American culture, many modern readers of the prophetic books assume that these texts excoriate a few venal individuals who deviated from norms otherwise observed in what was a healthy and just economic system." He avers that "little could be farther from the realities of Ancient Israel and Judah."[10]

Chaney characterizes the situation thusly: A period of rather impressive military power and territorial expansion, under the mostly concurrent reigns of Jeroboam II in the North and Uzziah in the South, occasioned an externally secure situation unlike Israel had known since the time of the Davidic-Solomonic United Monarchy. Royal administrations, hence, had the time and opportunity to adjust their economies to the increasing advantage of the elite. Peasants were regularly cheated in the marketplace. Judiciary corruption facilitated and accelerated the foreclosure of small plots, exorbitant interest rates, and peasant displacement from "the good and spacious land" promised to their ancestors. It is against this social and economic backdrop that the sharp critique and advocacy of eighth-century prophets, such as Amos, is to be heard:

> Hear this, you who trample upon the needy
> and destroy the poor of the land!
> "When will the new moon be over," you ask,
> "That we may sell our grain,
> And the Sabbath, that we may display the wheat?
> We will diminish the ephah,
> add to the shekel,
> and fix our scales for cheating!
> We will buy the lowly man for silver,
> and the poor man for a pair of sandals;
> even the refuse of the wheat we will sell!"
> (Amos 8:4–6)

He speaks of the high price to be paid for injustice. It is divine retribution visited on all the land, to be sure, but particularly on those who caused the suffering of the poor: "Therefore, now they shall be the first to go into exile, and their wanton revelry shall be done away with" (Amos 6:7). In a passage often quoted by Martin Luther King, Jr., Amos argues for the inextricable relationship between true pietistic praise and a commitment to justice: "Take away from me the noise of your songs; I will not listen to the melody of your harps. But let justice roll down like waters, and righteousness like an everflowing stream" (Amos 5:23–24).

Womanists have rightly framed this basic hermeneutical focus on "the sin of slavery" to include not just the theme of liberation but survival as evinced in other key passages, particularly the Hagar-Ishmael motif.[11] Finally, this understanding of liberation and *survival* as salvation's primary mission in the Old Testament is taken up in the New Testament by the gospel of Jesus, focused, as it is, on "Good News to the poor" (Luke 4:18*b*), and is expressed, in apocalyptic terms, by an early church community in an extreme situation of oppression as they hold out for God's judgment against systemic oppression and the coming of "a new heaven and a new earth" (Rev. 21:1*a*).

I posit all of this as an oppositional hermeneutic and the biblical basis on which the black church is called on to resist the encroachment of an uncritical biblicism that ignores that which is central to the mission of the church, reentering the biblical matrix of its own liberationist heritage as carried out by black churches during the first through the third moments of African American Christian resistance to racism. But if deeper engagement of the earlier moments (especially the third moment) by black churches lays a necessary foundation for the work ahead, the theological self-consciousness with which the work must proceed cannot be accomplished without reference to the fourth moment. Moreover, if the mission of the true church cannot be understood apart from the mission of Christ, then a black faith that truly sees truncated notions of God's salvation as a heresy against God and a sin against the poor must embrace a self-consciously oppositional thesis—a thesis signified by black theologians through the transvaluative meaning of the cross and "the Black Christ."[12]

Black Theologians and the Fourth Moment

THE BLACK CHRIST, posited by black theologians, stands in judgment *against* the theology of the white church. In that sense, it advises the black church of the depth of the *theological* difference between the religion that sacralized slavery and the religion that resisted it. Theologian James Cone, clearly the most prominent voice of the black theology movement, was the first to call the black church to a radical theological break with white Christianity. His emphasis on blackness as an ontological symbol, within the context of the black power movement, was an apt call on the church to stand where Christ stands, in unqualified solidarity with the poor of society, and to stake its claim with Christ as a divine witness *against* oppression.

In view of Cone's important contribution, I would call on the black church to hear the full theological import of his call in this new moment by moving beyond mere *political* over-againstness to *ontological over-againstness*. For in contradistinction to the Christ that it proclaims, the black church, like most churches, has a very difficult time giving its life over *fully* to the Christ who "bids [one] come and die," losing one's life for the sake of gaining it in principled and uncompromising struggle against "powers and principalities." Too often it is self-absorbed in the mundane work of self-preservation through meetings, budgets, and internal operational programming. Failing to incorporate a posture of principled over-againstness into the basic structure of its ecclesial self-understanding, its resistance is seen primarily in reaction to momentary political crises, glaring episodes of insult that bear witness to the ever-present disease of white supremacy in the body politic. In this sense, the black church has manifested a kind of over-againstness that is unduly limited to reacting to specific episodes and the machinations of electoral politics. There is little evidence that the churches have internalized the *fundamentally oppositional* character of the gospel as an ecclesial way of actually *being* the true church.

If *mission* is tied fundamentally to *being*, and the mission of the church is liberation, then the church is called to assume a posture of *ontological over-againstness* as the mark of an authentic Christian witness in every moment of its existence in a sinful and unjust world. As opposed to the reactionary, political over-againstness with which the black church typically has expressed itself in response to some immediate political stimulus (e.g., a protest march, participation in electoral politics), ontological over-againstness points to something deeper in the soul of the faith community. The former is episodic, while the latter is existential. It will therefore manifest itself during and in between extraordinary revolutionary moments in the proclamation, hymnody, programmatic thrust, and ministerial praxis of a church that resists the allure of "success," focusing instead on the concerns of the poor and standing visibly as a witness to God's solidarity with the most marginalized members of the human family.

But in order to embrace and sustain over-againstness as a profound, persistent, and ecclesial way of *being* in an inveterately unjust world, the black church will need to interrogate the meaning of its spirituality, and black theologians and black pastors will need to further clarify the relationship between piety and liberation. For it takes a profound spirituality to stand on the side of truth and to sustain resistance against evil and injustice against the overwhelming tide and tragic limits of history.

This is why the discipline of black theology must become much more attentive to the pietistic dimensions of black faith ensconced in the fabric of black churches. This faith is grounded in the revivalistic consciousness of the Second Great Awakening, during which large numbers of slaves—inspired by the embodied, interior freedom and liberating implications of a dynamic, evangelical faith—first became Christians. But with the turn of the twentieth century came the appearance of the Azusa Street Revival, the birth of Pentecostalism, and the rise of the "Sanctified Church." Moreover, with Pentecostalism's rapid growth among certain segments of the black church, particularly the poor, the evangelical faith embodied in Baptist, Methodist, and other mainline denominations was itself immersed in a movement that was decidedly more pneumatological in its theological emphasis, exuberant in its liturgical expression, and countercultural in its worldview. Zora Neale Hurston's classic interpretation is apt:

"The Sanctified Church is a protest against the high-brow tendency in Negro Protestant congregations as the Negroes gain more education and wealth."[13]

Yet more recently, Pentecostal and neo-Pentecostal piety has exploded as a global phenomenon, crossing racial, class, and denominational boundaries to become a rapidly growing movement among Christians, particularly the poor, worldwide.[14] This is why Theo Witvliet, who has demonstrated a deeper understanding and appreciation for black theology than hardly any other white theologian, has called attention to black theologians' need to more adequately engage this prominent pietistic side of black faith in their methodology and to probe its strengths and limitations for their liberationist agenda.[15]

Succinctly put, piety and protest must be held together because the biblical witness affirms that the gospel is the message of Jesus Christ to the poor who seek liberation and to the poor in spirit who seek transformation and meaning in a broken and sinful world. Moreover, this view is based on my reading of the nature of black Christian resistance in virtually every moment of black people's history. It is expressed in the testimony of slaves and by those who were deeply involved in the civil rights movement who speak of it as a time of personal and political transformation.[16] Its mass meetings were a profound display of a politically engaged piety, and the spirituality of its most celebrated leader, signified by a kitchen conversion experience, served as his existential anchor in the midst of real danger and human despair.

Moreover, the "spiritual militancy" examined by womanist sociologist of religion Cheryl Townsend Gilkes and evinced by the women and men of the Sanctified Church has exhibited both an otherworldly impulse and a counterworldly impulse that manifests itself primarily as a kind of *countercultural* resistance.[17] Clearly, ontological over-againstness would require an engagement of both politics *and* culture. All of this suggests that black theologians must ask themselves anew, "What does faithful proclamation to the poor and in response to their pain sound like during the daily silences *between* revolutionary moments?" I suggest that here the pietistic impulse, as it grounds those who faithfully struggle against evil in the mystery and reality of a sovereign God, is itself a work of liberation.

Black Theologians, Black Pastors, and the Fifth Moment

IF BLACK ACADEMIC theologians and black pastors are serious about black people's survival and liberation, then they ought to risk the comfort and prestige of their respective enclaves of academic and ecclesial privilege and commence a new moment, an *integrative moment* that brings together the revolutionary insights of black intellectuals and the institutional strength of the black church. The immediate aim is the development of a full-orbed pastoral and public theology of black liberation—one that is hermeneutically sophisticated in its engagement of biblical texts, historically conscious of the liberating heritage of the black church, multidimensional in its methodology, organically connected to meaningful social praxis, and sufficiently attentive to the latent spiritual militancy ensconced in the evangelical religion of the masses of black churches. In other words, what is most needed in the continuum of black religious resistance to oppression is *the flowering of a self-critical black liberationist community*.

Black theology stands to benefit from the commencement of this fifth moment because theology is critical reflection on the faith done on behalf of a community of faith. That is to say that part of what sets theology apart from other disciplines that may engage religion and religious discourse is its circle of critical accountability to and ongoing conversation with the faith community. For black theology, that community must be the black church. If it is not in the black church, then where is it? For black theology came out of the black church (NCBC), and it was born out of intense discussion among black pastors and black religious intellectuals regarding the distinctive meaning and mission of the black church (Joseph Washington's *Black Religion*). Moreover, its liberationist understanding of the gospel was largely inspired by a mass movement based in the church and led by a churchman (Martin Luther King, Jr.). Thus, the commencement of this new, fifth moment and the building of an institutional infrastructure, reminiscent of the NCBC or the black theology project, would actually reconnect black theology to its most militant roots and provide a regular forum in which to test the truth of its claims within the church community from which it emerged.

The black church would benefit because absent a critical and self-conscious theological principle against which to test its proclamation, the black church, precisely because it is largely an evangelical church, is likely to give itself over to the stealthy rhetoric of conservative evangelicalism, increasingly unaware of the significance of its own history of oppositional witness and the *theological* difference between that witness and the preaching of the most popular televangelists, white and black. Similarly, because the black church does place much emphasis on scripture, it would benefit greatly from a critical hermeneutics of collective memory regarding its historical approach to biblical texts.[18]

Finally, the black community would benefit from the commencement of this new moment because, at a moment of political and social crisis, in far too many instances, the gospel is not being heard. It is not being heard because the church born fighting for freedom needs to be clearer about what the gospel is and who it is as an instrument of its living manifestation in the world. Moreover, the black theology movement currently lacks an adequate institutional infrastructure and vision for a sustained public voice within the churches and the larger community. The resources for such an infrastructure can come perhaps only from a radical remnant within the churches themselves in partnership with scholars who possess a commitment to the life and social relevancy of the church.

Black theologians and black pastors must readdress their respective work to the reality and content of black suffering in this moment. It is there that the black church will rediscover its public voice and theologians and pastors will see that which makes a renewed dialogue and joint commitment between them not only desirable but urgent. For it was the urgent cry of black power, as it gave voice to black pain, that occasioned the rise of black theology and the work of the pastors and theologians who were its creators and earliest interlocutors. In fact, naming the impatience and heightened consciousness among black youth "the religion of black power," Vincent Harding suggested, in 1968, the need to explore its significance from the standpoint of faith: "It would be myopic to miss the central issues of human life and destiny which course through the current expression of blackness. Issues of anthropology, incarnation, the nature of the universe and of God, issues of hope and faith, questions of eschatology and of the nature of the kingdom, problems concerning love and its functions—all these and more are at stake in the present situation."[19] Clearly, Harding saw in the black power movement some hint of the truth of liberation's claim that God is hidden yet active in human history. But if Harding suggests that the black power movement was rife with theological questions, James Cone would be the first to set out to demonstrate this in a systematic way. Also, seeing black suffering as the context for doing theology and of God's revelatory action in history, he has this to say:

> It would seem that Black Power and Christianity have this in common: the liberation of man! If the work of Christ is that of liberating men from alien loyalties, and if racism is, as George Kelsey says, an alien faith, then there must be some correlation between Black Power and Christianity. For the gospel proclaims that God is with us now, actively fighting the forces which would make man captive. And it is the task of theology and the Church to know where God is at work so that we can join him in this fight against evil.[20]

Given this history in which black suffering provided the primary context in which academics such as Cone and Harding and the pastors of the NCBC considered their work, a sustained conversation among black theologians and black pastors regarding the social circumstances and contradictions that cry out today for critical reflection on "the central issues of human life" is well overdue. Among them are a politically motivated and profit-driven prison-industrial complex, HIV/AIDS, drug addiction and the so-called war on drugs, homelessness, glaring racial and class disparities in public education, and the stresses on millions of families trying to survive without a living wage. If the black church will not give itself over to this work, then it will prove that it indeed has lost sight of its liberating heritage and reason for being. And if that is so, it deserves to die. If white churches and their pastors will not stand in solidarity with the poor and against deep structures of racial injustice such as America's prison-industrial complex, "the new Jim Crow," then they will have demonstrated that they are every bit as much invested in the maintenance of white privilege and white supremacy as were their forebears of a different era. In this sense, a serious dialogue about the nature of piety and the content of protest must ultimately lead to praxis on the streets and in the world. Theology that is not lived is not theology at all.

If the foregoing analysis provides a basis for continuing dialogue and ongoing constructive work toward a lived theology of liberation in the American churches, some of which, such as the Ebenezer Baptist Church, are becoming increasingly racially and ethnically diverse, then this study has accomplished its goal. For even that increasing diversity and its potential as a signifier of what Martin Luther King, Jr., called "the beloved community" is itself best served by a memory of the black church, the antislavery church, which for reasons of history has had to stand vigil as the conscience of the American churches, a living testimony against America's original and ongoing sin: racism. The black church, however problematic that term may be for some people, must be clear about its mission because its soul and the nation's salvation depend on it.

That is why the black church cannot afford to be radical on the question of racial justice and reactionary when it comes to justice and equality for women, gays and lesbians, brown "illegal" immigrants, and just about everyone and everything else. It cannot fully live out its vocation as a liberationist church and be a xenophobic church at the same time. Moreover, if the black church truly believes in salvation, "the broadening of communal space," and "the good and spacious land" about which the scriptures speak, then its distinctive voice must be heard on the issue of ecology and ecological justice. A church that is vocal about race but silent or closed to honest dialogue on these issues because it does not see their interrelatedness loses its prophetic edge, theological integrity, and moral credibility.

The black church—a church I love, in which I was nurtured and raised, and to which I have given my entire life—is, for reasons of history and theology, a church with a divided mind. That is why it must be rigorously and lovingly challenged by both its theologians and its pastors to more fully integrate its pietistic and protest dimensions into a more holistic understanding of what it means to truly be a prophetic church and a liberationist community. Such a community sees that authentic piety and true liberation are inextricably linked, that sexism no less than racism is a heresy against a faith whose aim is liberation, that the mission of the true church is to save bodies and souls, and that the efforts to educate black children by churchwomen such as Arenia Mallory, no less than the civil disobedience of Martin Luther King, Jr., constitute a revolutionary act, bearing witness to "the beloved community" and the coming reign of God.

Notes

Notes to the Introduction

1. See St. Clair Drake and Horace R. Cayton, "A Bone of Contention," in *Black Metropolis: A Study of Negro Life in a Northern City*, rev. and enl. ed. (Chicago: University of Chicago Press, 1993), 418–429.

2. W. E. B. Du Bois, *The Negro Church; Report of a Social Study Made under the Direction of Atlanta University; Together with the Proceedings of the Eighth Conference for the Study of the Negro Problems, Held at Atlanta University, May 26th, 1903* (Atlanta: Atlanta University Press, 1903).

3. Carter Godwin Woodson, *The History of the Negro Church* (Washington, D.C.: Associated Publishers, 1921).

4. Benjamin Elijah Mays, Joseph William Nicholson, and Institute of Social and Religious Research, *The Negro's Church* (New York: Institute of Social and Religious Research, 1933).

5. E. Franklin Frazier, *The Negro Church in America*, in *The Negro Church in America / The Black Church since Frazier*, by E. Franklin Frazier and C. Eric Lincoln, Sourcebooks in Negro History (New York: Schocken Books, 1974).

6. Eddie Glaude, "The Black Church Is Dead," *Huffington Post*, February 24, 2010. Representing essentially the same kind of concern with the relationship between the black church and the struggle for liberation during the "black power" era, another black intellectual, C. Eric Lincoln, declared in the 1974 that "the Negro church . . . died." Frazier, *Negro Church in America*, 105–106.

7. Examples include James Cone's entire chapter devoted to the white church and black power in *Black Theology and Black Power* (1969; repr., Maryknoll, N.Y.: Orbis Books, 1989). Also, see his chapter "Church, World and Eschatology in Black Theology," in *A Black Theology of Liberation*, C. Eric Lincoln Series in Black Religion (Philadelphia: Lippincott, 1970). Also, see chapter 2 of Cone's *For My People: Black Theology and the Black Church*, Bishop Henry McNeal Turner Studies in North American Black Religion 1 (Maryknoll, N.Y.: Orbis Books, 1984); Gayraud S. Wilmore, "The White Church and the Search for Black Power," *Social Progress* 57, no. 4

(March–April 1967): 11–20. Moreover, see the "Black Power" statement published by the National Committee of Negro Churchmen, as it addresses a section of its message on the relationship between power and love "To White Churchmen" (*Renewal* 10, no. 7 [October–November 1970]: 14–16; reprinted in *Black Theology: A Documentary History*, vol. 1, *1966–1979*, 2nd ed., ed. James H. Cone and Gayraud S. Wilmore [Maryknoll, N.Y.: Orbis Books, 1993]).

8. Dale P. Andrews, *Practical Theology for Black Churches: Bridging Black Theology and African American Folk Religion* (Louisville, Ky.: Westminster John Knox Press, 2002).

9. James H. Harris, *Pastoral Theology: A Black-Church Perspective* (Minneapolis: Fortress, 1991).

10. Forrest E. Harris, Sr., with James T. Roberson and Larry D. George, eds., *What Does It Mean to Be Black and Christian? Pulpit, Pew, and Academy in Dialogue* (Nashville, Tenn.: Townsend, 1995).

11. Also, see Charles E. Booth, *Bridging the Breach: Evangelical Thought and Liberation in the African-American Preaching Tradition* (Chicago: Urban Ministries, 2000).

12. See Herbert O. Edwards, "Black Theology: Retrospect and Prospect," *Journal of Religious Thought* 32, no. 2 (Fall–Winter 1975): 46–59; and Dennis W. Wiley, "Black Theology, the Black Church, and the African-American Community," in *Black Theology: A Documentary History*, vol. 2, *1980–1992*, ed. James H. Cone and Gayraud S. Wilmore (Maryknoll, N.Y.: Orbis Books, 1993).

13. In *For My People: Black Theology and the Black Church*, James Cone proffers an outline of stages in the development of black theology (see chapter 5), including a third stage characterized by "a return to the black church and community as the primary workshop of black theology" (110). However, this conclusion has been challenged by black theologians actively engaged in pastoral ministry, and the question itself is serious enough to warrant a more sustained, systematic, and exclusive examination. See Harris, *Pastoral Theology*, chap. 3; and Wiley, "Black Theology."

14. Throughout the text, Andrews uses the term "black theology project" as a shorthand reference to the efforts and orientation of the black theology movement in general. At face value, this is perfectly legitimate. The only problem is that he does not address the actual "Black Theology Project" and its work under the auspices of "Theology in the Americas." Ironically, James Cone actually credits the Black Theology Project conference, held in Atlanta in August 1977, as a signal moment marking black theology's return to the black church (*For My People*, 110). Whether one agrees with Cone's assessment is beside the point. The glaring oversight just underscores the way in which even an adequate theological treatment of this problem requires more attention to historical details and to the places where black theologians and black pastors have attempted to engage each other.

15. E.g., Kelly Brown Douglas, *Sexuality and the Black Church: A Womanist Perspective* (Maryknoll, N.Y.: Orbis Books, 1999).

16. In this latter period of black theology's development, there are two texts that attempt to provide something of a general introduction and overview of the black theology movement. They are Dwight Hopkins's *Introducing Black Theology of*

Liberation (Maryknoll, N.Y.: Orbis Books, 1999) and Diana L. Hayes's *And Still We Rise: An Introduction to Black Liberation Theology* (New York: Paulist, 1996). While both engage the black church both as a source for the critical reflections of black and womanist theologians and as a conversation partner, their primary aim is to provide a broad interpretation of various theological concerns and intellectual developments within black theology itself. Hayes's work proceeds with an eye toward the articulation of a black Catholic theology. At each juncture of this project, my aim is to tease out the implications of the various methodological concerns for the relationship between the intellectual movement and the church and the prospects for a public and pastoral theology of black liberation.

17. Martin Luther King, Jr., "An Autobiography of Religious Development," in *The Papers of Martin Luther King, Jr.*, vol. 1, *Called to Serve, January 1929–June 1951*, ed. Clayborne Carson (Berkeley: University of California Press, 1992), 361.

18. See Martin Luther King, Jr., *Stride toward Freedom; the Montgomery Story* (New York: Harper, 1958); King, "Why Jesus Called a Man a Fool," sermon preached at Mount Pisgah Missionary Baptist Church, Chicago, Illinois, August 27, 1967, in *A Knock at Midnight: Inspiration from the Great Sermons of Martin Luther King, Jr.*, ed. Clayborne Carson and Peter Holloran (New York: Warner Books, 1998). Also, see Lewis V. Baldwin, *Never to Leave Us Alone* (Minneapolis: Fortress, 2010).

19. C. Eric Lincoln and Lawrence H. Mamiya, *The Black Church in the African American Experience* (Durham: Duke University Press, 1990), 1.

20. Delores S. Williams, *Sisters in the Wilderness: The Challenge of Womanist God-Talk* (Maryknoll, N.Y.: Orbis Books, 1993), 205, 206.

21. Albert J. Raboteau, *Slave Religion: The "Invisible Institution" in the Antebellum South* (New York: Oxford University Press, 1978); Raboteau, *A Fire in the Bones: Reflections on African-American Religious History* (Boston: Beacon, 1995); Raboteau, "The Black Experience in American Evangelism: The Meaning of Slavery," in *African-American Religion: Interpretive Essays in History and Culture*, ed. Timothy Earl Fulop and Albert J. Raboteau (New York: Routledge, 1997).

22. Joseph R. Washington, *Black Religion: The Negro and Christianity in the United States* (Boston: Beacon, 1964).

23. Emmanuel McCall, "Review of Allan A. Boesak's *Farewell to Innocence*," *Occasional Bulletin of Missionary Research* 2, no. 3 (July 1978): 110.

24. Gayraud S. Wilmore, "Introduction to Part IV," in *Black Theology: A Documentary History*, vol. 1, *1966–1979*, ed. Gayraud S. Wilmore and James H. Cone (Maryknoll, N.Y.: Orbis Books, 1979), 246.

Notes to Chapter 1

1. For examples of slave religion's oppositional witness against the religion of the slaveholders, see Clifton H. Johnson, ed., *God Struck Me Dead: Voices of Ex-Slaves* (Cleveland: Pilgrim, 1993); Norman R. Yetman, ed., *Life under the "Peculiar Institution": Selections from the Slave Narrative Collection* (New York: Holt, Rinehart and Winston, 1970). See William Canfield Emerson, *Stories and Spirituals of the Negro*

Slave (Boston: R. G. Badger, 1930). Also, see John Cade, "Out of the Mouths of Ex-Slaves," *Journal of Negro History* 20 (1935): 294–337. Albert J. Raboteau concludes from the testimony of slaves' own lips that they "distinguished the hypocritical religion of their masters from true Christianity and rejected the slaveholder's gospel of obedience to master and mistress." Raboteau, *Slave Religion*, 294. Black theologian James Cone argues that "the divine *liberation* of the oppressed from slavery is the central theological concept in the black spirituals." Cone, *The Spirituals and the Blues* (Maryknoll, N.Y.: Orbis Books, 1972), 32. Dwight Hopkins characterizes this underground hermeneutic and creative oppositional witness evinced in slave testimony and in the spirituals as the effort of slaves to "co-constitute the black self." He argues that "essentially, Africans and African Americans sowed the seeds for a systematic black theology by synthesizing a reinterpreted Christianity, everyday common sense wisdom, and remnants from West African indigenous religions." See especially chapter 2 of Hopkins, *Down, Up, and Over: Slave Religion and Black Theology* (Minneapolis: Fortress, 2000), 147.

2. The distinctive mission of the independent black churches and the conditions under which they were developed was summarized well by the bishops of the African Methodist Episcopal church in 1896: " 'God our Father; Christ our Redeemer; Man our Brother.' This is the official motto of the A.M.E. church, and her mission in the commonwealth of Christianity is to bring all denominations and races to acknowledge and practice the sentiments contained therein. When these sentiments are universal in theory and practice, then the mission of the distinctive colored organizations will cease." From the Quadrennial Address of the Bishops, *Journal of the 20th Quadrennial Session of the General Conference of the A.M.E. Church*, St. Stephens AME Church, Wilmington, N.C., May 4–22, 1896, 98. Also, see Carol V. R. George, *Segregated Sabbaths; Richard Allen and the Emergence of Independent Black Churches, 1760–1840* (New York: Oxford University Press, 1973); Stephen Ward Angell, *Bishop Henry McNeal Turner and African-American Religion in the South* (Knoxville: University of Tennessee Press, 1992); William E. Montgomery, *Under Their Own Vine and Fig Tree: The African-American Church in the South, 1865–1900* (Baton Rouge: Louisiana State University Press, 1993); Katharine L. Dvorak, *An African-American Exodus: The Segregation of the Southern Churches*, Chicago Studies in the History of American Religion 4 (Brooklyn, N.Y.: Carlson, 1991); and Stephen Ward Angell and Anthony B. Pinn, *Social Protest Thought in the African Methodist Episcopal Church, 1862–1939* (Knoxville: University of Tennessee Press, 2000). Also, see James Melvin Washington, *Frustrated Fellowship: The Black Baptist Quest for Social Power* (Macon, Ga.: Mercer University Press, 1986); and Evelyn Brooks Higginbotham, *Righteous Discontent: The Women's Movement in the Black Baptist Church, 1880–1920* (Cambridge: Harvard University Press, 1993). For an interpretation of the work of AME missionaries among the freedman in the South and their collective self-understanding as an ecclesial instrument imbued with a distinctive mission "to uplift the black race in America and then in the world," see Clarence E. Walker, *A Rock in a Weary Land: The African Methodist Episcopal Church during the Civil War and Reconstruction* (Baton Rouge: Louisiana

State University Press, 1982). Lawrence Little's work is an important addition to the literature inasmuch as he examines the AME Church's rhetoric of liberty, as black church leaders endeavored to respond, albeit in complex and sometimes contradictory ways, to oppression on a global scale within the context of the rise of the American empire in the world. See Little, *Disciples of Liberty: The African Methodist Episcopal Church in the Age of Imperialism, 1884–1916* (Knoxville: University of Tennessee Press, 2000).

3. Gayraud Wilmore has aptly identified the black churches' historic commitment to freedom as "an exceedingly *elastic* but *tenacious* thread [that] binds together the contributive and developmental factors of black religion in the United States as one distinctive social phenomenon." Calling it "radicalism," Wilmore sees it as "the defining characteristic of black Christianity and black religion in the United States." Wilmore, *Black Religion and Black Radicalism: An Interpretation of the Religious History of Afro-American People*, 2nd ed. (Maryknoll, N.Y.: Orbis Books, 1983), ix–x. Albert J. Raboteau concludes that black Christians essentially denied "the doctrinal basis of slaveholding Christianity by refusing to believe that God had made them inferior to whites." Raboteau, "Black Experience in American Evangelism," 95. His work shows the extent to which untutored black slaves developed their own hermeneutics of resistance and survival and an emphasis on freedom that made the difference between their faith and that of their masters "wide and deep." Raboteau, "African-Americans, Exodus, and the American Israel," in *African-American Christianity: Essays in History*, ed. Paul E. Johnson (Berkeley: University of California Press, 1994), 9. Cornel West and Eddie Glaude offer that "in some ways, the distinctive theology of black Christianity stood as a loud rebuke of white Christianity" through a "figural rereading of America" as Egypt, its slaveholders as Pharaoh, and themselves as the children of Israel even while white Christians saw America as the "shining city on the hill" and themselves as "the New Israel." Cornel West and Eddie S. Glaude, "Introduction: Towards New Visions and New Approaches in African American Religious Studies," in *African American Religious Thought: An Anthology*, ed. Cornel West and Eddie S. Glaude (Louisville, Ky.: Westminster John Knox Press, 2003), xxi, xxii. Eugene D. Genovese writes, regarding the slaveholders' Christianity, that "the black slaves of the New World made it their own, they transformed it into a religion of resistance." Genovese, *Roll, Jordan, Roll: The World the Slaves Made* (New York: Vintage Books, 1976), 254.

4. Wilmore, *Black Religion and Black Radicalism*, ix.

5. See Manning Marable, "The Ambiguous Politics of the Black Church," in *How Capitalism Underdeveloped Black America: Problems in Race, Political Economy, and Society* (Boston: South End, 1983).

6. Students of the spirituals observe that during slavery the spirituals often had double meanings. In the case of this spiritual, what is evinced is both an eschatological expectation of egalitarianism in the divine economy or afterlife and, by implication, even if not by direct assertion, a sharp critique of the political conditions that left the slaves without "shoes" and within the narrow circumscriptions of a so-called

Christian slavocracy. Over against this reality, the spiritual declares, "When I get to heaven, I'm gonna put on my shoes and *shout all over God's heaven.*" The protest continues, "Everybody talkin' 'bout heaven ain't a-goin' dere.'"

7. James H. Cone, "Theology's Great Sin: Silence in the Face of White Supremacy," *Union Seminary Quarterly Review* 55, nos. 3–4 (2001): 3.

8. From *The Doctrines and Disciplines of the African Methodist Episcopal Church* (Philadelphia, 1817), 14.

9. Ironically, the layperson and slave abolitionist Frederick Douglass saw clearly and stated passionately the difference between what he saw as true Christianity and "the slaveholding religion of this land" but still opposed the idea of an independent black church.

> For between the Christianity of this land, and the Christianity of Christ, I recognize the widest possible difference—so wide that to receive the one as good, pure and holy, is of necessity to reject the other as bad, corrupt, and wicked. . . . Indeed, I can see no reason, but the most deceitful one, for calling the religion of this land Christianity. I look upon it as the climax of all misnomers, the boldest of all frauds, and the grossest of all libels. . . . I mean by the religion of this land, that which is revealed in the words, deeds, and actions, of those bodies, north and south, calling themselves Christian churches, and yet in union with slave-holders.

Douglass, *Narrative of the Life of Frederick Douglass, An American Slave* (Boston: Anti-Slavery Office, 1835).

10. Peter Paris offers an insightful discussion of this point in his chapter titled "Moral Agency in Conflict," in *The Social Teaching of the Black Churches* (Philadelphia: Fortress, 1985). It is instructive to note that according to C. Eric Lincoln and Lawrence Mamiya's landmark sociological study *The Black Church in the African American Experience*, while black churches were usually more politically active, most black clergy saw the essential mission of the black church as no different from that of the white churches. Among the possible explanations for this offered by Lincoln and Mamiya "is that the majority of black clergy tend to follow the orthodox understanding that the main purpose of Christian churches is to spread the Word and to save souls. To the extent that this is the case, certainly black clergy would see their mission as no different from white clergy" (170–171; also, see chart on 169).

11. Paris, *Social Teaching of the Black Churches*, 76.

12. Among the Europeans, the insightful work of Theo Witvliet has represented an important exception. See Witvliet, *The Way of the Black Messiah: The Hermeneutical Challenge of Black Theology as a Theology of Liberation* (Oak Park, Ill.: Meyer-Stone Books, 1987).

13. James H. Cone, *God of the Oppressed* (San Francisco: Harper, 1975), 52–53. Also, see his discussion in *Black Theology and Black Power*, 31; J. Cone, *A Black Theology of Liberation*, 4–20; J. Cone, "Theology's Great Sin." Moreover, see his discussion of Jürgen Moltmann's "theology of hope" and black theologians' engagement of it and other European political theologies in J. Cone, *For My People*, 68–72.

14. Frederick Herzog, *Liberation Theology: Liberation in the Light of the Fourth Gospel* (New York: Seabury, 1972). Also, see Herzog, "The Liberation of White Theology," *Christian Century*, March 20, 1974, 316–319.

15. Witvliet, *Way of the Black Messiah*, 219–220.

16. Helmut Gollwitzer, "Why Black Theology?," in Wilmore and Cone, *Black Theology*, vol. 1, 159. Appearing first in *Evangelische Theologie* and in the *Union Seminary Quarterly Review*, this essay was written as part of a symposium and as a response to James Cone's "Black Theology on Revolution, Violence and Reconciliation" (in *Black Theology and Black Power*).

17. One infamous example is a text written by Dutch Reformed minister and former president of Dickinson College Samuel B. How. See Samuel Blanchard How, *Slaveholding Not Sinful. Slavery, the Punishment of Man's Sin, Its Remedy, the Gospel of Christ*, Black Heritage Library Collection (Freeport, N.Y.: Books for Libraries Press, 1971). For a discussion of this history of interpretation and slaveholding *apologia*, see H. Shelton Smith, *In His Image, but . . . : Racism in Southern Religion, 1780–1910* (Durham: Duke University Press, 1972). See especially his chapters titled "In Defense of Bondage" and "The Triumph of Racial Orthodoxy." Also, see John Patrick Daly, *When Slavery Was Called Freedom: Evangelicalism, Proslavery, and the Causes of the Civil War*, Religion in the South (Lexington: University Press of Kentucky, 2002).

18. Theophus Smith has emphasized the *cultural* dimension of black religious resistance. Utilizing the concept of "conjure" as a "root metaphor," his work underscores the broad cultural and hermeneutical means through which African Americans have sought to "magically" transform the reality of a race-conscious society through biblical notions of chosenness and peoplehood. See Smith, *Conjuring Culture: Biblical Formations of Black America* (New York: Oxford University Press, 1994). Gayraud Wilmore also hints at the need to be more attentive to "deep-lying cultural transformations" rather than "electoral politics" and "segmental political action" as the key to measuring the black church's faithfulness to its vocation as oppositional witness in American culture. See his essay "Spirituality and Social Transformation as the Vocation of the Black Church," in *Churches in Struggle: Liberation Theologies and Social Change in North America*, ed. William K. Tabb (New York: Monthly Review Press, 1986).

19. See Lewis V. Baldwin, *There Is a Balm in Gilead: The Cultural Roots of Martin Luther King, Jr.* (Minneapolis: Fortress, 1991). Also, see James H. Cone, *Martin and Malcolm and America: A Dream or a Nightmare* (Maryknoll, N.Y.: Orbis Books, 1991); J. Cone, "Martin Luther King, Jr., Black Theology–Black Church," *Theology Today* 40, no. 4 (1984): 409–420; J. Cone, "The Theology of Martin Luther King, Jr.," *Union Seminary Quarterly Review* 40, no. 4 (1986): 21–40.

20. Adam Fairclough, *To Redeem the Soul of America: The Southern Christian Leadership Conference and Martin Luther King, Jr.* (Athens: University of Georgia Press, 1987).

21. Raboteau, "African-Americans, Exodus, and the American Israel," 9.

22. Howard Thurman, *Deep River* (Mills College, Calif.: Eucalyptus, 1945), 34.

23. For a book-length treatment of the meaning of the difference between black

religion before and after black power, see Mark L.. Chapman, *Christianity on Trial: Black Religious Thought before and after Black Power* (Maryknoll, N.Y.: Orbis Books, 1996).

24. Orlando Patterson, *Freedom in the Making of Western Culture* (New York: HarperCollins, 1991); Patterson, *Slavery and Social Death: A Comparative Study* (Cambridge: Harvard University Press, 1982). Also, see David Brion Davis's essay "Slavery and Sin: The Ancient Legacy," in *The Problem of Slavery in Western Culture* (New York: Oxford University Press, 1966). For a discussion of the theological debate over slavery in the American South, also see H. Smith, *In His Image*.

25. Raboteau, *Slave Religion*; Raboteau, *Fire in the Bones*; Hayes, *And Still We Rise*, chap. 2.

26. Paris, *Social Teaching of the Black Churches*, 42.

27. Raboteau, *Slave Religion*, 98.

28. James D. Essig, *The Bonds of Wickedness: American Evangelicals against Slavery, 1770– 1808* (Philadelphia: Temple University Press, 1982); Sidney Kaplan, *The Black Presence in the Era of the American Revolution* (Washington, D.C.: Smithsonian Institute Press, 1973); Mark A. Noll, *A History of Christianity in the United States and Canada* (Grand Rapids, Mich.: Eerdmans, 1992); Noll, *Christians in the American Revolution* (Grand Rapids, Mich.: Eerdmans, 1977). No one has articulated the irony of the rhetoric of freedom surrounding the American Revolution in relationship to American chattel slavery more powerfully than the nineteenth-century abolitionist Frederick Douglass. See his speech given, on the anniversary of Independence Day 1852, to the Ladies Anti-Slavery Society of Rochester, New York. Douglass asks, "What to the American slave, is your 4th of July? . . . You boast of your love of liberty, your superior civilization and your pure Christianity, while the whole political power of the nation . . . is solemnly pledged to support and perpetuate the enslavement of three millions of your countrymen. . . . The existence of slavery in this country brands your republicanism as a sham, your humanity as a base pretense, and your Christianity as a lie."

29. Qtd. in Raboteau, *Slave Religion*, 99.

30. Qtd. in ibid., 103.

31. Dorothy Sterling, *Freedom Train: The Story of Harriet Tubman* (Garden City, N.Y.: Doubleday, 1954); Sterling, *We Are Your Sisters: Black Women in the Nineteenth Century* (New York: Norton, 1984). Also, see Edward P. Wimberly and Anne Streaty Wimberly, *Liberation and Human Wholeness: The Conversion Experiences of Black People in Slavery and Freedom* (Nashville, Tenn.: Abingdon, 1986).

32. Wimberly and Wimberly, *Liberation and Human Wholeness*, 31.

33. Harvey Gallagher Cox, *Fire from Heaven: The Rise of Pentecostal Spirituality and the Reshaping of Religion in the Twenty-First Century* (Reading, Mass.: Addison-Wesley, 1995).

34. See their discussion of "The Dialectical Model of the Black Church," in *Black Church in the African American Experience*, 10–16. In developing a sociology of the black church, they posit six pairs of polar opposites that are dialectically related: "'The dialectic between priestly and prophetic functions," "other-worldly versus

this-worldly," "universalism and particularism," "communal and privatistic," "charismatic versus bureaucratic," and "resistance versus accommodation."

35. Among the more recent studies, see Eddie S. Glaude's insightful examination of its creative use among African Americans in the National Negro Convention movement between 1830 and 1843. Glaude, *Exodus! Religion, Race, and Nation in Early Nineteenth-Century Black America* (Chicago: University of Chicago Press, 2000).

36. Vincent Harding, "The Uses of the Afro-American Past," *Negro Digest* 17 (February 1968): 4–9, 81–84.

37. J. Cone, *Spirituals and the Blues*.

38. Slaves made a sharp distinction between their moral obligations to each other and that owed slaveholders. For example, it was a common view in the slave community that the commandment not to steal from whites did not apply to them since they were themselves stolen property. "Puttin' on ol' massa," that is, expressing one sentiment while harboring another, was another common form of survival in a brutal system. See Raboteau, *Slave Religion*, chap. 6.

39. Raboteau, "African-Americans, Exodus, and the American Israel," 9.

40. Patterson, *Slavery and Social Death*.

41. Lucretia Alexander, in *The American Slave: A Composite Autobiography*, vol. 8, *Arkansas Narratives*, ed. George P. Rawick (Westport, Conn.: Greenwood, 1972), 35.

42. Gayraud S. Wilmore, *Black Religion and Black Radicalism: An Interpretation of the Religious History of African Americans*, 3rd ed. (Maryknoll, N.Y.: Orbis Books, 1998), chap. 5, 78.

43. See James Washington, *Frustrated Fellowship*, especially chapter 2, "Abolitionism and the Quest for a Prophetic Polity."

44. See J. Cone, *Black Theology of Liberation*, 130–132.

45. A bishop of the AME Church with a decidedly nationalist bent, Turner, who declared that "God is a Negro," was one of the most controversial figures of his time (*The Voice of Missions*, February 1, 1898, qtd. in Wilmore, *Black Religion and Black Radicalism*, 3rd ed., 152). He was an early advocate of reparations for the enslavement of blacks and suggested that a modest $100 million be given to blacks for the purpose of building a nation in Africa. Decades before the United States and other Western nations brokered the founding of the modern state of Israel, Turner imagined "a highway made across the Atlantic; upon which regular social and economic intercourse between Black America and Africa could be carried on and self-reliant, energetic Black people could be permanently settled if they chose to do so" (Henry M. Turner, "The Races Must Separate," in *The Possibilities of the Negro in Symposium*, ed. Willis B. Park [Atlanta: Franklin, 1904], 91–92). For a discussion of Turner's life and its significance for those who decades later developed a systematic black theology, see Wilmore, *Black Religion and Black Radicalism*, 3rd ed., 149–167. Also, see Edwin S. Redkey, *Black Exodus: Black Nationalist and Back to Africa Movements, 1890–1910* (New Haven: Yale University Press, 1969); and Redkey, *Respect Black: The Writings and Speeches of Henry McNeal Turner* (New York: Arno / New York Times, 1971).

46. Nathaniel Paul is just one example of a prominent Baptist minister who combined the pastoral activities of organizing churches and the work of abolitionism. The role of faith in his militant abolitionist stance is eloquently expressed in "An Address, Delivered on the Celebration of the Abolition of Slavery, in the State of New York, July 5, 1827."

   The captive must be liberated, the oppressed go free, and slavery must be revert back to its original chaos of darkness, and be forever annihilated from the earth. Did I believe that it would always continue, . . . I would disallow any allegiance or obligation I was under to my fellow creatures, or any submission that I owed to the laws of my country; I would deny the superintending power of divine providence in the affairs of this life; I would ridicule the religion of the Saviour of the world, and treat as the worst of men the ministers of the everlasting gospel; I would consider my Bible as a book of false and delusive fables; I would at once confess myself an atheist, and deny the existence of the holy God.

   In *Negro Protest Pamphlets: A Compendium*, ed. Dorothy Porter (New York: Arno, 1969), 62–63.

47. For an account of Harvey Johnson's role in the organizing of black Marylanders against lynching and discrimination and a discussion of his eloquent argumentation on behalf of the separatist movement of black Baptists toward the establishment of an independent denomination, see James Washington, *Frustrated Fellowship*, 147, 189–190, 192–193.

48. See Jarena Lee's autobiography in *Sisters of the Spirit: Three Black Women's Autobiographies of the Nineteenth Century*, ed. William L. Andrews (Bloomington: Indiana University Press, 1986).

49. Ibid.

50. Hilah F. Thomas and Rosemary Skinner Keller, eds., *Women in New Worlds* (Nashville, Tenn.: Abingdon, 1981). See Smith's autobiography: Amanda Berry Smith, *Amanda Smith the Colored Evangelist* (Chicago: Christian Witness Company, 1921).

51. See Jualynne Dodson's "Nineteenth Century AME Preaching Women," in Thomas and Keller, *Women in New Worlds*.

52. Little, *Disciples of Liberty*.

53. J. Cone, *Black Theology of Liberation*, 131.

54. E.g., the Quakers, the short-lived efforts of Methodist abolitionists. See Timothy Lawrence Smith, *Revivalism and Social Reform: American Protestantism on the Eve of the Civil War* (Baltimore: Johns Hopkins University Press, 1980). Also, see Essig, *Bonds of Wickedness*.

55. Hans Baer and Merrill Singer, *African-American Religion in the Twentieth Century: Varieties of Protest and Accommodation* (Knoxville: University of Tennessee Press, 1992), 27.

56. Manning Marable, "The Ambiguous Politics of the Black Church," chap. 7 in *How Capitalism Underdeveloped Black America*.

57. Zora Neale Hurston, *The Sanctified Church* (Berkeley, Calif.: Turtle Island Foundation, 1981).

58. Iain MacRobert, *The Black Roots and White Racism of Early Pentecostalism in the USA* (New York: St. Martin's, 1988).

59. George Whitefield, letter dated May 10, 1740, in Frank Lambert, "'I Saw the Book Talk': Slave Readings of the First Great Awakening," *Journal of Negro History* 77, no. 4 (1992), qtd. in Winthrop D. Jordan, *White over Black: American Attitudes toward the Negro, 1550–1812* (Chapel Hill: University of North Carolina Press, 2012), 213.

60. See J. Cone, "Martin Luther King, Jr., Black Theology–Black Church."; J. Cone, "Theology of Martin Luther King, Jr."; J. Cone, *Martin and Malcolm and America.*

61. I am borrowing from the Latin American context the term *conscientizing*, associated with the thinking and work of Paulo Freire and described in his book *The Pedagogy of the Oppressed* (New York: Seabury, 1973). Also, see his reflections in his essay "Conscientizing as a Way of Liberating" (1970), in *Liberation Theology: A Documentary History*, ed. Alfred T. Hennelly (Maryknoll, N.Y.: Orbis Books, 1990). By "conscientization," I am suggesting that the civil rights movement engaged ordinary masses of poor black folk in a heightened sense of critical awareness of themselves as potential agents in history. Indeed, the mass meetings, voter education, and other efforts by SCLC, SNCC, and others provided what Freire describes in his context as "education for freedom," praxis that leads to reflection that gives way to deeper praxis.

62. In the nineteenth century, examples include Henry Highland Garnett and less known figures such as the Baptist preacher and activist Harvey Johnson. But King stands directly in the line of twentieth-century black social gospelers such as Reverdy Ransom and Adam Powell, Sr., and Adam Powell, Jr. King's own father led a voter-rights campaign in Atlanta, the heart of the Confederacy, in 1935. Also, see Gary Dorrien's discussion titled "Benjamin E. Mays and the Theology of Racial Justice," in *The Making of American Liberal Theology: Idealism, Realism, and Modernity, 1900–1950* (Louisville, Ky.: Westminster John Knox Press, 2003), 415–425. Also, see Chapman, *Christianity on Trial.*

63. James Cone identifies the civil rights movement as one of three contexts for the emergence of black theology. See J. Cone, *For My People*, 6–11. The other two contexts are the black power movement and the publication of Joseph Washington's *Black Religion: The Negro and Christianity in the United States.*

64. Martin Luther King, Jr., "Letter from Birmingham Jail," in *Why We Can't Wait* (New York: Harper and Row, 1963), 92.

65. See Peter J. Paris, *Black Religious Leaders: Conflict in Unity* (Louisville, Ky.: Westminster John Knox Press, 1991). Also, see Robert Michael Franklin, *Liberating Visions: Human Fulfillment and Social Justice in African-American Thought* (Minneapolis: Fortress, 1990). For an understanding of Malcolm X's influence on the theological development of James Cone, see Cone's *Martin and Malcolm and America.*

66. See Dwight Hopkins's chapter "From Sundown to Sunup: The African American Co-constitute the Black Self," in *Down, Up, and Over.*

67. Frazier, *Negro Church in America*, chap. 3.

68. Taylor Branch, *Parting the Waters: America in the King Years, 1954–63* (New York:

Simon and Schuster, 1988); Branch, *Pillar of Fire: America in the King Years, 1963–65* (New York: Simon and Schuster, 1998); Stewart Burns, *To the Mountaintop: Martin Luther King, Jr.'s Sacred Mission to Save America, 1955–1968* (New York: HarperCollins, 2004); Marshall Frady, *Martin Luther King, Jr.* (New York: Penguin, 2002); David J. Garrow, *Bearing the Cross: Martin Luther King, Jr., and the Southern Christian Leadership Conference* (New York: Morrow, 1986); Peter J. Ling, *Martin Luther King, Jr.* (New York: Routledge, 2002); Fredrik Sunnemark, *Ring Out Freedom! The Voice of Martin Luther King, Jr. and the Making of the Civil Rights Movement* (Bloomington: Indiana University Press, 2004).

69. David L. Chappell, *A Stone of Hope: Prophetic Religion and the Death of Jim Crow* (Chapel Hill: University of North Carolina Press, 2004), 87. See especially the chapter titled "The Civil Rights Movement as a Religious Revival."

70. Aldon Morris, *The Origins of the Civil Rights Movement: Black Communities Organizing for Change* (New York: Free Press, 1984), 98.

71. Raboteau, *Fire in the Bones*, 59.

72. Richard King, *Civil Rights and the Idea of Freedom* (New York: Oxford University Press, 1992), 202–207.

73. Burns, *To the Mountaintop*, 56–57.

74. Chappell, *Stone of Hope*, 97.

75. Here I am in agreement with "the dialectical model of the black church" proffered by C. Eric Lincoln and Lawrence Mamiya in their groundbreaking study *Black Church in the African American Experience* (10–19). Also, see Larry Murphy's "Piety and Liberation: A Historical Exploration of African American Religion and Social Justice," in *Blow the Trumpet in Zion! Global Vision and Action for the Twenty-First-Century Black Church*, ed. Iva E. Carruthers, Frederick D. Haynes, and Jeremiah A. Wright (Minneapolis: Fortress, 2005).

76. Murphy, "Piety and Liberation," 51.

77. The Apostle Paul's description of Abraham's faith in the promise of geopolitical salvation and abundance to his descendants as he will become "the father of many nations." Romans 4:18*a*.

78. Nat Turner's eschatological visions led him to violent revolt against the system of slavery. See Gayraud Wilmore's chapter "'Three Generals in the Lord's Army," in *Black Religion and Black Radicalism*. David Walker's "Appeal to the Coloured Citizens of the World" is another example. Wilmore also discusses this radical side of black eschatological faith in a chapter titled "Eschatology in Black," in *Last Things First* (Philadelphia: Westminster, 1982). Also, see James Cone's chapter "'The Meaning of Heaven in the Black Spirituals," in *Spirituals and the Blues*.

79. Baldwin, *There Is a Balm in Gilead*; Lewis V. Baldwin, *To Make the Wounded Whole: The Cultural Legacy of Martin Luther King, Jr.* (Minneapolis: Fortress, 1992); Burns, *To the Mountaintop*; J. Cone, "Theology of Martin Luther King, Jr."; J. Cone, *Martin and Malcolm and America*; David J. Garrow, "The Intellectual Development of Martin Luther King, Jr.: Influences and Commentaries," *Union Seminary Quarterly Review*

40, no. 4 (1986): 5–20; Richard Lischer, *The Preacher King: Martin Luther King, Jr. and the Word That Moved America* (New York: Oxford University Press, 1995).

80. M. King, "Autobiography of Religious Development," 361, 363.

81. M. King, "Why Jesus Called a Man a Fool."

82. M. King, "Autobiography of Religious Development," 361.

83. See James H. Cone, "Martin Luther King: The Source of His Courage to Face Death," *Concilium* 183 (1983): 74–79.

84. This was clearly a turning point in King's personal spiritual development and prophetic vocation. Among the places where the account is given is his sermon "Why Jesus Called a Man a Fool," 161. Also, see his earlier account in chapter 8 of his first book, *Stride toward Freedom: The Montgomery Story*.

85. M. King, "Why Jesus Called a Man a Fool," 161.

86. Ibid., 162.

87. Garrow, *Bearing the Cross*, 57.

88. Burns, *To the Mountaintop*, 151.

89. J. Cone, *Martin and Malcolm and America*, 124.

90. J. Cone, "Theology of Martin Luther King, Jr.," 27. Also, see J. Cone, "Martin Luther King: The Source of His Courage to Face Death."

91. J. Cone, "Martin Luther King: The Source of His Courage to Face Death."

92. J. Cone, "Theology of Martin Luther King, Jr.," 27.

93. Wimberly and Wimberly, *Liberation and Human Wholeness*, 31.

94. M. King, "Why Jesus Called a Man a Fool," 162–163.

95. Martin Luther King, Jr., "Discerning the Signs of History, November 15, 1964," sermon, King Center Archives, Atlanta, Georgia.

96. M. King, "Letter from Birmingham Jail," 85; Luther D. Ivory, *Toward a Theology of Radical Involvement: The Theological Legacy of Martin Luther King, Jr.* (Nashville, Tenn.: Abingdon, 1997).

97. Martin Luther King, Jr., "A Walk through the Holy Land, " sermon, March 29, 1959, King Center Archives, Atlanta, Georgia.

98. Martin Luther King, Jr., "Revolution and Redemption," August 16, 1964, King Center Archives, Amsterdam.

99. Martin Luther King, Jr., "Suffering and Faith" (1960), in *A Testament of Hope: The Essential Writings and Speeches of Martin Luther King, Jr.*, ed. James M. Washington (San Francisco: Harper and Row, 1986), 41–42.

100. M. King, "Why Jesus Called a Man a Fool," 141–142. There is a variation of this same rhetorical hook in his final speech, "I See the Promised Land," given at Mason Temple, headquarters of the Church of God in Christ, on April 3, 1968, in Memphis, Tennessee. In what the historian James Melvin Washington called his "most apocalyptic sermon," King intones, "It's alright to talk about 'long white robes over yonder,' in all of its symbolism. But ultimately people want some suits and dresses and shoes to wear down here. It's alright to talk about 'streets flowing with milk and honey,' but God has commanded us to be concerned about the slums down here,

and his children who can't eat three square meals a day. It's alright to talk about the new Jerusalem, but one day, God's preacher must talk about the New York, the new Atlanta, the new Philadelphia, the new Los Angeles, the new Memphis, Tennessee." In *Testament of Hope*, 282.

101. King was reared in the social milieu of politically active black clergy. His father and pastor of Atlanta's Ebenezer Baptist Church, Rev. Martin Luther King, Sr., was very active in the NAACP, had led a voter-rights campaign in 1935, and fought for the equalization of black teachers' salaries. Prior to that, his maternal grandfather and pastor of Ebenezer fought for Atlanta's first public high school for colored children, Booker T. Washington High School, a school King later attended. It is through this lens that King later read Walter Rauschenbush's *Christianity and the Social Crisis* (New York: Macmillan, 1913).

102. Martin Luther King, Jr., "Recommendations to the Dexter Avenue Baptist Church for the Fiscal Year 1954–1955," in *The Papers of Martin Luther King, Jr.*, vol. 2, *Rediscovering Precious Values, July 1951–November 1955*, ed. Clayborne Carson (Berkeley: University of California Press, 1994), 290.

103. M. King, *Stride toward Freedom*, 116–117.

104. Ibid., 36.

105. See M. King, "Why Jesus Called a Man a Fool," 160–162.

106. Cf. the account in M. King, *Stride toward Freedom*, 134–135. In *Stride toward Freedom*, King does not mention the Spirit's having called him by name. Also, King apparently did not immediately share this experience with his wife, since she was not aware of it until reading a publisher's draft of *Stride toward Freedom*. Burns, *To the Mountaintop*, 466n. 213.

107. M. King, *Why We Can't Wait*, 88.

108. Williston Walker, Richard A. Norris, David W. Lotz, and Robert T. Handy, *A History of the Christian Church* (New York: Scribner's, 1985), 437.

109. Martin Luther, "The Freedom of the Christian," in *Luther's Works*, ed. Jaroslav Pelikan (St. Louis: Concordia, 1961), vol. 31.

110. Martin Luther, "Temporal Authority: To What Extent It Should Be Obeyed," in ibid., vol. 21.

111. For a good discussion of Luther's "Two Kingdoms" doctrine and its implications for African American faith and struggle, see James Kenneth Echols, "The Two Kingdoms: A Black American Perspective," in *Theology and the Black Experience: The Lutheran Heritage Interpreted by African and African American Theologians*, ed. Albert Pero and Ambrose Moyo (Minneapolis: Fortress, 1988).

112. Martin Luther, "Admonition to Peace," in *Luther's Works*, vol. 46, 20.

113. Martin Luther King, Jr., "Who Is Their God?," *Nation*, October 13, 1962.

114. Paul R. Garber, "King Was a Black Theologian," *Journal of Religious Thought* 31, no. 2 (Fall–Winter 1975): 16–32. Also, see Garber, "Black Theology: Latter Day Legacy of Martin Luther King, Jr.," *Journal of the International Theological Center* 2 (1975): 100–113.

115. J. Cone, "Theology of Martin Luther King, Jr."; James H. Cone, review of *Ring Out*

Freedom! The Voice of Martin Luther King, Jr. and the Making of the Civil Rights Movement, by Fredrik Sunnemark, *Journal of Southern Religion* 7 (2004).

116. Garber, "King Was a Black Theologian," 18. Also, see James H. Smylie, "On Jesus, Pharaohs, and the Chosen People: Martin Luther King as Biblical Interpreter and Humanist," *Interpretation* 24 (1970): 74–91.

117. Garrow, *Bearing the Cross*; Garrow, "Intellectual Development of Martin Luther King, Jr."

118. J. Cone, "Theology of Martin Luther King, Jr."; J. Cone, *Martin and Malcolm and America*.

119. Baldwin, *There Is a Balm in Gilead*; Baldwin, *To Make the Wounded Whole*.

120. Joseph R. Washington, "Are American Negro Churches Christian?," *Theology Today* 20 (April 1963): 82–83.

121. In *For My People*, James Cone identifies the publication of Washington's *Black Religion: The Negro and Christianity in the United States* and the divergent response to it in the white and black church and scholarly communities as one of "three contexts of the origin of black theology" (8–10). Washington served at the time as Dean of the Chapel and Associate Professor of Religion at Albion College, Albion, Michigan. He earned a B.A. degree in sociology (1952) from the University of Wisconsin, a B.D. at Andover Newton Theological School (1957), where he was already reflecting on the issues he would raise in his first book, having written as his thesis "Segregation, Integration and Christian Fellowship." He received a Th.D. in social ethics from Boston University (1961) with a dissertation titled "The Social Ethics of Lewis O. Hartman, 1920–1945." He went on to write several books, including *The Politics of God: The Future of the Black Churches*, retiring as a religion professor at the University of Pennsylvania in 1994.

122. J. Cone, *For My People*, 8–10.

Notes to Chapter 2

1. Joseph Washington, "Are American Negro Churches Christian?," 83, 81, 76.

2. Joseph Washington, *Black Religion*, vii.

3. Joseph Washington, "Are American Negro Churches Christian?," 76.

4. Joseph Washington, *Black Religion*, 27.

5. Joseph Washington, "Are American Negro Churches Christian?," 85.

6. Ibid.

7. Ibid., 85–86.

8. Joseph Washington, *Black Religion*, 22.

9. Neither would it be proper, in my estimation, to refer to Gandhi, as some might, as an "anonymous Christian," a term made popular by the Roman Catholic theologian Karl Rahner. See Rahner, "Observation on the Problem of the 'Anonymous Christian,'" in *Theological Investigations*, vol. 14 (New York: Seabury, 1976); Rahner, "The One Christ and the Universality of Salvation," in *Theological Investigations*, vol. 16 (New York: Crossroads, 1983). The problem with such a designation is that while it is an ostensibly inclusivist term that, at least, welcomes and affirms the light

in non-Christian traditions, it harbors a christological imperialism that imposes on others what they do not claim for themselves. Also, it suggests that the christological lens affords a superior view, through which Christians understand the ultimate implications of the truth in other faith traditions better than their respective adherents do.

10. Joseph Washington, *Black Religion*, 22.

11. Joseph Washington, "Are American Negro Churches Christian?," 79.

12. Ibid., 86.

13. Ibid., 83.

14. Joseph Washington, *Black Religion*, 30.

15. Ibid., 271, 289.

16. See Acts 8:26–40.

17. Joseph Washington, *Black Religion*, 162.

18. No less prominent white liberal scholar than Martin E. Marty hailed the book as authored by one who "more than any other Negro interpreter to date, has been informed by the Christian theological renewal of the 20th Century." See Marty's review reprinted in the Beacon paperback edition: ibid., xiii–xiv. Culbert G. Rutenber, professor of philosophy of religion and social ethics at Andover Newton, Washington's alma mater, reviewed the book favorably (*Andover Newton Quarterly*, September 1964, 47), and Elmer G. Million, characterizing Washington's work as a "protean, impressive essay on black religion," remarked that "one must admire the candor, courage, and creativity of his effort." See *Church History* 34 (Spring 1965): 364.

19. E.g., see Jerome Long's review in *Foundations*, October 1964. Also, see Carleton Lee's review in *Christian Scholar*, Fall 1965, 242–47.

20. J. Cone, *For My People*, 9. See also Gayraud Wilmore's discussion of the book and his summary regarding its impact on the rise of black theology in "Black Theology: Its Significance for Christian Mission Today," *International Review of Mission* 63, no. 250 (April 1974): 211–231.

21. M. King, "Who Is Their God?"

22. Martin Luther King, Jr., "The Role of the Church in Facing the Nation's Chief Moral Dilemma, April 23–25, 1957," address to Conference on Christian Faith and Human Relations, Nashville, Tennessee, King Center Archives, Atlanta.

23. See Martin Luther King, Jr., "Paul's Letter to American Christians," in *Strength to Love* (1963; repr., Philadelphia: Fortress, 1981), 140, 141.

24. For a good discussion on SNCC, the rise of the "Black Power" slogan, the negative response that it received in the media and the white community, and the confusion and debate that it created within the civil rights community itself, see J. Cone, *Martin and Malcolm and America*, 227–232. For a more critical view of "black power" and its meaning for SNCC and the movement, see Charles Marsh, *God's Long Summer: Stories of Faith and Civil Rights* (Princeton: Princeton University Press, 1997), 172–191. John Lewis, now a U.S. congressman from Georgia, resigned from SNCC in the wake of the black power controversy and an internal struggle for the soul and direction of the organization. For his personal reminiscences, see John Lewis

with Michael D'Orso, *Walking with the Wind: A Memoir of the Movement* (New York: Simon and Schuster, 1998), 369–374. But no one within the civil rights movement was more severe in their criticism of black power than Roy Wilkins. Comparing it to Nazism, he called it "the father of hatred and the mother of violence," "a reverse Mississippi, a reverse Hitler, a reverse Ku Klux Klan." See *New York Times*, 6 July 1966, 8; *New York Times*, 10 July 1966, sec. 4, 1.

25. Lewis with D'Orso, *Walking with the Wind*, 371. Also, it should be noted that Powell authored a book titled *Marching Blacks*, his reflections and insights on the black struggle in 1944, a time when the nomenclature "black" was not widely embraced and, as he notes, "was almost an insult to the average Negro, because blackness had not come of age." See Adam Clayton Powell, Jr., *Marching Blacks* (1945; repr., New York: Dial, 1973), v. Also, see Adam Clayton Powell, Jr., "Black Power in the Church," *Black Scholar* 2, no. 4 (December 1970): 32–34.

26. John Lewis observes that the phrase, made popular by Carmichael, had actually been around for years. In addition to Adam Powell, the novelist Richard Wright had used it (see Richard Wright, *Black Power: A Record of Reactions in a Land of Pathos* [New York: Harper, 1954]), and the performer Paul Robeson used it in response to the 1957 crisis in Little Rock, Arkansas. Lewis also notes that SNCC members had used a longer version of the phrase during the Alabama campaigns: "Black Power for Black People." But it was the timing and sharp punctuation of the phrase, first by Willie Ricks and then by Carmichael, that created the air of frenzy among the marchers and subsequent controversy in the media and broader community. See Lewis with D'Orso, *Walking with the Wind*, 370–371.

27. Wilmore, *Black Religion and Black Radicalism*, 3rd ed., 210–213; J. Cone, *For My People*, 10–11.

28. For a more detailed accounting of this history, see Wilmore, *Black Religion and Black Radicalism*, 2nd ed., chap. 9; and J. Cone, *For My People*, 11–19.

29. At the time, Benjamin Payton was serving as executive director of the Commission on Religion and Race and the Department of Social Justice of the National Council of Churches in the USA and director of the Office of Church and Race of the Protestant Council of the City of New York. A 1955 honors graduate of the University of South Carolina, Payton received a B.D. from Harvard University (1958), an M.A. degree from Columbia University (1960), and a Ph.D. in ethics from Yale University, under the tutelage of H. Richard Niebuhr, in 1963. He has served as president of Tuskegee University since 1981.

30. Reinhold Niebuhr, *Moral Man and Immoral Society: A Study in Ethics and Politics*, Library of Theological Ethics (Louisville, Ky.: Westminster John Knox Press, 2001). See especially Reinhold Niebuhr, "Morality and Power," chap. 2 in *Reinhold Niebuhr: Theologian of Public Life*, ed. Larry L. Rasmussen (Minneapolis: Fortress, 1991).

31. See J. Cone, "Revolution, Violence, and Reconciliation in Black Theology," in *Black Theology and Black Power*.

32. National Committee of Negro Churchmen, "Black Power," in Cone and Wilmore, *Black Theology*, vol. 1, 2nd ed., 21.

33. Leon Watts, "The National Committee of Black Churchmen," *Christianity and Crisis* 30, no. 18 (1970): 239.

34. See Nathan Wright, Jr., *Black Power and Urban Unrest: Creative Possibilities* (New York: Hawthorn Books, 1967). Wright also chaired the steering committee of the very first National Black Power Conference, Newark, New Jersey, July 10–23, 1967. For an account of the conference, see *Life* magazine, August 4, 1967, 26–28. Also, see Floyd B. Barbour, "The National Conference on Black Power," in *The Black Power Revolt* (Boston: Extending Horizon, 1968), 189–198.

35. Smith was the pastor of the First Baptist Church, Capital Hill (Nashville, Tennessee). Smith had been a founding member of Martin Luther King, Jr.'s Southern Christian Leadership Conference and onetime president of its Nashville arm. See Marcia Riggs, ed., *The Kelly Miller Smith Papers* (Nashville, Tenn.: Jean and Alexander Heard Library, Vanderbilt University, 1989); Kelly Miller Smith, "Pursuit of a Dream (the Nashville Story)," Kelly Miller Smith Papers, Vanderbilt University, Nashville; K. Smith, *Social Crisis Preaching: The Lyman Beecher Lectures, 1983* (Macon, Ga.: Mercer University Press, 1984). Also, see Raymond R. Sommerville, *An Ex-Colored Church: Social Activism in the CME Church, 1870–1970*, Voices of the African Diaspora (Macon, Ga.: Mercer University Press, 2004), 115–121. Smith became very active in the NCBC, serving as its last president (1978–1984). Following his untimely death, an NCBC that was already waning ceased to meet. Mary Sawyer observes that King directed SCLC staff members to attend NCBC meetings. Several of them joined, including Wyatt Tee Walker, who had served as King's chief of staff and later joined the NCBC's board of directors. King also asked for the NCBC's assistance in training urban clergy for the Poor People's Campaign. Mary R. Sawyer, *Black Ecumenism: Implementing the Demands of Justice* (Valley Forge, Pa.: Trinity, 1984), 69–70, 182. For more on the relationship between SCLC and the NCBC, see Wilmore, *Black Religion and Black Radicalism*, 2nd ed., 200; and Wilmore and Cone, "General Introduction," in Cone and Wilmore, *Black Theology*, vol. 2, 11n. 1.

36. Lawrence E. Lucas, *Black Priest / White Church: Catholics and Racism* (New York: Random House, 1970). For a sense of the militant spirit emerging among a remnant of black Catholics during this period, also see "A Statement of the Black Catholic Clergy Caucus, April 18, 1968." Two weeks after Dr. King's assassination, the statement was first published by the National Office of Black Catholics' magazine, *Freeing the Spirit* 1, no. 3 (Summer 1972), reprinted in Wilmore and Cone, *Black Theology*, vol. 1.

37. National Committee of Black Churchmen, "Black Theology," in Cone and Wilmore, *Black Theology*, vol. 1, 2nd ed., 38.

38. The NCBC ceased to meet following the death of its last president, Kelly Miller Smith, in 1983. See Mary Sawyer's discussion of its origins, development, and demise in *Black Ecumenism*, chap. 3.

39. For a collection of the key documents in the early history of the NCBC, see the October–November 1970 issue of *Renewal*. Included in the issue is a critical article on the NCBC by Vincent Harding: "No Turning Back."

40. Gayraud S. Wilmore, *A Summary Report* (NCNC Theological Commission Project, Fall 1968), 5.

41. Ibid., 11, 12.

42. Ibid., 11.

43. Ibid., 17.

44. Gayraud Wilmore discusses "a critical turning point" in September 1967 which would help to catalyze the development of black caucuses in white denominations. At a meeting sponsored by the NCC Division of Christian Life and Work and focused on the urban crisis in America, black delegates proposed dividing into separate sessions, one black and the other white, and coming together for the final plenary session. Such a format had never before been proposed in the history of the ecumenical movement in the United States. After some weak resistance from the white delegates, each group met separately for the remaining three days. The black caucus developed a statement which supported black power, called for the formation of black caucuses in all predominantly white churches, and urged greater involvement by all churches in the crises confronting American cities. Wilmore observes that most of the black delegates were members of the newly formed NCNC and that the formation of black caucuses in some nine denominations, representing more than half of white Protestants in America, is directly traceable to this meeting. See Wilmore, *Black Religion and Black Radicalism*, 2nd ed., 229–233.

45. Gilbert Caldwell, "Black Folk in White Churches," *Christian Century*, February 12, 1969, 211.

46. J. Cone, *Black Theology and Black Power*, 89.

47. Martin Luther King, Jr., for example, asserts in his famous Holt Street address at the outset of the Montgomery Bus Boycott that, because of black people's disciplined Christian witness, history will have to pause and say, "There lived a great people, a black people who injected new meaning into the veins of civilization." For a discussion on King and black messianism, see Baldwin, *There Is a Balm in Gilead*, chap. 4.

48. Joseph R. Washington, *The Politics of God: The Future of Black Churches* (1967; repr., Boston: Beacon, 1969), 201.

49. Joseph R. Washington, "How Black Is Black Religion?," in *Quest for a Black Theology*, ed. James J. Gardiner and J. Deotis Roberts (Philadelphia: Pilgrim, 1971), 28.

50. Ibid., 39–40. Also, see his essay "The Roots and Fruits of Black Theology," *Theology Today* 30 (July 1973): 121–129.

51. Joseph Washington, "Roots and Fruits of Black Theology," 128.

52. See J. Deotis Roberts, *From Puritanism to Platonism in Seventeenth Century England* (The Hague: Martinus Nijhoff, 1969).

53. For a sense of the spirited and sometimes caustic tone of their debates, see James Cone, "A Critique of J. Deotis Roberts, Sr.'s *A Black Political Theology*," *Journal of International Theological Center* 3, no. 1 (1975): 55–57; J. Deotis Roberts, "A Critique of James H. Cone's *God of the Oppressed*," *Journal of International Theological Center* 3, no. 1 (Fall 1975): 58–63. Also, see J. Cone, "An Interpretation of the Debate among Black Theologians," in Wilmore and Cone, *Black Theology*, vol. 1.

54. See J. Deotis Roberts, *The Prophethood of Black Believers: An African American Political Theology for Ministry* (Louisville, Ky.: Westminster John Knox Press, 1994); Roberts, *Africentric Christianity: A Theological Appraisal for Ministry* (Valley Forge, Pa.: Judson, 2000); and Roberts, *Roots of a Black Future: The Black Family and the Church*, 2nd ed. (Silver Spring, Md.: Strebor Books, 2001). In addition to his teaching posts, Roberts has served as the dean of the School of Theology, Virginia Union University, and president of the Interdenominational Theological Center, both predominantly black seminaries that train scores of ministers for the black churches.

55. See Henry H. Mitchell, *Black Belief: Folk Beliefs of Blacks in America and West Africa* (New York: Harper and Row, 1975); and Mitchell, *Black Preaching* (Philadelphia: Lippincott, 1970). Also, see Mitchell, "Black Power and the Christian Church," *Foundations*, April–July 1968, 99–109.

56. Gayraud S. Wilmore, *The Secular Relevance of the Church* (Philadelphia: Westminster, 1962).

57. Wilmore made this comment to the author during an interview, September 29, 2003, Washington, D.C.

58. James H. Cone, *Risks of Faith: The Emergence of a Black Theology of Liberation, 1968–1998* (Boston: Beacon, 1999), xxi–xxii.

59. M. King, "Autobiography of Religious Development," 361.

60. Burns, *To the Mountaintop*, 151.

61. J. Cone, *Risks of Faith*, xxii.

Notes to Chapter 3

1. E.g., D. Andrews, *Practical Theology for Black Churches*.

2. I agree with Gayraud Wilmore, who says that often "the criticism [of the black church] is not misplaced." Yet he opines, "The radicals who deprecate the black church, the black professionals who avoid it, and the black television comedians who mimic it, need to know how facilely they have absorbed white ignorance and how they have sewn themselves up in that bag. Black pride and power, black nationalism and pan-Africanism have had no past without the black church and black religion, and without them may well have no enduring future." Wilmore, *Black Religion and Black Radicalism*, 2nd ed., x.

3. To be sure, Du Bois uses this phrase in his famed discussion regarding the "double-consciousness" of African American people, in general, and the way in which they are viewed by the dominant culture as essentially a problem. See W. E. B. Du Bois, "Of Our Spiritual Strivings," in *The Souls of Black Folk* (1903; repr., New York: New American Library, 1969).

4. See Drake and Cayton, "The Church as a Race Institution," in *Black Metropolis*, 424.

5. Mays, Nicholson, and Institute of Social and Religious Research, *Negro's Church*,

6. Hamilton offers a helpful summary of the widespread phenomenon of social actions by black preachers and their varied approaches of negotiating the white power structure from the time of Reconstruction until the emergence of black theology. See his chapter titled "Preachers and Political Action," in *The Black Preacher*

in America (New York: Morrow, 1972). Charles Shelby Rooks discusses the need to further clarify this often "unexamined expectation" of the minister's involvement in the work of racial uplift. Rooks, "The Minister as a Change Agent," *Journal of the ITC* 4, no. 1 (Fall 1977): 12–23.

7. See Du Bois, *Negro Church*; Du Bois, *The Philadelphia Negro: A Social Study* (Philadelphia: University of Pennsylvania Press, 1996). Also, see Du Bois's classic essay "Of the Faith of the Fathers," in *Souls of Black Folk*.

8. See Jacqueline M. Moore, *Booker T. Washington, W. E. B. Du Bois, and the Struggle for Racial Uplift* (Wilmington, Del.: Scholarly Resources, 2003).

9. Woodson, *History of the Negro Church*.

10. Drake and Cayton, *Black Metropolis*.

11. Gunnar Myrdal, *An American Dilemma: The Negro Problem and Modern Democracy*, Black and African-American Studies (New Brunswick, NJ: Transaction, 1996).

12. Mays, Nicholson, and Institute of Social and Religious Research, *Negro's Church*.

13. Frazier, *Negro Church in America*.

14. See Du Bois, "Of the Faith of the Fathers," in *Souls of Black Folk*.

15. For a good interpretation of Du Bois, see David Levering Lewis, *W. E. B. Du Bois: Biography of a Race, 1868–1919* (New York: Owl Books, 1994); Lewis, *W. E. B. Du Bois: The Fight for Equality and the American Century, 1919–1963* (New York: Owl Books, 2001). Also, see Manning Marable, *W. E. B. Du Bois, Black Radical Democrat*, Twayne's Twentieth-Century American Biography Series 3 (Boston: Twayne, 1986).

16. Du Bois, *Negro Church*, 85.

17. Ibid., 86.

18. For a good socio-ethical analysis of their contrasting visions of racial uplift, see R. Franklin, *Liberating Vision*. Also, see J. Moore, *Booker T. Washington*.

19. Booker T. Washington, *The Future of the American Negro* (Boston, 1899).

20. Orishatukeh Faduma, "The Defects of the Negro Church" (American Negro Academy Occasional Paper 10, 1904). Born September 15, 1857, in British Guyana, Faduma (Christened William J. Davis in honor of the Welsh missionary) settled, with his parents, in Sierra Leone before moving to the United States in 1891. Influenced by the AME Church while in Sierra Leone, he became the first native African to enroll at the Yale Divinity School in 1891. Graduating with honors in 1894, he passed the rigorous ordination examinations and was ordained as a Congregational minister in 1895. He was a strong advocate of theological liberalism and wrote about it in the *AME Church Review* before arriving to the United States. Becoming a naturalized citizen of the United States in 1902, Faduma became an African missionary to African Americans in the South. He was elected, in 1899, as a member of the American Negro Academy and used its platform as an opportunity to call for reform in the black church. See Moses N. Moore, *Orishatukeh Faduma: Liberal Theology and Evangelical Pan-Africanism, 1857–1946* (Lanham, Md.: Scarecrow, 1996).

21. Faduma, "Defects of the Negro Church," 3.

22. Ibid., 4–5, 15, 7.

23. Du Bois, *Souls of Black Folk*, 140–141.

24. William Wells Brown, "Black Religion in the Post-Reconstruction South," in *Afro-American Religious History: A Documentary Witness*, ed. Milton C. Sernett (Durham: Duke University Press, 1985), 243. For a discussion of the efforts of both white and black denominational leaders to root out the folk practices of a southern religiosity from their churches and to introduce the masses to "intelligent worship" and middle-class virtues, see Paul Harvey, "'These Untutored Masses': The Campaign for Respectability among White and Black Evangelicals in the American South, 1870–1930," *Journal of Religious History* 21, no. 3 (1997): 302–317.

25. Joseph Washington, *Black Religion*, 51.

26. Frazier, *Negro Church in America*, 90.

27. Martin Luther King, Jr., "A Knock at Midnight," in *A Knock at Midnight*, 73–74.

28. Burns, *To the Mountaintop*, 56.

29. Baldwin, *There Is a Balm in Gilead*. Also see Aldon Morris's discussion of King's "refocusing of the cultural content of the church" (*Origins of the Civil Rights Movement*, 94).

30. Gary T. Marx, "Religion: Opiate or Inspiration of Civil Rights Militancy?," in *Protest and Prejudice: A Study of Belief in the Black Community*, rev. ed., Patterns of American Prejudice 3 (New York: Harper and Row, 1969), 105. The book is the third volume in a series titled *Patterns of American Prejudice*, a five-year study on anti-Semitism sponsored by the Anti-Defamation League of B'nai B'rith and conducted by the Survey Research Center of the University of California at Berkeley.

31. Nascent black theology's encounter with Marxist class analysis came initially as a result of the strained dialogue between black theologians and Latin American liberation theologians. In their initial dialogue, theologians from Latin America, such as Hugo Assmann, emphasized Marxist class analysis while ignoring the problem of race in their own context. James Cone emphasized the issue of race but had yet to incorporate Marxist class analysis into his theological framework. For an account of this World Council of Churches symposium, see *Risk* 9, no. 2 (1973). Cone discusses the growing impact of class analysis on his emerging theological consciousness in *For My People*, 92–96 and the chapter titled "Black Christians and Marxism." Also, see chapters 4 and 5 of J. Cone, *My Soul Looks Back: Journeys in Faith* (Nashville, Tenn.: Abingdon, 1982); J. Cone, "The Black Church and Marxism: What Do They Have to Say to Each Other?" (occasional paper, Institute for Democratic Socialism, 1980); J. Cone, "Black Christians and Marxism," *Voices from the Third World* 9, no. 1 (1986): 1–12; J. Cone, "Black Theology and Marxism," *Voices from the Third World* 9, no. 3 (1986). But no one had a greater impact on the incorporation of Marxist analysis into the black theological framework than Cornel West. West and Cone were colleagues at Union Theological Seminary in the 1980s, and they taught several classes together on "black theology and Marxist thought." West was a member of EATWOT (the Ecumenical Association of Third World Theologians) and TIA (Theology in the Americas). See Cornel West, *Prophesy Deliverance! An Afro-American Revolutionary Christianity* (Philadelphia: Westminster, 1982); C. West, "Black Theology and Marxist Thought," in West and Glaude, *African American Religious Thought*;

C. West, "Black Theology of Liberation as Critique of Capitalist Civilization," in Cone and Wilmore, *Black Theology*, vol. 2. Also, see second-generation black theologian Dwight N. Hopkins's "Black Theology and Third World Liberation Theologies," in *Introducing Black Theology of Liberation*. Among the studies of the black struggle in America and Marxist thought are Michael C. Dawson, "Black Marxists in White America," in *Black Visions: The Roots of Contemporary African-American Political Ideologies* (Chicago: University of Chicago Press, 2001); Mark Naison, *Communists in Harlem during the Depression* (Urbana: University of Illinois Press, 1983); Cedric J. Robinson, *Black Marxism: The Making of the Black Radical Tradition* (Chapel Hill: University of North Carolina Press, 2000); Alan M. Wald, *Exiles from a Future Time: The Forging of the Mid-Twentieth-Century Literary Left* (Chapel Hill: University of North Carolina Press, 2002); Philip S. Foner, *American Socialism and Black Americans: From the Age of Jackson to World War II* (Westport, Conn.: Greenwood, 1977).

32. For a very insightful critique of Gary Marx's flawed analysis, see Hart M. Nelsen and Anne Kusener Nelsen, *Black Church in the Sixties* (Lexington: University Press of Kentucky, 1975), 122–123.

33. For an interesting discussion of this issue among intellectuals within the context of the AME Church prior to the rise of black theology, see Dennis Dickerson, "The Black Church and Black Intellectuals," *AME Church Review*, 1986, 22–29. Also, see Harold Cruse, *The Crisis of the Negro Intellectual: A Historical Analysis of the Failure of Black Leadership* (New York: New York Review Books, 2005).

34. C. Eric Lincoln, *The Black Church since Frazier*, in Frazier and Lincoln, *The Negro Church in America / The Black Church since Frazier*, 105–106.

35. For further study, see Thomas J. J. Altizer, *The Gospel of Christian Atheism* (London: Collins, 1967); Altizer, *The Descent into Hell: A Study of the Radical Reversal of the Christian Consciousness* (Philadelphia: Lippincott, 1970); Thomas J. J. Altizer and William Hamilton, *Radical Theology and the Death of God*, new ed. (Harmondsworth, UK: Penguin, 1968); Kenneth Hamilton, *God Is Dead: The Anatomy of a Slogan* (Grand Rapids, Mich.: Eerdmans, 1966); K. Hamilton, *What's New in Religion? A Critical Study of New Theology, New Morality, and Secular Christianity* (Grand Rapids, Mich.: Eerdmans, 1968).

36. J. Cone, *Black Theology and Black Power*, chap. 4.

37. J. Cone, *Black Theology of Liberation*, 131.

38. J. Cone, "Christianity and Black Power," in *Risks of Faith*; first published in *Is Anybody Listening to Black America?*, ed. C. Eric Lincoln (New York: Seabury, 1968).

39. See James H. Cone, "The Doctrine of Man in the Theology of Karl Barth" (Ph.D. diss., Northwestern University, 1965). Cone's major adviser was William Hordern. An expert on Karl Barth and twentieth-century theology, among Hordern's writings are *Christianity, Communism, and History* (Nashville, Tenn.: Abingdon, 1954), *The Case for a New Reformation Theology* (Philadelphia: Westminster, 1959), *New Directions in Theology Today* (Philadelphia: Westminster, 1966), and *A Layman's Guide to Protestant Theology*, rev. ed. (New York: Macmillan, 1968). See Cone and Hordern, "Dialogue on Black Theology," *Christian Century* 88 (1971): 1079–1085.

40. J. Cone, "Doctrine of Man," 1. One of Cone's professors, P. S. Watson, had spoken
    of Luther's "Copernican Revolution." See P. S. Watson, *Let God Be God* (Philadel-
    phia: Muhlenberg Press, 1947), 33.
41. J. Cone, *Black Theology of Liberation*, 121.
42. Statement during an interview with the author, March 1, 2005. One of the best
    treatments of Barth's revolt against the liberal theology of his teachers in the wake
    of their capitulation to a so-called Religious War Experience and the definitive role
    that Barth plays in the development and debates of twentieth-century theology is
    Gary Dorrien's *The Barthian Revolt in Modern Theology: Theology without Weapons*
    (Louisville, Ky.: Westminster John Knox Press, 2000).
43. J. Cone, *Risks of Faith*, xxii.
44. J. Cone, "Christianity and Black Power," in ibid., 3.
45. Ibid., 3.
46. Ibid.
47. J. Cone, *Black Theology and Black Power*, 73.
48. J. Cone, "Doctrine of Man," 51–52, 158.
49. J. Cone, *Black Theology and Black Power*, 73.
50. Qtd. in J. Cone, "Christianity and Black Power," in *Risks of Faith*, 8.
51. Karl Barth, *The Epistle to the Romans* (New York: Oxford University Press, 1968), 10.
    For a dialogue on the problem of Christian theology and ideology between James
    Cone and sympathetic critics of black theology on this issue, see the Fall 1975 issue
    of the *Union Seminary Quarterly Review*. Also, see Harry H. Singleton's discussion
    of Cone's theology in the light of Juan Segundo's methodology and critique of the
    uncritical ideological presuppositions and ahistorical naivete of Western theology.
    Singleton sees Cone's theology as an important corrective, completing Segundo's
    "hermeneutic circle" and unmasking the way in which theology participates in the
    legitimization of structures of oppression. Harry H. Singleton, *Black Theology and
    Ideology: Deideological Dimensions in the Theology of James H. Cone* (Collegeville, Minn.:
    Liturgical, 2002).
52. J. Cone, "Christianity and Black Power," in *Risks of Faith*, 10.
53. J. Cone, *Black Theology and Black Power*, 94.
54. Josiah's reform is part of the Deuteronomistic history and redaction found in the
    Old Testament. See 2 Kings 22–23.
55. Victor Anderson, as part of his overall critique of "the black theology project," has
    labeled this methodological move, among first- and second-generation black theo-
    logians, to locate black theology along an historical continuum of resistance "a cult
    of black heroic genius." Anderson, *Beyond Ontological Blackness: An Essay on African
    American Religious and Cultural Criticism*. New York: Continuum, 1995), 100. Among
    Anderson's concerns are that within this "oppression-liberation circle," too much
    of the radically differentiated character of black identity (relative privilege, sexual
    orientation, political orientation) fades into black. Similarly, he argues that woman-
    ist theology is caught up in the same discursive bind of suffering and resistance.

Requiring white racism for legitimacy, both are trapped, Anderson argues, in "the blackness that whiteness created" (117).

56. J. Cone, *Black Theology and Black Power*, 103.

57. Ibid., 105.

58. Joseph Washington, qtd. in ibid.

59. Ibid., 106.

60. James H. Cone, "Black Consciousness and the Black Church: An Historical-Theological Interpretation," in *The Sixties: Radical Change in American Religion*, vols. 387–392 of *The Annals of the American Academy of Political and Social Science*, January 1970, 49. Written during the same period, also see J. Cone, "Christian Theology and the Afro-American Revolution," *Christianity and Crisis* 30 (1970): 123–125.

61. J. Cone, *Black Theology of Liberation*, 134.

62. Ibid., 108, 134.

63. James H. Cone, "What Does It Mean to Be Saved?," in *Preaching the Gospel*, ed. Henry J. Young and William Holmes Borders (Philadelphia: Fortress, 1976), 21.

64. Ibid. Cone marshals the same basic argument in "Black Theology: Tears, Anguish and Salvation," *Circuit Rider*, May 1978, 3–6.

65. James H. Cone, "Christian Faith and Political Praxis," *Bulletin de théologie africaine* 2, no. 4 (1980): 210–211.

66. J. Cone, "Black Theology: Tears, Anguish and Salvation," 22.

67. See J. Cone, "What Does It Mean to Be Saved?" Also see J. Cone, "Christian Theology and Scripture as the Expression of God's Liberating Activity for the Poor," *Bangalore Theological Forum* 22, no. 2 (1990): 26–39.

68. James H. Cone, "The Mission of Black Churches: Saving Souls or Saving Bodies?," unpublished lecture.

69. James H. Cone, "What Time Is It for the AME Church?," *AME Church Review*, January–March 1987, 32.

70. E.g., J. Cone, *For My People*; James H. Cone, "God Our Father, Christ Our Redeemer, Man Our Brother: A Theological Interpretation of the AME Church," *AME Church Review*, January–March 1991, 25–33.

71. Wilmore, *Black Religion and Black Radicalism*, 2nd ed., ix–x.

72. See David Noel Freedman, "Deuteronomistic History," in *The Anchor Bible Dictionary*, 6 vols. (New York: Doubleday, 1992), 2:160–168.

73. An ordained minister and former executive in the United Presbyterian Church in the USA, Wilmore has remained very active in this church while pursuing his deep scholarly interests in the historical and theological meaning of the independent black church movement.

74. See his first two books: J. Deotis Roberts, *Liberation and Reconciliation: A Black Theology* (Philadelphia: Westminster, 1971); Roberts, *A Black Political Theology* (Philadelphia: Westminster, 1974).

75. J. Deotis Roberts, "Black Ecclesiology of Involvement," *Journal of Religious Thought* 32 (Spring–June 1975), reprinted in *Black Religion, Black Theology: The Collected*

Essays of J. Deotis Roberts, ed. David Emmanuel Goatley, African American Religious Thought and Life (Harrisburg, Pa.: Trinity, 2003), 73. Page cites refer to the reprint edition.

76. Ibid., 75, 80, 73.

77. For a more nuanced view of the black church during this period, see Lincoln and Mamiya, *Black Church in the African American Experience*, 121, 209–212. Also see 438n. 41.

78. Wilmore, "Introduction to Part IV," in Wilmore and Cone, *Black Theology*, vol. 1, 246.

79. Baer and Singer, *African-American Religion in the Twentieth Century*, 27.

80. Cecil Wayne Cone, *The Identity Crisis in Black Theology* (Nashville, Tenn.: AMEC, 1975), 101.

81. Charles H. Long, *Significations: Signs, Symbols, and Images in the Interpretation of Religion* (Philadelphia: Fortress, 1986); Long, "Perspectives for a Study of Afro-American Religion in the United States," *History of Religions* 11 (August 1974): 54–66.

82. Cf. Frazier, *Negro Church in America*; Melville J. Herskovits, *The Myth of the Negro Past* (Boston: Beacon, 1958). Also, see the discussion regarding this debate concerning the extent to which there are African retentions among blacks in the North American context in Raboteau, *Slave Religion*, part 1; and Peter J. Paris, *The Spirituality of African Peoples: The Search for a Common Moral Discourse* (Minneapolis: Fortress, 1995).

83. For a brief overview of the debate on this issue, see James Cone's essay "An Interpretation of the Debate among Black Theologians," in Wilmore and Cone, *Black Theology*, vol. 1.

84. C. Cone, *The Identity Crisis in Black Theology*, 37.

85. Ibid., 72.

86. James H. Cone, *Speaking the Truth: Ecumenism, Liberation, and Black Theology* (Grand Rapids, Mich.: Eerdmans, 1986), 18.

87. Ibid., 20.

88. For a good discussion of James Cone's own view about how vigorous debate, not only with his brother Cecil but with Wilmore, Roberts, Long, Jones, and others, helped to shape the development of his perspective, see "An Interpretation of the Debate among Black Theologians," in Wilmore and Cone, *Black Theology*, vol. 1.

89. J. Cone, *God of the Oppressed*, iii.

90. Ibid., 13.

91. Ibid., 53.

92. Ibid., 55.

93. Albert B. Cleage, *Black Christian Nationalism: New Directions for the Black Church* (New York: Morrow, 1972), 33.

94. Ibid.

95. Ibid., 32.

96. Ibid., 34.

97. Ibid., 30.

98. For Cleage, Nat Turner was one exception. Ibid., 32.

99. Cleage elaborates on this theme in his first book, a collection of sermons preached during the uprisings in Detroit: *The Black Messiah* (Trenton, N.J.: Africa World, 1989).

100. Cleage, *Black Christian Nationalism*, 39.

101. Ibid., 35.

102. For a countervailing pastoral view of Paul's theology and its implications for black liberation, see Amos Jones, *Paul's Message of Freedom: What Does It Mean to the Black Church?* (Valley Forge, Pa.: Judson, 1984). The text is based on Jones's 1975 doctor of ministry thesis at Vanderbilt University, "In Defense of Paul: A Discussion with James Cone and Albert Cleage."

103. Cleage, *Black Christian Nationalism*, 39.

104. William Jones argues that given the misdistribution, enormity, and longevity of black suffering, theodicy must be the controlling category of black theology. Black theologians must seriously ask, "Is God a white racist?" Furthermore, black theologians must demonstrate, not assume, that God is not a racist. He proffers a framework of humanistic existentialism as the most viable framework for black theology. See W. Jones, "Suffering Servants and Wounded Warriors: A Description of Major Themes in Black Theology," *AME Church Review*, 1993, 19–27; W. Jones, "Theodicy and Methodology in Black Theology: A Critique of Washington, Cone and Cleage," *AME Church Review*, 1993, 28–39; and W. Jones, "Theodicy: The Controlling Category for Black Theology," *AME Church Review*, 1993, 9–17.

105. Cleage, *Black Christian Nationalism*, xvii.

106. Hopkins, *Introducing Black Theology of Liberation*, 122–124.

107. Ibid., 123.

108. Dwight N. Hopkins, *Shoes That Fit Our Feet: Sources for a Constructive Black Theology* (Maryknoll, N.Y.: Orbis Books, 1993); Hopkins, *Down, Up, and Over*; Dwight N. Hopkins and George C. L. Cummings, *Cut Loose Your Stammering Tongue: Black Theology in the Slave Narratives* (Maryknoll, N.Y.: Orbis Books, 1991). Cummings's other manuscript work, based on his doctoral dissertation ("A Comparative Analysis of the Origins and Development of Black Theology in the United States of America and Latin American Liberation Theology, 1968–1986" [Ph.D. diss., Union Theological Seminary, 1989]), focuses on the relationship between black theology in the United States and Latin American liberation theology. See Cummings, *A Common Journey: Black Theology (USA) and Latin American Liberation Theology*, Bishop Henry McNeal Turner Studies in North American Black Religion 6 (Maryknoll, N.Y.: Orbis Books, 1993).

109. Hopkins, *Shoes That Fit Our Feet*, 4, 5.

110. Hopkins, *Down, Up, and Over*, 147.

111. See J. Kameron Carter, *Race: A Theological Account* (Oxford: Oxford University Press, 2008). Also, see Willie J. Jennings, *The Christian Imagination: Theology and the Origins of Race* (New Haven: Yale University Press, 2010); and Brian Bantum, *Redeeming Mulatto: A Theology of Race and Christian Hybridity* (Waco, Tex.: Baylor University Press, 2010).

112. Carter, *Race*, 35.
113. Cf. W. Jones, "Theodicy and Methodology in Black Theology"; W. Jones, "Theodicy"; W. Jones, *Is God a White Racist? A Preamble to Black Theology* (Boston: Beacon, 1998); and Anthony B. Pinn, *Why, Lord? Suffering and Evil in Black Theology* (New York: Continuum, 1995).
114. Cf. Long, "Perspectives for a Study of Afro-American Religion; Anthony B. Pinn, *Varieties of African American Religious Experience* (Minneapolis: Fortress, 1998); and Pinn, *Terror and Triumph: The Nature of Black Religion* (Minneapolis: Fortress, 2003).
115. Pinn's title is a spin on the classic by William James, *The Varieties of Religious Experience: A Study in Human Nature: Being the Gifford Lectures on Natural Religion Delivered at Edinburgh in 1901–1902* (Mineola, N.Y.: Dover, 2002).
116. Ibid., 6, 1. Also, see Sylvester A. Johnson, "The 'Children of Ham' in America: Divine Identity and the Hamitic Idea in Nineteenth-Century American Christianity" (Ph.D. diss., Union Theological Seminary, 2002).
117. Wiley, "Black Theology," 127. Also, see Wiley, "The Concept of the Church in the Works of Howard Thurman" (Ph.D. diss., Union Theological Seminary, 1988).
118. Wiley, "Black Theology," 129.
119. Ibid.
120. Ibid., 130.
121. Harris received his master of divinity degree (1976) from the School of Theology at Virginia Union University (now the Samuel Dewitt Proctor School of Theology at Virginia Union). J. Deotis Roberts was the dean of the School of Theology at the time. Harris earned an M.A. degree in philosophy and religious studies (1981) and a Ph.D. in urban studies from Old Dominion University. Harris received a D.Min. degree from United Theological Seminary. His areas of concentration were African American church studies and homiletics. Samuel Proctor directed his doctor of ministry thesis.
122. James H. Harris, "Practicing Liberation in the Black Church," *Christian Century*, 1990, 599–602; Gayraud S. Wilmore, "Connecting Two Worlds: A Response to James Henry Harris by Gayraud Wilmore," *Christian Century*, 1990, 602–604.
123. J. Harris, *Pastoral Theology*, 57.
124. Ibid., 62.
125. James H. Harris, *Preaching Liberation* (Minneapolis: Fortress, 1995), 8.
126. Harris, Roberson, and George, *What Does It Mean to Be Black and Christian?*
127. E.g., Wiley's Covenant Baptist Church sponsors the ChristAfrican Community-Based Theological Institute, an effort to situate the insights of black theology in the churches, "empowering the people to do theology from the bottom up." Wiley, "Black Theology," 134. A 1994 Community Institute and Revival, with the theme "Breaking down the Barriers That Divide Us" and also held at Covenant, endeavored to accomplish the same end. Mark L. Chapman, "Christianity on Trial: African-American Religious Thought before and after Black Power, 1945–1992" (Ph.D. diss., Union Theological Seminary, 1993), 179. James Harris, sourced by his experience as a pastor and reflections as a theologian, has offered practical suggestions for a

pastoral theology committed to the work of liberation. See J. Harris, *Pastoral Theology*; J. Harris, *Preaching Liberation.*

128. Gayraud S. Wilmore, "Black Theology: Review and Assessment," *Voices from the Third World* 5, no. 2 (December 1982): 6.

129. James H. Evans, *We Have Been Believers: An African-American Systematic Theology* (Minneapolis: Fortress, 1992), 1.

Notes to Chapter 4

1. For a historical interpretation of how American Protestantism, confronted with the complex challenges of modernity, split into two distinct groups (liberals and evangelicals) and how the debate between those who emphasized "saving souls" and those who sought to transform individuals and the social order calcified into "two Protestantisms," see Jean Miller Schmidt, *Souls or the Social Order: The Two-Party System in American Protestantism*, Chicago Studies in the History of American Religion 18 (Brooklyn, N.Y.: Carlson, 1991). Schmidt argues that "by 1912, there were two parties in American Protestantism, one asserting that the church must seek to transform the social order, the other claiming that the church's principal task is saving individuals" (155).

2. McCall, "Review of Allan A. Boesak's *Farewell to Innocence.*"

3. Wilmore, "Introduction to Part IV," in Wilmore and Cone, *Black Theology*, vol. 1, 246.

4. See Herbert O. Edwards, "The Third World and the Problem of God-Talk," *Harvard Theological Review* 6, no. 4 (1971); and Edwards, "Racism and Christian Ethics in America," *Katallegete*, Winter 1971.

5. Edwards, "Black Theology," 55–56. For an excellent example of a positive interpretation of black theology by a white scholar, see Witvliet, *Way of the Black Messiah.* For a negative response by a liberal white theologian, early in black theology's development, see Paul Holmer, "Remarks Excerpted from 'The Crisis in Rhetoric,'" *Theological Education* 7, no. 3 (Spring 1971): 211. Also, see Holmer's "About Black Theology," along with varying responses by white theologians, in Wilmore and Cone, *Black Theology*, vol. 1, part 3.

6. Wilmore, "Black Theology: Review and Assessment," 10.

7. For good examples of how black clergy articulated the message of black theology as a public theology, see Black Theology Project, "Message to the Black Church and Community," *Journal of Religious Thought* 34 (Fall–Winter 1977): 23–28. Also, see the documents edited by Leon Watts and critiqued by Vincent Harding in the October–November 1970 edition of *Renewal* (vol. 10, no. 7): National Committee of Black Churchmen, "Black Declaration of Independence," 21–23; National Committee of Black Churchmen, "A Message to the Churches from Oakland," 19–20; National Committee of Negro Churchmen, "Black Power," 14–16; National Committee of Negro Churchmen, "Racism and the Elections: The American Dilemma of 1966, 17–18"; as well as National Conference of Black Churchmen, *Spiritual Alienation: The Self-Destruction of Black Community* (Atlanta, May 11, 1973). Black clergy also joined with black theologians to articulate a public theology in global terms, addressing

apartheid in South Africa, American domestic racism and imperialism abroad, and the ways in which all were inextricably connected. For an example of the work of the African Commission of the NCBC, see National Committee of Black Churchmen, *Philadelphia Proclamation of 1972* (New York, 1972). Reverends Maynard L. Catchings and Metz Rollins served as the media contacts for this statement, which read, in part,

> The grim reality in 1972 for Black people in America is to be seen in the continuing policy of colonialism and neo-colonialism in Africa and its relationship to the muffling of the drums of freedom on that continent. It involves an understanding of the indivisibility of African people around the world. It involves the understanding that Attica and Sharpsville are caused by the same forces. It involves an understanding that Marks, Mississippi and Namibia are exploited by the same forces, . . . that the forces that murdered El Haj Malik [*sic*] and Lumumba are the same, . . . that the backbone of the American dollar is the bloodstained, downtrodden shoulders of the people of Harlem, Selma, Latin America, South America, Asia and Africa. It is because of this duality that the African Commission of the National Committee of Black Churchmen calls upon all concerned people to raise the cry of African Liberation and to support movements against colonialism, apartheid and neo-colonialism.

8. Lincoln and Mamiya point out in their landmark study that as late as the late 1980s, only about 10 to 20 percent of black clergy had completed professional training at an accredited divinity school or seminary (*Black Church in the African American Experience*, 129). Unfortunately, the rate of actual completion of seminary training, as evidenced in this estimate, does not represent substantial improvement since the time of the Mays and Nicholson study (1933).

9. For an example of the dialogue that has taken place, see Harris, Roberson, and George, *What Does It Mean to Be Black and Christian?* Also, see the debate between piety and liberation in the *Atlanta Journal-Constitution*'s coverage of the Samuel DeWitt Proctor Conference, a conference of pastors and black theologians that emphasized the liberationist side of the black church's heritage, and the response by Eddie Long and Creflo Dollar, Atlanta pastors with megachurch ministries emphasizing individual salvation and a gospel of personal prosperity. John Blake, "Pastors Choose Sides over Direction of Black Church," *Atlanta Journal-Constitution*, February 15, 2005.

10. See James H. Cone, "In Search of a Definition of Violence," *Church and Society* (Presbyterian Church, USA) (January–February 1995): 5–7.

11. Wilmore, "Introduction to Part IV," in Wilmore and Cone, *Black Theology*, vol. 1, 246.

12. Sommerville, *Ex-Colored Church*, 116. Also, see K. Smith, "Pursuit of a Dream (the Nashville Story)."

13. Joseph A Johnson, Jr., "The Need for a Black Christian Theology," *Journal of the International Theological Center* 2, no. 2 (Fall 1974): 19–29.

14. See Johnson's essay (originally a sermon) "Jesus, the Liberator," in Gardiner and Roberts, *Quest for a Black Theology*, esp. 102ff.

15. See Joseph Harrison Jackson, *A Story of Christian Activism: The History of the National Baptist Convention, U.S.A., Inc.* (Nashville, Tenn.: Townsend, 1980), 271–276. Also, see Jackson, *Unholy Shadows and Freedom's Holy Light* (Nashville, Tenn.: Townsend, 1967); and Peter J. Paris, *Black Leaders in Conflict: Joseph H. Jackson, Martin Luther King, Jr., Malcolm X, Adam Clayton Powell, Jr.* (New York: Pilgrim, 1978).

16. See Jackson's severe critique of black theology in a chapter titled "A Theology of Polarization," in Jackson, *Nairobi: A Joke, a Junket, or a Journey?* (Nashville, Tenn.: Townsend, 1976).

17. Years later, Smith served on the NCBC's board of directors (1974–1976) and became its last president (1978–1984). A waning organization entered its demise following Smith's death.

18. Sommerville, *Ex-Colored Church*, 116. A 1938 graduate of Texas College, Johnson had already earned a master of theology degree (1943) and a doctor of theology degree (1945) from the Illiff School of Theology. Recognized within his denomination as a leading pastor/scholar, he served as president of its Phillips School of Theology in Jackson, Tennessee, before his move to Nashville.

19. For more on Lawson's extraordinary commitment and courage as a devotee to the philosophy of nonviolent confrontation, see Branch, *Parting the Waters*, 204–205. Also, see Chappell, "James Lawson," in *Stone of Hope*, 67–71. King initially went to Memphis to support sanitation workers at the request of James Lawson. See Burns, *To the Mountaintop*, 423–425.

20. Joseph A Johnson, Jr., "My Other Assignments, 1977," memo, Henry C. Bunton Papers, Schomburg Center for Research in Black Culture, New York.

21. J. Johnson, "Jesus, the Liberator," 99.

22. The conference was held May 2–3, 1969. Johnson was not a participant in the actual conference, but his essay was later added. It also appears as "Jesus: The Liberator [Limitations of White Theology]," *Anderson Newton Quarterly* 10 (January 1970): 85–96. Other presenters at the Georgetown conference were Albert Cleage, James Cone, Joseph Washington, Walter Yates, J. Deotis Roberts, and Preston Williams. See Cone, *For My People*, 23.

23. J. Johnson, "Jesus, the Liberator," 101.

24. J. Cone, *Black Theology and Black Power*, 68.

25. J. Johnson, "Jesus, the Liberator," 103, 102.

26. Ibid., 104.

27. Ibid., 105. Also, see Kelly Brown Douglas, "'Who Do They Say That I Am?' A Critical Examination of the Black Christ" (Union Theological Seminary, 1988); Douglas, *The Black Christ*, Bishop Henry McNeal Turner Studies in North American Black Religion 9 (Maryknoll, N.Y.: Orbis Books, 1993); Jacquelyn Grant, *White Women's Christ and Black Women's Jesus: Feminist Christology and Womanist Response* (Atlanta: Scholars, 1989).

28. Jackson, *Nairobi*, chap. 5.

29. Joseph H. Jackson, "The Basic Theological Position of the National Baptist Convention, U.S.A., Inc.," in Cone and Wilmore, *Black Theology*, vol. 1, 2nd ed., 248.

30. Ibid., 247.

31. Jackson, *Story of Christian Activism*, 586.

32. Jackson, *Nairobi*, 63.

33. Ibid., 73.

34. Joseph Harrison Jackson, *Many, but One: The Ecumenics of Charity* (New York: Sheen and Ward, 1964).

35. Jackson, *Nairobi*, 84.

36. Leon Watts, "'The Black Church Yes! COCU No!,'" *Renewal* 10, no. 3 (March 1970): 11.

37. For more on the history of the NCBC and other ecumenical movements among African Americans in the twentieth century, from the Fraternal Council of Negro Churches to the Congress of National Black Churches, see Mary R. Sawyer's *Black Ecumenism: Implementing the Demands of Justice*.

38. Cf. Lincoln and Mamiya, *Black Church in the African-American Experience*.

39. From a copy of an NCBC pamphlet in the author's possession: "NCBC: What Is It?"

40. Paris, *Black Religious Leaders*.

41. Jackson, *Story of Christian Activism*, 273.

42. Joseph H. Jackson, "A Call for National Unity," from the Record of the 86th Annual Session of the National Baptist Convention, USA, Inc., 1966, reprinted in Paris, *Black Leaders in Conflict*, appendix C.

43. See Eve Evans, "Olivet's Star Attraction," *Renewal*, Winter 1975.

44. Gardner C. Taylor, "The Power of Blackness," the President's Message at the Progressive National Baptist Convention, September 1968, Washington, D.C., in *The Words of Gardner Taylor*, vol. 4, *Special Occasion and Expository Sermons*, ed. Edward L. Taylor (Valley Forge, Pa.: Judson, 2001), 20–21.

45. For an early explication of this issue in black theology, see Warner R. Traynham, "The Scandal of Particularity," in *Christian Faith in Black and White: A Primer in Theology from the Black Perspective* (Wakefield, Mass.: Parameter, 1973).

46. A. Roger Williams, "A Black Pastor Looks at Black Theology," *Harvard Theological Review* 64 (1971): 564, 566.

47. J. Cone, *Black Theology and Black Power*, 69.

48. A. Williams, "Black Pastor Looks at Black Theology," 566.

49. Samuel Proctor, "The Metes and Bounds of Black Theology," *United Theological Seminary* 96 (1992): 34.

50. Ibid., 36–37, 40, 41.

51. Samuel D. Proctor, *Samuel Proctor: My Moral Odyssey* (Valley Forge, Pa.: Judson, 1989), 77–78.

52. See J. Alfred Smith, Sr., "Black Theology and the Parish Ministry," in *Black Faith and Public Talk: Critical Essays on James H. Cone's "Black Theology and Black Power,"* ed. Dwight N. Hopkins (Maryknoll, N.Y.: Orbis Books, 1999).

53. J. Alfred Smith, with Harry Louis Williams II, *On the Jericho Road: A Memoir of Racial Justice, Social Action and Prophetic Ministry* (Downers Grove, Ill.: InterVarsity, 2004), 154.

54. J. Smith, "Black Theology and the Parish Ministry," 90.

55. J. Cone, "Christianity and Black Power," in *Risks of Faith*, 3.

56. Powell, "Black Power in the Church," 34.

57. Barbour, "The National Conference on Black Power," in *Black Power Revolt*, 189–198.

58. N. Wright, *Black Power and Urban Unrest*, 136. Also, see Nathan Wright, Jr., "Power and Reconciliation," *Concern* 9, no. 16 (1967): 22.

59. E.g., Columbus Salley and Ronald Behm, *Your God Is Too White* (Downers Grove, Ill.: InterVarsity, 1970); Salley and Behm, *What Color Is Your God? Black Consciousness and the Christian Faith*, rev. ed. (Downers Grove, Ill.: InterVarsity, 1981).

60. Anthony Tyrone Evans, "A Biblical Critique of Selected Issues in Black Theology" (Ph.D. diss., Dallas Theological Seminary, 1982), 274.

61. Lincoln and Mamiya, *The Black Church in the African-American Experience*, 168–169, 170.

62. Martin Luther King, Jr., "Advice for Living," *Ebony*, October 1957, reprinted in *The Papers of Martin Luther King, Jr.*, vol. 4, *Symbol of the Movement*, ed. Clayborne Carson (Berkeley: University of California Press, 2000), 279–280.

63. Cone, *Martin and Malcolm and America*, 231. See Martin Luther King, Jr., "To Minister to the Valley," February 23, 1968, King Center Archives, Atlanta, Georgia.

64. M. King, "To Minister to the Valley."

65. Cone, *Martin and Malcolm and America*, 231.

66. Cone, *God of the Oppressed*, 136. Also, see Cone's discussion on "the fallacy of colorlessness," in "Black Consciousness and the Black Church," *Christianity and Crisis* 30 (1970): 244–250.

67. See Robert E. Hood, *Begrimed and Black: Christian Traditions on Blacks and Blackness* (Minneapolis: Fortress, 1994), xii.

68. Anderson, *Beyond Ontological Blackness*, 117. Scholars of black religion who have raised similar methodological concerns include Theophus Smith (*Conjuring Culture*, 178–182), Cornel West ("Black Theology and Marxist Thought," in West and Glaude, *African American Religious Thought*, 878–879), Dale Andrews (*Practical Theology for Black Churches*, 85–88), and Cheryl J. Sanders (*Empowerment Ethics for a Liberated People: A Path to African American Social Transformation* [Minneapolis: Fortress, 1995], 1–9).

69. Roberts, *Africentric Christianity*. Molefi Kete Asante, chair of the African American Studies Department at Temple University, is the founder of the Africentric movement. Born one of sixteen children in Valdosta, Georgia, Asante, the grandson of a minister, was also a preacher early in life. While a student at UCLA, where he was awarded a doctoral degree at age twenty-six, he led the Student Nonviolent Coordinating Committee (SNCC). He is the author of dozens of books, including *The Afrocentric Idea* (Philadelphia: Temple University Press, 1987), *Afrocentricity* (Trenton, N.J.: Third World, 1988), and *Afrocentricity and Knowledge* (Trenton, N.J.: Third World, 1992). Also, several leading womanist scholars respond to Afrocentrism and its implications for black women in Cheryl J. Sanders, ed., *Living the Intersection:*

Womanism and Afrocentrism in Theology (Minneapolis: Fortress, 1995). Among the responses in the edited work, Delores Williams's critique of Afrocentrism is perhaps the most severe. She avers,

> The gravest limitation of Asante's Afrocentrism is that its sexism and its support of male dominance make it a convenient instrument (along with white feminism) for helping to hold white male supremacy in place in the United States. An illustration can be given here. Because of its racist emphasis upon white women's experience and its way of ignoring racism as it achieves opportunities and advancement for white women, the white feminist movement has helped hold white supremacy in place in American society. . . . Thus white male power can manipulate white supremacy (supported by white feminism) and male dominance (supported by Afrocentrism) so that it serves the interest of white males and keeps most women and most black oppressed.

Williams, "Afrocentrism and Male-Female Relations in Church and Society," in ibid., 53. Also, see Julia Speller's study of "Africentric spirituality" in three congregations: *Walkin' the Talk: Keepin' the Faith in Africentric Congregations* (Cleveland: Pilgrim, 2005).

70. For a discussion of this relatively late development (1940s–1950s) in African American readings of the Bible, see Vincent L. Wimbush, *The Bible and African Americans: A Brief History* (Minneapolis: Fortress, 2003), chap. 5. Also, see Albert G. Miller, "The Construction of a Black Fundamentalist Worldview: The Role of Bible School," in *African Americans and the Bible: Sacred Texts and Social Textures*, ed. Vincent L. Wimbush and Rosamond C. Rodman (New York: Continuum, 2000); and William H. Bentley, "Bible Believers in the Black Community," in *The Evangelicals: What They Believe, Who They Are, Where They Are Changing*, ed. David F. Wells and John D. Woodbridge (Grand Rapids, Mich.: Baker Book House, 1977).

71. George M. Marsden, *Fundamentalism and American Culture: The Shaping of Twentieth-Century Evangelicalism, 1870–1925* (New York: Oxford University Press, 1980), 228.

72. Wimbush, *Bible and African Americans*, 65.

73. Ibid., 66.

74. Kathleen C. Boone, *The Bible Tells Them So: The Discourse of Protestant Fundamentalism* (Albany: SUNY Press, 1989).

75. Wimbush, *Bible and African Americans*, 68.

76. Bentley, "Bible Believers in the Black Community," 138.

77. Anthony T. Evans, qtd. in Jimmy Locklear, "'Theology-Culture Rift Surfaces among Black Evangelicals," *Christianity Today* 24, no. 44 (1980). See also Thabiti M. Anyabwile, *The Decline of African American Theology: From Biblical Faith to Cultural Captivity* (Downers Grove, Ill.: InterVarsity, 2007).

78. Clarice J. Martin, "The *Haustafeln* (Household Codes) in African American Biblical Interpretation: 'Free Slaves' and 'Subordinate Women,'" in *Stony the Road We Trod: African American Biblical Interpretation*, ed. Cain Hope Felder (Minneapolis: Fortress, 1991), 225.

79. Ibid., 231.

80. No recent work has more clearly and systematically shown the depth, resourcefulness, and intractable character of racism in America than Michelle Alexander's examination of the criminal justice system and young African American men, *The New Jim Crow: Mass Incarceration in the Age of Colorblindness* (New York: New Press, 2010). In this very important book, she demonstrates how old forms of discrimination putatively banished by the victories of the civil rights movement are reinscribed in a "postracial" era, as persons who enter the system are stigmatized long after they leave, facing a life of legalized discrimination in employment, voting, public benefits, and financial aid toward the pursuit of higher education.

81. See Renee L. Hill, "Who Are We for Each Other? Sexism, Sexuality and Womanist Theology," in Cone and Wilmore, *Black Theology*, vol. 2.

82. Among the scriptures used by those who argued in support of slavery on biblical grounds were Gen. 9:25–27, Deut. 20:10–11, 1 Cor. 7:21–24, the household codes of Eph. 6:5–9, Col. 3:22–4:1, and 1 Tim. 6:1–5.

83. Calling race "one of the fault lines in American culture and American politics from the start," Barack Obama himself remarked, "I never bought into the notion that by electing me, somehow we were entering into a post-racial period. On the other hand, I've seen in my own lifetime how racial attitudes have changed and improved." Jann S. Wenner, "Ready for the Fight: Rolling Stone Interview with Barack Obama," *Rolling Stone* April 25, 2012. For a window into the national conversation on this issue at the time, see Randall Kennedy, *The Persistence of the Color Line: Racial Politics and the Obama Presidency* (New York: Pantheon Books, 2011); ibid.; Walter Rodgers, "A Year into Obama's Presidency, Is America Post-Racial?," *Christian Science Monitor*, January 5, 1010; "Under Obama, Is America 'Post-Racial'?," *New York Times*, September 21, 2011; Thomas J. Sugrue, *Not Even Past: Barack Obama and the Burden of Race* (Princeton: Princeton University Press, 2010); Tim Wise, *Between Barack and a Hard Place: Racism and White Denial in the Age of Obama*, Open Media Series (San Francisco: City Lights Books, 2009).

84. "Reverend Wright at the National Press Club," *New York Times*, April 28, 2008.

85. The relationship between "God and Caesar," as it is put in the New Testament, is a classic theological question as old as the Church itself. Among other Christian thinkers, Augustine explores the question in *City of God*, and Luther lays out his famous "two kingdoms" doctrine in "Temporal Authority: To What Extent It Should Be Obeyed." Standing in the Lutheran tradition, Bonhoeffer wrestled with it in the context of the Church struggle in Germany. Wright raises the question from his perspective as an African American preacher who sees concern for the poor as central to the meaning of the gospel and its demand on its adherents in particular and the society in general.

86. Jeremiah A. Wright, "Confusing God and Government" (Chicago: Trinity United Church of Christ).

87. Ibid.

88. Jeremiah A. Wright, "An Underground Theology," in Hopkins, *Black Faith and Public Talk*; J. Wright, "Doing Black Theology in the Black Church," in *Living Stones in the*

Household of God: The Legacy and Future of Black Theology, ed. Linda E. Thomas (Minneapolis: Fortress, 2004).

89. J. Wright, "Doing Black Theology in the Black Church," 13–14.

90. Ibid., 18, 19, 22.

91. Glorya Askew and Gayraud Wilmore, eds., *Reclamation of Black Prisoners: A Challenge to the African American Church*, Black Church Scholars Series 3 (Atlanta: ITC, 1992); Askew and Wilmore, eds., *From Prison Cell to Church Pew*, Black Church Scholars Series 5 (Atlanta: ITC, 1993); Wilmore, ed., *Black Men in Prison: The Response of the African American Church*, Black Church Scholars Series 2 (Atlanta: ITC, 1990).

92. J. Wright, "Doing Black Theology in the Black Church," 18.

93. Prathia Hall-Wynn, "The Challenge of True Kinship," in Harris, Roberson, and George, *What Does It Mean to Be Black and Christian?*, 116.

94. Karen E. Mosby-Avery, "Black Theology and the Black Church," in Thomas, *Living Stones in the Household of God*, 35.

95. Wiley, "Black Theology," 130.

Notes to Chapter 5

1. Burns, *To the Mountaintop*, 56.

2. See Harvey, "These Untutored Masses."

3. Emilie M. Townes, ed., *Embracing the Spirit: Womanist Perspectives on Hope, Salvation and Transformation* (Maryknoll, N.Y.: Orbis Books, 1997). Also, see Rosetta E. Ross, *Witnessing and Testifying: Black Women, Religion, and Civil Rights* (Minneapolis: Fortress, 2003); Emilie M. Townes, *In a Blaze of Glory: Womanist Spirituality as Social Witness* (Nashville, Tenn.: Abingdon, 1995).

4. Karen Baker-Fletcher, "The Strength of My Life," in Townes, *Embracing the Spirit*, 125.

5. Ibid.

6. Delores S. Williams, "Straight Talk, Plain Talk: Womanist Words about Salvation in a Social Context," in Townes, *Embracing the Spirit*, 118.

7. James Cone, in particular, deserves much credit for this. See his "Preface to the 1986 Edition," his afterword, and the critical reflections he invites from other respondents in the Twentieth Anniversary Edition of his second book, *A Black Theology of Liberation*, 20th anniversary ed. (Maryknoll, N.Y.: Orbis Books, 1990).

8. James Cone, "New Roles in the Ministry: A Theological Appraisal," in Wilmore and Cone, *Black Theology*, vol. 1, 395.

9. Demetrius Williams would agree with this point. He writes, "The final assessment of the roles and challenges of African American women in black churches cannot be written by black men, no matter how sympathetic we might be to the struggle against racism and sexism." Yet, he insists, "The effects of black sexism in the black churches in America will end only when black men begin to seriously challenge and uproot the patriarchal assumptions and institutions that still dominate black religious, civil and political society." Demetrius K. Williams, *An End to This Strife: The Politics of Gender in African American Churches* (Minneapolis: Fortress, 2004), 190.

10. J. Cone, *For My People*, 134.

11. Frances Beale, "Double Jeopardy: To Be Black and Female," in Cone and Wilmore, *Black Theology*, vol. 1, 2nd ed., 286. Also, see Theressa Hoover's "Black Women and the Churches: Triple Jeopardy," in ibid.

12. For a general introduction to the discipline, see Stephanie Y. Mitchem, *Introducing Womanist Theology* (Maryknoll, N.Y.: Orbis Books, 2002).

13. Pauli Murray, "Black Theology and Feminist Theology: A Comparative View," in Cone and Wilmore, *Black Theology*, vol. 1, 2nd ed., 304, 307, 319. The essay first appeared in the *Anglican Theological Review* 60, no. 1 (January 1978).

14. For example, see Douglas, *Sexuality and the Black Church*.

15. Douglas, *Black Christ*, 114.

16. Traci C. West, *Wounds of the Spirit: Black Women, Violence, and Resistance Ethics* (New York: NYU Press 1999).

17. Daphne Wiggins, *Righteous Content: Black Women's Perspectives of Church and Faith, Religion, Race, and Ethnicity* (New York: NYU Press, 2005), 178, 179.

18. Teresa L. Fry Brown, "Avoiding Asphyxiation: A Womanist Perspective on Intrapersonal and Interpersonal Transformation," in Townes, *Embracing the Spirit*.

19. Wiggins, *Righteous Content*, 181.

20. Jacquelyn Grant, "Epistle to the Black Church: What a Womanist Would Want to Say to the Black Church," *AME Church Review*, April–June 1991, 49–58. Also, see Grant, "Women and Theology: Black Women's Experience as a Source for Doing Theology, with Special Reference to Christology," *AME Church Review*, 1987, 41–57; Grant, *White Women's Christ and Black Women's Jesus*.

21. See Jacquelyn Grant, "The Sin of Servanthood and the Deliverance of Discipleship," in *A Troubling in My Soul: Womanist Perspectives on Evil and Suffering*, ed. Emilie M. Townes (Maryknoll, N.Y.: Orbis Books, 1993), 200. Grant offers some further elaboration and musings on this theme in "Servanthood Revisited: Womanist Explorations of Servanthood Theology," in Hopkins, *Black Faith and Public Talk*.

22. Jacquelyn Grant, "Sin of Servanthood," 204.

23. Ibid., 200.

24. Ibid., 209.

25. Ibid., 214, 216.

26. Frances E. Wood, "'Take My Yoke upon You': The Role of the Church in the Oppression of African-American Women," in Townes, *Troubling in My Soul*, 37.

27. See Matt. 11:28–30.

28. Wood, "Take My Yoke upon You," 39, 46.

29. Delores S. Williams, "Black Women's Surrogacy Experience and the Christian Notion of Redemption," in *After Patriarchy: Feminist Transformations of the World Religions*, ed. Paula M. Cooey, William R. Eakin, and Jay Byrd McDaniel (Maryknoll, N.Y.: Orbis Books, 1991).

30. Ibid., 11, 13.

31. See James Cone's discussion in *Spirituals and the Blues*, 46–52. Also, see his and other essays from various contexts, including Asia, Africa, and Latin America in

Yacob Tesfai, ed., *The Scandal of a Crucified World* (Maryknoll, N.Y.: Orbis Books, 1994).

32. James H. Cone, *The Cross and the Lynching Tree* (Maryknoll, N.Y.: Orbis Books, 2011).

33. JoAnne Marie Terrell, *Power in the Blood? The Cross in the African American Experience*, Bishop Henry McNeal Turner / Sojourner Truth Series in Black Religion 15 (Maryknoll, N.Y.: Orbis Books, 1998), 121, 124, 125.

34. Kelly Brown Douglas, *What's Faith Got to Do with It? Black Bodies/Christian Souls* (Maryknoll, N.Y.: Orbis Books, 2005), 100, 96.

35. Schalom Ben-Chorin, *Die Antwort des Jona* (Hamburg, 1956), 99; and *Die Christusfrage an die Juden* (Jerusalem, 1941), 25, qtd. in Jürgen Moltmann, *The Way of Jesus Christ: Christology in Messianic Dimensions* (Minneapolis: Fortress, 1993), 29.

36. Qtd. in Dietrich Bonhoeffer, "Christ the Center," in *A Testament to Freedom: The Essential Writings of Dietrich Bonhoeffer*, ed. Geffrey B. Kelly and F. Burton Nelson (San Francisco: HarperCollins, 1990), 117. In *Imperial Designs: Neoconservatism and the New Pax Americana* (New York: Routledge, 2004), Gary Dorrien discusses the ideology put forward by neoconservatives, in the wake of the end of the Cold War, that America should actually expand its military spending and its military reach to the end of establishing its global preeminence and the institution of a new *Pax Americana*. Dorrien sees the Bush doctrine of preemptive war which led to the invasion of Iraq as a manifestation of this. See especially his chapter "Benevolent Global Hegemony."

37. See his 1933 christology lectures: Dietrich Bonhoeffer, *Christ the Center*, trans., Edwin H. Robertson (San Francisco: HarperCollins, 1978), 33, 35.

38. Renate Wind, *Dietrich Bonhoeffer: A Spoke in the Wheel*, trans. John Bowden (Grand Rapids, Mich.: Eerdmans, 1990), 50–52.

39. Dietrich Bonhoeffer, *Letters and Papers from Prison* (New York: Macmillan, 1972), 17.

40. Distinguishing black radicalism from the radicalism that emerged in Europe following the 1848 publication of the *Communist Manifesto*, the rise of the Soviet Union, communism, and communist parties, Gayraud Wilmore observes that black radicalism

> has been less political, less obsessed with ideology on the grand scale, and somewhat less committed to violence as a revolutionary strategy. From time to time it has flirted with socialist ideas but without submitting to doctrinaire Marxism. At times it has been violent, but without the misanthropic and genocidal tendencies that frequently accompany radical political movements in the West. Black radicalism has certainly fomented revolution, but usually without the anarchistic nihilism and terrorism that have characterized the most extreme forms of fascism and communism, or even some of the strategies of the New Left of the post–civil rights period.

Wilmore, *Black Religion and Black Radicalism*, 3rd ed., 196–197.

41. Cheryl Townsend Gilkes, *If It Wasn't for the Women: Black Women's Experience and Womanist Culture in Church and Community* (Maryknoll, N.Y.: Orbis Books, 2001), 7, 5. By focusing on the lives of seven religious black women who were activists,

Rosetta E. Ross addresses her work to the religious consciousness and activism of black women during the civil rights movement, in part, as a historical corrective to the androcentrism that has dominated most studies in the field. See Ross, *Witnessing and Testifying*. Among the studies that she cites in an emerging field of literature in this area are Zita Allen, *Black Women Leaders of the Civil Rights Movement* (New York: Franklin Watts, 1996); Bettye Collier-Thomas and V. P. Franklin, eds., *Sisters in the Struggle: African American Women in the Civil Rights–Black Power Movement* (New York: NYU Press, 2001); Cynthia Griggs Fleming, *Soon We Will Not Cry: The Liberation of Ruby Doris Smith Robinson* (Lanham, Md.: Rowman and Littlefield, 1998); Joanne Grant, *Ella Baker: Freedom Bound* (New York: Wiley, 1998); Chana Kai Lee, *For Freedom's Sake: The Life of Fannie Lou Hamer* (Urbana: University of Illinois Press, 1999); Lynn Olson, *Freedom's Daughters: The Unsung Heroines of the Civil Rights Movement from 1830 to 1970* (New York: Scribner's, 2001).

42. E.g., Franklin, *Liberating Visions*; Paris, *Black Religious Leaders*.

43. Gilkes, *If It Wasn't for the Women*, 213n. 11. On the Sanctified or Pentecostal-Holiness Church tradition, see Anthea D. Butler, *Women in the Church of God in Christ: Making a Sanctified World* (Chapel Hill: University of North Carolina Press, 2007).

44. Gilkes, *If It Wasn't for the Women*, 43.

45. Barbara A. Holmes, *Joy Unspeakable: Contemplative Practices of the Black Church* (Minneapolis: Fortress, 2004).

46. Hurston, *Sanctified Church*, 103.

47. Gilkes, *If It Wasn't for the Women*, 44.

48. Ibid., 46.

49. For an analysis of Pentecostal piety as a response to racism within the context of the United Kingdom, see Robert Beckford, *Dread and Pentecostal: A Political Theology for the Black Church in Britain* (London: SPCK, 2000). Beckford proffers a Dread Pentecostal Theology, as the British black church reconnects with the radical side of its ministry in a postmodern context.

50. Gilkes, *If It Wasn't for the Women*, 47.

51. Qtd. in ibid., 49.

52. Ibid., 47, 51.

53. See Dovie Marie Simmons and Olivia L. Martin, *Down behind the Sun: The Story of Arenia Conelia Mallory* ([Lexington, Miss.?]: D. M. Simmons and O. L. Martin, 1983).

54. Emilie M. Townes, *Womanist Justice, Womanist Hope*, American Academy of Religion Academy Series 79 (Atlanta: Scholars, 1993). Also, see Townes's doctor of ministry thesis on black theology: "The Kingdom of God in Black Preaching: An Analysis and Critique of James H. Cone" (D.Min. diss., University of Chicago, 1982); and Townes, *In a Blaze of Glory*.

55. Townes, *Womanist Justice, Womanist Hope*, 11.

56. Ibid., 12.

57. Ida B. Wells, *Crusade for Justice*, ed. Alfreda Duster (Chicago: University of Chicago Press, 1970), 299, qtd. in ibid., 186.

58. Terrell, *Power in the Blood?*, 66–67.

Notes to the Conclusion

1. C. Cone, *Identity Crisis in Black Theology*; Edwards, "Black Theology."
2. Milmon Harrison, *Righteous Riches: The Word of Faith Movement in Contemporary African American Religion* (Oxford: Oxford University Press, 2005); Shayne Lee, *T. D. Jakes: America's New Preacher* (New York: NYU Press, 2005); Jonathan L. Walton, *Watch This! The Ethics and Aesthetics of Black Televangelism*, Religion, Race, and Ethnicity (New York: NYU Press, 2009).
3. M. King, *Stride toward Freedom*, 36.
4. Lincoln and Mamiya, *Black Church in the African American Experience*, 170.
5. Vincent L. Wimbush, "The Bible and African Americans: An Outline of an Interpretive History," in Felder, *Stony the Road We Trod*.
6. Freedman, "Salvation," in *Anchor Bible Dictionary*, 5:907.
7. See Cone, *Black Theology of Liberation*; Atilio Rene Dupertuis, "Liberation Theology: A Study in Its Soteriology" (Ph.D. diss., Andrews University Seminary, 1982); Gustavo Gutiérrez, *A Theology of Liberation: History, Politics and Salvation* (New York: Orbis Books, 1973); Olin P. Moyd, *Redemption in Black Theology* (Valley Forge, Pa.: Judson, 1979).
8. Freedman, "Salvation," in *Anchor Bible Dictionary*, 5:907–908.
9. See Brevard S. Childs, *Biblical Theology of the Old and New Testaments: Theological Reflection on the Christian Bible* (Minneapolis: Fortress, 1993), 131.
10. Marvin L. Chaney, "Bitter Bounty: The Dynamics of Political Economy Critiqued by the Eighth-Century Prophets," in *The Bible and Liberation: Political and Social Hermeneutics*, ed. Norman K. Gottwald and Richard A. Horsley (Maryknoll, N.Y.: Orbis Books, 1993), 251.
11. See Delores Williams, *Sisters in the Wilderness*.
12. J. Cone, *Cross and the Lynching Tree*.
13. Hurston, *Sanctified Church*, 103.
14. See Cox, *Fire from Heaven*.
15. Witvliet, *Way of the Black Messiah*, 219–220.
16. See Chappell's chapter "The Civil Rights Movement as a Religious Revival," in *Stone of Hope*. Also, see Morris, *Origins of the Civil Rights Movement*, 98, Raboteau, *Fire in the Bones*, 59; R. King, *Civil Rights and the Idea of Freedom*, 200–207.
17. Cheryl Townsend Gilkes, "The Role of Women in the Sanctified Church," *Journal of Religious Thought* 43, no. 1 (Spring–Summer 1986): 24–41; Gilkes, *If It Wasn't for the Women*.
18. Felder, *Stony the Road We Trod*; Terrell, *Power in the Blood?*; Delores Williams, *Sisters in the Wilderness*.
19. Vincent Harding, "The Religion of Black Power," in Cone and Wilmore, *Black Theology*, vol. 1, 2nd ed., 41.
20. Cone, *Black Theology and Black Power*, 39–40.

BIBLIOGRAPHY

Alexander, Michelle. *The New Jim Crow: Mass Incarceration in the Age of Colorblindness*. New York: New Press, 2010.

Allen, Zita. *Black Women Leaders of the Civil Rights Movement*. New York: Franklin Watts, 1996.

Altizer, Thomas J. J. *The Descent into Hell: A Study of the Radical Reversal of the Christian Consciousness*. Philadelphia: Lippincott, 1970.

————. *The Gospel of Christian Atheism*. London: Collins, 1967.

Altizer, Thomas J. J., and William Hamilton. *Radical Theology and the Death of God*. New ed. Harmondsworth, UK: Penguin, 1968.

Anderson, Victor. *Beyond Ontological Blackness: An Essay on African American Religious and Cultural Criticism*. New York: Continuum, 1995.

Andrews, Dale P. *Practical Theology for Black Churches: Bridging Black Theology and African American Folk Religion*. Louisville, Ky.: Westminster John Knox Press, 2002.

Andrews, William L., ed. *Sisters of the Spirit: Three Black Women's Autobiographies of the Nineteenth Century*. Bloomington: Indiana University Press, 1986.

Angell, Stephen Ward. *Bishop Henry McNeal Turner and African-American Religion in the South*. Knoxville: University of Tennessee Press, 1992.

Angell, Stephen Ward, and Anthony B. Pinn. *Social Protest Thought in the African Methodist Episcopal Church, 1862–1939*. Knoxville: University of Tennessee Press, 2000.

Anyabwile, Thabiti M. *The Decline of African American Theology: From Biblical Faith to Cultural Captivity*. Downers Grove, Ill.: InterVarsity, 2007.

Asante, Molefi Kete. *The Afrocentric Idea*. Philadelphia: Temple University Press, 1987.

————. *Afrocentricity*. Trenton, N.J.: Third World, 1988.

————. *Afrocentricity and Knowledge*. Trenton, N.J.: Third World, 1992.

Askew, Glorya, and Gayraud Wilmore, eds. *From Prison Cell to Church Pew*. Black Church Scholars Series 5. Atlanta: ITC, 1993.

————, eds. *Reclamation of Black Prisoners: A Challenge to the African American Church*. Black Church Scholars Series 3. Atlanta: ITC, 1992.

Baer, Hans, and Merrill Singer. *African-American Religion in the Twentieth Century: Varieties of Protest and Accommodation*. Knoxville: University of Tennessee Press, 1992.

Baker-Fletcher, Karen. "The Strength of My Life." In Townes, *Embracing the Spirit*, 122–139.

Baldwin, Lewis V. *Never to Leave Us Alone*. Minneapolis: Fortress, 2010.

———. *There Is a Balm in Gilead: The Cultural Roots of Martin Luther King, Jr.* Minneapolis: Fortress, 1991.

———. *To Make the Wounded Whole: The Cultural Legacy of Martin Luther King, Jr.* Minneapolis: Fortress, 1992.

Bantum, Brian. *Redeeming Mulatto: A Theology of Race and Christian Hybridity*. Waco, Tex.: Baylor University Press, 2010.

Barbour, Floyd B. *The Black Power Revolt*. Boston: Extending Horizon, 1968.

Barth, Karl. *The Epistle to the Romans*. New York: Oxford University Press, 1968.

Beale, Frances. "Double Jeopardy: To Be Black and Female." In Cone and Wilmore, *Black Theology*, vol. 1, 2nd ed., 284–292.

Beckford, Robert. *Dread and Pentecostal: A Political Theology for the Black Church in Britain*. London: SPCK, 2000.

Bentley, William H. "Bible Believers in the Black Community." In *Evangelicals: What They Believe, Who They Are, Where They Are Changing*, edited by David F. Wells and John D. Woodbridge, 108–121. Grand Rapids, Mich.: Baker Book House, 1977.

Black Theology Project. "Message to the Black Church and Community." *Journal of Religous Thought* 34 (Fall–Winter 1977): 23–28.

Blake, John. "Pastors Choose Sides over Direction of Black Church." *Atlanta Journal-Constitution*, February 15, 2005.

Bonhoeffer, Dietrich. *Christ the Center*. Translated by Edwin H. Robertson. San Francisco: HarperCollins, 1978.

———. *Letters and Papers from Prison*. New York: Macmillan, 1972.

———. *A Testament to Freedom: The Essential Writings of Dietrich Bonhoeffer*. Edited by Geffrey B. Kelly and F. Burton Nelson. San Francisco: HarperCollins, 1990.

Boone, Kathleen C. *The Bible Tells Them So: The Discourse of Protestant Fundamentalism*. Albany: SUNY Press, 1989.

Booth, Charles E. *Bridging the Breach: Evangelical Thought and Liberation in the African-American Preaching Tradition*. Chicago: Urban Ministries, 2000.

Branch, Taylor. *Parting the Waters: America in the King Years, 1954–63*. New York: Simon and Schuster, 1988.

———. *Pillar of Fire: America in the King Years, 1963–65*. New York: Simon and Schuster, 1998.

Brown, Teresa L. Fry. "Avoiding Asphyxiation: A Womanist Perspective on Intrapersonal and Interpersonal Transformation." In Townes, *Embracing the Spirit*, 72–94.

Brown, William Wells. "Black Religion in the Post-Reconstruction South." In *Afro-American Religious History: A Documentary Witness*, edited by Milton C. Sernett, 239–243. Durham: Duke University Press, 1985.

Burns, Stewart. *To the Mountaintop: Martin Luther King, Jr.'s Sacred Mission to Save America, 1955–1968*. New York: HarperCollins, 2004.

Butler, Anthea D. *Women in the Church of God in Christ: Making a Sanctified World.* Chapel Hill: University of North Carolina Press, 2007.

Cade, John. "Out of the Mouths of Ex-Slaves." *Journal of Negro History* 20 (1935): 294–337.

Caldwell, Gilbert. "Black Folk in White Churches." *Christian Century*, February 12, 1969, 209–211.

Carter, J. Kameron. *Race: A Theological Account.* Oxford: Oxford University Press, 2008.

Chaney, Marvin L. "Bitter Bounty: The Dynamics of Political Economy Critiqued by the Eighth-Century Prophets." In *The Bible and Liberation: Political and Social Hermeneutics*, edited by Norman K. Gottwald and Richard A. Horsley, 250–263. Maryknoll, N.Y.: Orbis Books, 1993.

Chapman, Mark L. "Christianity on Trial: African-American Religious Thought before and after Black Power, 1945–1992." Ph.D. diss., Union Theological Seminary, 1993.

———. *Christianity on Trial: Black Religious Thought before and after Black Power.* Maryknoll, N.Y.: Orbis Books, 1996.

Chappell, David L. *A Stone of Hope: Prophetic Religion and the Death of Jim Crow.* Chapel Hill: University of North Carolina Press, 2004.

Childs, Brevard S. *Biblical Theology of the Old and New Testaments: Theological Reflection on the Christian Bible.* Minneapolis: Fortress, 1993.

Cleage, Albert B. *Black Christian Nationalism: New Directions for the Black Church.* New York: Morrow, 1972.

———. *The Black Messiah.* Trenton, N.J.: Africa World, 1989.

Collier-Thomas, Bettye, and V. P. Franklin, eds. *Sisters in the Struggle: African American Women in the Civil Rights–Black Power Movement.* New York: NYU Press, 2001.

Cone, Cecil Wayne. *The Identity Crisis in Black Theology.* Nashville, Tenn.: AMEC, 1975.

Cone, James H. "Black Christians and Marxism." *Voices from the Third World* 9, no. 1 (1986): 1–12.

———. "The Black Church and Marxism: What Do They Have to Say to Each Other?" Occasional paper, Institute for Democratic Socialism, 1980).

———. "Black Consciousness and the Black Church." *Christianity and Crisis* 30 (1970): 244–250.

———. "Black Consciousness and the Black Church: An Historical-Theological Interpretation." In *The Sixties: Radical Change in American Religion.* Vols. 387–392 of *The Annals of the American Academy of Political and Social Science*, January 1970, 49–55.

———. *Black Theology and Black Power.* New York: Seabury, 1969. Reprint, Maryknoll, N.Y.: Orbis Books, 1989.

———. "Black Theology and Marxism." *Voices from the Third World* 9, no. 3 (1986).

———. *A Black Theology of Liberation.* C. Eric Lincoln Series in Black Religion. Philadelphia: Lippincott, 1970.

———. "Black Theology: Tears, Anguish and Salvation." *Circuit Rider*, May 1978, 3–6.

———. "Christian Faith and Political Praxis." *Bulletin de théologie africaine* 2, no. 4 (1980): 205–218.

———. "Christian Theology and Scripture as the Expression of God's Liberating Activity for the Poor." *Bangalore Theological Forum* 22, no. 2 (1990): 26–39.

Cone, James H. "Christian Theology and the Afro-American Revolution." *Christianity and Crisis* 30 (1970): 123–125.

———. "A Critique of J. Deotis Roberts, Sr.'s *A Black Political Theology.*" *Journal of International Theological Center* 3, no. 1 (1975): 55–57.

———. *The Cross and the Lynching Tree.* Maryknoll, N.Y.: Orbis Books, 2011.

———. "The Doctrine of Man in the Theology of Karl Barth." Ph.D. diss., Northwestern University, 1965.

———. *For My People: Black Theology and the Black Church.* Bishop Henry McNeal Turner Studies in North American Black Religion 1. Maryknoll, N.Y.: Orbis Books, 1984.

———. *God of the Oppressed.* San Francisco: Harper, 1975.

———. "God Our Father, Christ Our Redeemer, Man Our Brother: A Theological Interpretation of the AME Church." *AME Church Review,* January–March 1991, 25–33.

———. "In Search of a Definition of Violence." *Church and Society* (Presbyterian Church, USA) (January–February 1995): 5–7.

———. "An Interpretation of the Debate among Black Theologians." In Wilmore and Cone, *Black Theology,* vol. 1, 609–623.

———. *Martin and Malcolm and America: A Dream or a Nightmare.* Maryknoll, N.Y.: Orbis Books, 1991.

———. "Martin Luther King, Jr., Black Theology–Black Church." *Theology Today* 40, no. 4 (1984): 409–420.

———. "Martin Luther King: The Source of His Courage to Face Death." *Concilium* 183 (1983): 74–79.

———. "The Mission of Black Churches: Saving Souls or Saving Bodies?" Unpublished lecture.

———. *My Soul Looks Back: Journeys in Faith.* Nashville, Tenn.: Abingdon, 1982.

———. Review of *Ring Out Freedom! The Voice of Martin Luther King, Jr. and the Making of the Civil Rights Movement,* by by Fredrik Sunnemark. *Journal of Southern Religion* 7 (2004).

———. *Risks of Faith: The Emergence of a Black Theology of Liberation, 1968–1998.* Boston: Beacon, 1999.

———. *Speaking the Truth: Ecumenism, Liberation, and Black Theology.* Grand Rapids, Mich.: Eerdmans, 1986.

———. *The Spirituals and the Blues.* Maryknoll, N.Y.: Orbis Books, 1972.

———. "The Theology of Martin Luther King, Jr." *Union Seminary Quarterly Review* 40, no. 4 (1986): 21–40.

———. "Theology's Great Sin: Silence in the Face of White Supremacy." *Union Seminary Quarterly Review* 55, nos. 3–4 (2001): 1–14.

———. "What Does It Mean to Be Saved?" In *Preaching the Gospel,* edited by Henry J. Young and William Holmes Borders, 20–24. Philadelphia: Fortress, 1976.

———. "What Time Is It for the AME Church?" *AME Church Review,* January–March 1987, 32–41.

Cone, James H., and William Hordern. "Dialogue on Black Theology." *Christian Century* 88 (1971): 1079–1085.

Cone, James H., and Gayraud S. Wilmore, eds. *Black Theology: A Documentary History.* Vol. 1, *1966–1979.* 2nd ed. Maryknoll, N.Y.: Orbis Books, 1993.

———, eds. *Black Theology: A Documentary History.* Vol. 2, *1980–1992.* Maryknoll, N.Y.: Orbis Books, 1993.

Cox, Harvey Gallagher. *Fire from Heaven: The Rise of Pentecostal Spirituality and the Reshaping of Religion in the Twenty-First Century.* Reading, Mass.: Addison-Wesley, 1995.

Cruse, Harold. *The Crisis of the Negro Intellectual: A Historical Analysis of the Failure of Black Leadership.* New York: New York Review Books, 2005.

Cummings, George C. L. *A Common Journey: Black Theology (USA) and Latin American Liberation Theology.* Bishop Henry McNeal Turner Studies in North American Black Religion 6. Maryknoll, N.Y.: Orbis Books, 1993.

———. "A Comparative Analysis of the Origins and Development of Black Theology in the United States of America and Latin American Liberation Theology, 1968–1986." Ph.D. diss., Union Theological Seminary, 1989.

Daly, John Patrick. *When Slavery Was Called Freedom: Evangelicalism, Proslavery, and the Causes of the Civil War.* Religion in the South. Lexington: University Press of Kentucky, 2002.

Davis, David Brion. *The Problem of Slavery in Western Culture.* New York: Oxford University Press, 1966.

Dawson, Michael C. *Black Visions: The Roots of Contemporary African-American Political Ideologies.* Chicago: University of Chicago Press, 2001.

Dickerson, Dennis. "The Black Church and Black Intellectuals." *AME Church Review,* 1986, 22–29.

Doctrines and Disciplines of the African Methodist Episcopal Church, The. Philadelphia, 1817.

Dorrien, Gary J. *The Barthian Revolt in Modern Theology: Theology without Weapons.* Louisville, Ky.: Westminster John Knox Press, 2000.

———. *Imperial Designs: Neoconservatism and the New Pax Americana.* New York: Routledge, 2004.

———. *The Making of American Liberal Theology: Idealism, Realism, and Modernity, 1900–1950.* Louisville, Ky.: Westminster John Knox Press, 2003.

Douglas, Kelly Brown. *The Black Christ.* Bishop Henry McNeal Turner Studies in North American Black Religion 9. Maryknoll, N.Y.: Orbis Books, 1993.

———. *Sexuality and the Black Church: A Womanist Perspective.* Maryknoll, N.Y.: Orbis Books, 1999.

———. *What's Faith Got to Do with It? Black Bodies / Christian Souls.* Maryknoll, N.Y.: Orbis Books, 2005.

———. "'Who Do They Say That I Am?': A Critical Examination of the Black Christ." Union Theological Seminary, 1988.

Douglass, Frederick. *Narrative of the Life of Frederick Douglass, An American Slave.* Boston: Anti-Slavery Office, 1835.

Drake, St. Clair, and Horace R. Cayton. *Black Metropolis: A Study of Negro Life in a Northern City.* Rev. and enl. ed. Chicago: University of Chicago Press, 1993.

Du Bois, W. E. B. *The Negro Church; Report of a Social Study Made under the Direction of*

Atlanta University; Together with the Proceedings of the Eighth Conference for the Study of the Negro Problems, Held at Atlanta University, May 26th, 1903. Atlanta: Atlanta University Press, 1903.

Du Bois, W. E. B. *The Philadelphia Negro: A Social Study*. Philadelphia: University of Pennsylvania Press, 1996.

———. *The Souls of Black Folk*. 1903. Reprint, New York: New American Library, 1969.

Dupertuis, Atilio Rene. "Liberation Theology: A Study in Its Soteriology." Ph.D. diss., Andrews University Seminary, 1982.

Dvorak, Katharine L. *An African-American Exodus: The Segregation of the Southern Churches*. Chicago Studies in the History of American Religion 4. Brooklyn, N.Y.: Carlson, 1991.

Echols, James Kenneth. "The Two Kingdoms: A Black American Perspective." In *Theology and the Black Experience: The Lutheran Heritage Interpreted by African and African American Theologians*, edited by Albert Pero and Ambrose Moyo, 110–132. Minneapolis: Fortress, 1988.

Edwards, Herbert O. "Black Theology: Retrospect and Prospect." *Journal of Religious Thought* 32, no. 2 (Fall–Winter 1975): 46–59.

———. "Racism and Christian Ethics in America." *Katallegete*, Winter 1971.

———. "The Third World and the Problem of God-Talk." *Harvard Theological Review* 6, no. 4 (1971).

Emerson, William Canfield. *Stories and Spirituals of the Negro Slave*. Boston: R. G. Badger, 1930.

Essig, James D. *The Bonds of Wickedness: American Evangelicals against Slavery, 1770–1808*. Philadelphia: Temple University Press, 1982.

Evans, Anthony Tyrone. "A Biblical Critique of Selected Issues in Black Theology." Ph.D. diss., Dallas Theological Seminary, 1982.

Evans, Eve. "Olivet's Star Attraction." *Renewal*, Winter 1975.

Evans, James H. *We Have Been Believers: An African-American Systematic Theology*. Minneapolis: Fortress, 1992.

Faduma, Orishatukeh. "The Defects of the Negro Church." American Negro Academy Occasional Paper 10, 1904.

Fairclough, Adam. *To Redeem the Soul of America: The Southern Christian Leadership Conference and Martin Luther King, Jr*. Athens: University of Georgia Press, 1987.

Felder, Cain Hope, ed. *Stony the Road We Trod: African American Biblical Interpretation*. Minneapolis: Fortress, 1991.

Fleming, Cynthia Griggs. *Soon We Will Not Cry: The Liberation of Ruby Doris Smith Robinson*. Lanham, Md.: Rowman and Littlefield, 1998.

Foner, Philip S. *American Socialism and Black Americans: From the Age of Jackson to World War II*. Westport, Conn.: Greenwood, 1977.

Frady, Marshall. *Martin Luther King, Jr*. New York: Penguin, 2002.

Franklin, Robert Michael. *Liberating Visions: Human Fulfillment and Social Justice in African-American Thought*. Minneapolis: Fortress, 1990.

Frazier, E. Franklin, and C. Eric Lincoln. *The Negro Church in America* / The Black Church since Frazier. Sourcebooks in Negro History. New York: Schocken Books, 1974.

Freedman, David Noel. *The Anchor Bible Dictionary*. New York: Doubleday, 1992.

Freire, Paulo. "Conscientizing as a Way of Liberating." In *Liberation Theology: A Documentary History*, edited by Alfred T. Hennelly, 5–13. Maryknoll, N.Y.: Orbis Books, 1990.

———. *The Pedagogy of the Oppressed*. New York: Seabury, 1973.

Garber, Paul R. "Black Theology: Latter Day Legacy of Martin Luther King, Jr." *Journal of the International Theological Center* 2 (1975): 100–113.

———. "King Was a Black Theologian." *Journal of Religious Thought* 31, no. 2 (Fall–Winter 1975): 16–32.

Gardiner, James J., and J. Deotis Roberts, eds. *Quest for a Black Theology*. Philadelphia: Pilgrim, 1971.

Garrow, David J. *Bearing the Cross: Martin Luther King, Jr., and the Southern Christian Leadership Conference*. New York: Morrow, 1986.

———. "The Intellecual Development of Martin Luther King, Jr.: Influences and Commentaries." *Union Seminary Quarterly Review* 40, no. 4 (1986): 5–20.

Genovese, Eugene D. *Roll, Jordan, Roll: The World the Slaves Made*. New York: Vintage Books, 1976.

George, Carol V. R. *Segregated Sabbaths; Richard Allen and the Emergence of Independent Black Churches, 1760–1840*. New York: Oxford University Press, 1973.

Gilkes, Cheryl Townsend. *If It Wasn't for the Women: Black Women's Experience and Womanist Culture in Church and Community*. Maryknoll, N.Y.: Orbis Books, 2001.

———. "The Role of Women in the Sanctified Church." *Journal of Religious Thought* 43, no. 1 (Spring–Summer 1986): 24–41.

Glaude, Eddie S. "The Black Church Is Dead." *Huffington Post*, February 24, 2010.

———. *Exodus! Religion, Race, and Nation in Early Nineteenth-Century Black America*. Chicago: University of Chicago Press, 2000.

Gollwitzer, Helmut. "Why Black Theology?" In Wilmore and Cone, *Black Theology*, vol. 1, 152–173.

Grant, Jacquelyn. "Epistle to the Black Church: What a Womanist Would Want to Say to the Black Church." *AME Church Review*, April–June 1991, 49–58.

———. "Servanthood Revisited: Womanist Explorations of Servanthood Theology." In Hopkins, *Black Faith and Public Talk*, 126–137.

———. "The Sin of Servanthood and the Deliverance of Discipleship." In Townes, *Troubling in My Soul*, 199–218.

———. *White Women's Christ and Black Women's Jesus: Feminist Christology and Womanist Response*. Atlanta: Scholars, 1989.

———. "Women and Theology: Black Women's Experience as a Source for Doing Theology, with Special Reference to Christology." *AME Church Review*, 1987, 41–57.

Grant, Joanne. *Ella Baker: Freedom Bound*. New York: Wiley, 1998.

Gutiérrez, Gustavo. *A Theology of Liberation: History, Politics and Salvation*. Maryknoll, N.Y.: Orbis Books, 1973.

Hall-Wynn, Prathia. "The Challenge of True Kinship." In Harris, Roberson, and George, *What Does It Mean to Be Black and Christian?*

Hamilton, Charles V. *The Black Preacher in America*. New York: Morrow, 1972.

Hamilton, Kenneth. *God Is Dead: The Anatomy of a Slogan.* Grand Rapids, Mich.: Eerdmans, 1966.

———. *What's New in Religion? A Critical Study of New Theology, New Morality, and Secular Christianity.* Grand Rapids, Mich.: Eerdmans, 1968.

Harding, Vincent. "No Turning Back." *Renewal* 10, no. 7 (1970): 7–13.

———. "The Religion of Black Power." In Cone and Wilmore, *Black Theology,* vol. 1, 2nd ed., 40–65.

———. "The Uses of the Afro-American Past." *Negro Digest* 17 (February 1968): 4–9, 81–84.

Harris, Forrest E., Sr., with James T. Roberson and Larry D. George, eds. *What Does It Mean to Be Black and Christian? Pulpit, Pew, and Academy in Dialogue.* Nashville, Tenn.: Townsend, 1995.

Harris, James H. *Pastoral Theology: A Black-Church Perspective.* Minneapolis: Fortress, 1991.

———. "Practicing Liberation in the Black Church." *Christian Century,* 1990, 599–602.

———. *Preaching Liberation.* Minneapolis: Fortress, 1995.

Harrison, Milmon. *Righteous Riches: The Word of Faith Movement in Contemporary African American Religion.* Oxford: Oxford University Press, 2005.

Harvey, Paul. "'These Untutored Masses': The Campaign for Respectability among White and Black Evangelicals in the American South, 1870–1930." *Journal of Religous History* 21, no. 3 (1997): 302–317.

Hayes, Diana L. *And Still We Rise: An Introduction to Black Liberation Theology.* New York: Paulist, 1996.

Herskovits, Melville J. *The Myth of the Negro Past.* Boston: Beacon, 1958.

Herzog, Frederick. "The Liberation of White Theology." *Christian Century,* March 20, 1974, 316–319.

———. *Liberation Theology: Liberation in the Light of the Fourth Gospel.* New York: Seabury, 1972.

Higginbotham, Evelyn Brooks. *Righteous Discontent: The Women's Movement in the Black Baptist Church, 1880–1920.* Cambridge: Harvard University Press, 1993.

Hill, Renee L. "Who Are We for Each Other? Sexism, Sexuality and Womanist Theology." In Cone and Wilmore, *Black Theology,* vol. 2, 345–351.

Holmer, Paul. "Remarks Excerpted from 'The Crisis in Rhetoric,'" *Theological Education* 7, no. 3 (Spring 1971): 211.

Holmes, Barbara A. *Joy Unspeakable: Contemplative Practices of the Black Church.* Minneapolis: Fortress, 2004.

Hood, Robert E. *Begrimed and Black: Christian Traditions on Blacks and Blackness.* Minneapolis: Fortress, 1994.

Hoover, Theressa. "Black Women and the Churches: Triple Jeopardy." In Cone and Wilmore, *Black Theology,* vol. 1, 2nd ed., 293–303.

Hopkins, Dwight N., ed. *Black Faith and Public Talk: Critical Essays on James H. Cone's "Black Theology and Black Power."* Maryknoll, N.Y.: Orbis Books, 1999.

———. *Down, Up, and Over: Slave Religion and Black Theology.* Minneapolis: Fortress, 2000.

———. *Introducing Black Theology of Liberation.* Maryknoll, N.Y.: Orbis Books, 1999.

————. *Shoes That Fit Our Feet: Sources for a Constructive Black Theology*. Maryknoll, N.Y.: Orbis Books, 1993.

Hopkins, Dwight N., and George C. L. Cummings. *Cut Loose Your Stammering Tongue: Black Theology in the Slave Narratives*. Maryknoll, N.Y.: Orbis Books, 1991.

Hordern, William. *The Case for a New Reformation Theology*. Philadelphia: Westminster, 1959.

————. *Christianity, Communism, and History*. Nashville, Tenn.: Abingdon, 1954.

————. *A Layman's Guide to Protestant Theology*. Rev. ed. New York: Macmillan, 1968.

————. *New Directions in Theology Today*. Philadelphia: Westminster, 1966.

How, Samuel Blanchard. *Slaveholding Not Sinful: Slavery, the Punishment of Man's Sin, Its Remedy, the Gospel of Christ*. Black Heritage Library Collection. Freeport, N.Y.: Books for Libraries Press, 1971.

Hurston, Zora Neale. *The Sanctified Church*. Berkeley, Calif.: Turtle Island Foundation, 1981.

Ivory, Luther D. *Toward a Theology of Radical Involvement: The Theological Legacy of Martin Luther King, Jr.* Nashville, Tenn.: Abingdon, 1997.

Jackson, Joseph Harrison. "The Basic Theological Position of the National Baptist Convention, U.S.A., Inc." In Cone and Wilmore, *Black Theology*, vol. 1, 2nd ed., 245–249.

————. *Many, but One: The Ecumenics of Charity*. New York: Sheen and Ward, 1964.

————. *Nairobi: A Joke, a Junket, or a Journey?* Nashville, Tenn.: Townsend, 1976.

————. *A Story of Christian Activism: The History of the National Baptist Convention, U.S.A., Inc.* Nashville, Tenn.: Townsend, 1980.

————. *Unholy Shadows and Freedom's Holy Light*. Nashville, Tenn.: Townsend, 1967.

James, William. *The Varieties of Religious Experience: A Study in Human Nature: Being the Gifford Lectures on Natural Religion Delivered at Edinburgh in 1901–1902*. Mineola, N.Y.: Dover, 2002.

Jennings, Willie J. *The Christian Imagination: Theology and the Origins of Race*. New Haven: Yale University Press, 2010.

Johnson, Clifton H., ed. *God Struck Me Dead: Voices of Ex-Slaves*. Cleveland: Pilgrim, 1993.

Johnson, Joseph A., Jr. "Jesus, the Liberator." In Gardiner and Roberts, *Quest for a Black Theology*, 97–111.

————. "Jesus: The Liberator [Limitations of White Theology]." *Anderson Newton Quarterly* 10 (January 1970): 85–96.

————. "My Other Assignments." Memo. Henry C. Bunton Papers, Schomburg Center for Research in Black Culture, New York.

————. "The Need for a Black Christian Theology." *Journal of the International Theological Center* 2, no. 2 (Fall 1974): 19–29.

Johnson, Sylvester A. "The 'Children of Ham' in America: Divine Identity and the Hamitic Idea in Nineteenth-Century American Christianity." Ph.D. diss., Union Theological Seminary, 2002.

Jones, Amos. *Paul's Message of Freedom: What Does It Mean to the Black Church?* Valley Forge, Pa.: Judson, 1984.

Jones, William R. *Is God a White Racist? A Preamble to Black Theology.* Boston: Beacon, 1998.

———. "Suffering Servants and Wounded Warriors: A Description of Major Themes in Black Theology." *AME Church Review*, 1993, 19–27.

———. "Theodicy and Methodology in Black Theology:A Critique of Washington, Cone and Cleage." *AME Church Review*, 1993, 28–39.

———. "Theodicy: The Controlling Category for Black Theology." *AME Church Review*, 1993, 9–17.

Jordan, Winthrop D. *White over Black: American Attitudes toward the Negro, 1550–1812.* Chapel Hill: University of North Carolina Press, 2012.

Kaplan, Sidney. *The Black Presence in the Era of the American Revolution.* Washington, D.C.: Smithsonian Institute Press, 1973.

Kennedy, Randall. *The Persistence of the Color Line: Racial Politics and the Obama Presidency.* New York: Pantheon Books, 2011.

King, Martin Luther, Jr. "Advice for Living." *Ebony*, October 1957. Reprinted in *The Papers of Martin Luther King, Jr.*, vol. 4, *Symbol of the Movement*, edited by Clayborne Carson, 305–306. Berkeley: University of California Press, 2000.

———. "An Autobiography of Religious Development." In *The Papers of Martin Luther King, Jr.*, vol. 1, *Called to Serve January, 1929–June 1951*, edited by Clayborne Carson, 359–363. Berkeley: University of California Press, 1992.

———. "Discerning the Signs of History, November 15, 1964." Sermon. King Center Archives, Atlanta, Georgia.

———. "I See the Promised Land." 1968. In *A Testament of Hope: The Essential Writings and Speeches of Martin Luther King, Jr.*, edited by James M. Washington, 279–286. San Francisco: Harper and Row, 1986.

———. "A Knock at Midnight." In *A Knock at Midnight: Inspiration from the Great Sermons of Martin Luther King, Jr.*, edited by Clayborne Carson and Peter Holloran, 61–78. New York: Warner Books, 1998.

———. "Letter from Birmingham Jail." In *Why We Can't Wait*, 85–110. New York: Harper and Row, 1963.

———. "Recommendations to the Dexter Avenue Baptist Church for the Fiscal Year 1954–1955." In *The Papers of Martin Luther King, Jr.*, vol. 2, *Rediscovering Precious Values, July 1951–November 1955*, edited by Clayborne Carson, 287–294. Berkeley: University of California Press, 1994.

———. "Revolution and Redemption." August 16, 1964. King Center Archives, Amsterdam.

———. "The Role of the Church in Facing the Nation's Chief Moral Dilemma, April 23–25, 1957." Address to Conference on Christian Faith and Human Relations, Nashville, Tennessee. King Center Archives, Atlanta, Georgia.

———. *Strength to Love.* 1963. Reprint, Philadelphia: Fortress, 1981.

———. *Stride toward Freedom: The Montgomery Story.* New York: Harper, 1958.

———. "Suffering and Faith." 1960. In *A Testament of Hope: The Essential Writings and Speeches of Martin Luther King, Jr.*, edited by James M. Washington, 41–42. San Francisco: Harper and Row, 1986.

———. "To Minister to the Valley." February 23, 1968. King Center Archives, Atlanta, Georgia.

———. "A Walk through the Holy Land." Sermon, March 29, 1959. King Center Archives, Atlanta, Georgia.

———. "Who Is Their God?" *Nation*, October 13, 1962, 210.

———. "Why Jesus Called a Man a Fool." In *A Knock at Midnight: Inspiration from the Great Sermons of Martin Luther King, Jr.*, edited by Clayborne Carson and Peter Holloran, 141–164. New York: Warner Books, 1998.

———. *Why We Can't Wait.* New York: Harper and Row, 1963.

King, Richard. *Civil Rights and the Idea of Freedom.* New York: Oxford University Press, 1992.

Lambert, Frank. " 'I Saw the Book Talk': Slave Readings of the First Great Awakening." *Journal of Negro History* 77, no. 4 (1992): 185–198.

Lee, Chana Kai. *For Freedom's Sake: The Life of Fannie Lou Hamer.* Urbana: University of Illinois Press, 1999.

Lee, Shayne. *T. D. Jakes: America's New Preacher.* New York: NYU Press, 2005.

Lewis, David Levering. *W. E. B. Du Bois: Biography of a Race, 1868–1919.* New York: Owl Books, 1994.

———. *W. E. B. Du Bois: The Fight for Equality and the American Century, 1919–1963.* New York: Owl Books, 2001.

Lewis, John, with Michael D'Orso. *Walking with the Wind: A Memoir of the Movement.* New York: Simon and Schuster, 1998.

Lincoln, C. Eric, ed. *Is Anybody Listening to Black America?* New York: Seabury, 1968.

Lincoln, C. Eric, and Lawrence H. Mamiya. *The Black Church in the African American Experience.* Durham: Duke University Press, 1990.

Ling, Peter J. *Martin Luther King, Jr.* New York: Routledge, 2002.

Lischer, Richard. *The Preacher King: Martin Luther King, Jr. and the Word That Moved America.* New York: Oxford University Press, 1995.

Little, Lawrence S. *Disciples of Liberty: The African Methodist Episcopal Church in the Age of Imperialism, 1884–1916.* Knoxville: University of Tennessee Press, 2000.

Locklear, Jimmy. "Theology-Culture Rift Surfaces among Black Evangelicals." *Christianity Today* 24, no. 44 (1980).

Long, Charles H. "Perspectives for a Study of Afro-American Religion in the United States." *History of Religions* 11 (August 1974): 54–66.

———. *Significations: Signs, Symbols, and Images in the Interpretation of Religion.* Philadelphia: Fortress, 1986.

Lucas, Lawrence E. *Black Priest / White Church: Catholics and Racism.* New York: Random House, 1970.

Luther, Martin. "Admonition to Peace." In *Luther's Works*, edited by Jaroslav Pelikan, vol. 46. St. Louis: Concordia, 1961.

———. "The Freedom of the Christian." In *Luther's Works*, edited by Jaroslav Pelikan, vol. 31. St. Louis: Concordia, 1961.

———. "Temporal Authority: To What Extent It Should Be Obeyed." In *Luther's Works*, edited by Jaroslav Pelikan, vol. 21. St. Louis: Concordia, 1961.

MacRobert, Iain. *The Black Roots and White Racism of Early Pentecostalism in the USA.* New York: St. Martin's, 1988.

Marable, Manning. *How Capitalism Underdeveloped Black America: Problems in Race, Political Economy, and Society.* Boston: South End, 1983.

———. *W. E. B. Du Bois, Black Radical Democrat.* Twayne's Twentieth-Century American Biography Series 3. Boston: Twayne, 1986.

Marsden, George M. *Fundamentalism and American Culture: The Shaping of Twentieth-Century Evangelicalism, 1870–1925.* New York: Oxford University Press, 1980.

Marsh, Charles. *God's Long Summer: Stories of Faith and Civil Rights.* Princeton: Princeton University Press, 1997.

Martin, Clarice J. "'The *Haustafeln* (Household Codes) in African American Biblical Interpretation: 'Free Slaves' and 'Subordinate Women.'" In Felder, *Stony the Road We Trod,* 206–231.

Marx, Gary T. *Protest and Prejudice: A Study of Belief in the Black Community.* Rev. ed. Patterns of American Prejudice 3. New York: Harper and Row, 1969.

Mays, Benjamin Elijah, Joseph William Nicholson, and Institute of Social and Religious Research. *The Negro's Church.* New York: Institute of Social and Religious Research, 1933.

McCall, Emmanuel. "Review of Allan A. Boesak's *Farewell to Innocence.*" *Occasional Bulletin of Missionary Research* 2, no. 3 (July 1978).

Miller, Albert G. "The Construction of a Black Fundamentalist Worldview: The Role of Bible School." In *African Americans and the Bible: Sacred Texts and Social Textures,* edited by Vincent L. Wimbush and Rosamond C. Rodman, 712–727. New York: Continuum, 2000.

Mitchell, Henry H. *Black Belief: Folk Beliefs of Blacks in America and West Africa.* New York: Harper and Row, 1975.

———. "Black Power and the Christian Church." *Foundations,* April–July 1968, 99–109.

———. *Black Preaching.* Philadelphia: Lippincott, 1970.

Mitchem, Stephanie Y. *Introducing Womanist Theology.* Maryknoll, N.Y.: Orbis Books, 2002.

Moltmann, Jürgen. *The Way of Jesus Christ: Christology in Messianic Dimensions.* Minneapolis: Fortress, 1993.

Montgomery, William E. *Under Their Own Vine and Fig Tree: The African-American Church in the South, 1865–1900.* Baton Rouge: Louisiana State University Press, 1993.

Moore, Jacqueline M. *Booker T. Washington, W. E. B. Du Bois, and the Struggle for Racial Uplift.* Wilmington, Del.: Scholarly Resources, 2003.

Moore, Moses N. *Orishatukeh Faduma: Liberal Theology and Evangelical Pan-Africanism, 1857–1946.* Lanham, Md.: Scarecrow, 1996.

Morris, Aldon. *The Origins of the Civil Rights Movement: Black Communities Organizing for Change.* New York: Free Press, 1984.

Mosby-Avery, Karen E. "Black Theology and the Black Church." In Thomas, *Living Stones in the Household of God,* 33–36.

Moyd, Olin P. *Redemption in Black Theology.* Valley Forge, Pa.: Judson, 1979.

Murphy, Larry. "Piety and Liberation: A Historical Exploration of African American Religion and Social Justice." In *Blow the Trumpet in Zion! Global Vision and Action for the Twenty-First-Century Black Church*, edited by Iva E. Carruthers, Frederick D. Haynes, and Jeremiah A. Wright, 35–56. Minneapolis: Fortress, 2005.

Murray, Pauli. "Black Theology and Feminist Theology: A Comparative View." In Cone and Wilmore, *Black Theology*, vol. 1, 2nd ed., 304–322.

Myrdal, Gunnar. *An American Dilemma: The Negro Problem and Modern Democracy*. Black and African-American Studies. New Brunswick, NJ: Transaction, 1996.

Naison, Mark. *Communists in Harlem during the Depression*. Urbana: University of Illinois Press, 1983.

National Committee of Black Churchmen. "Black Declaration of Independence." *Renewal* 10, no. 7 (October–November 1970): 21–23.

———. "Black Theology." In Cone and Wilmore, *Black Theology*, vol. 1, 2nd ed., 37–39.

———. "A Message to the Churches from Oakland." *Renewal* 10, no. 7 (October–November 1970): 19–20.

———. *Philadelphia Proclamation of 1972*. New York, 1972.

National Committee of Negro Churchmen. "Black Power." *Renewal* 10, no. 7 (October–November 1970): 14–16. Reprinted in Cone and Wilmore, *Black Theology*, vol. 1, 2nd ed., 19–26.

———. "Racism and the Elections: The American Dilemma of 1966." *Renewal* 10, no. 7 (October–November 1970): 17–18.

National Conference of Black Churchmen. *Spiritual Alienation: The Self-Destruction of Black Community*. Atlanta, May 11, 1973.

Nelsen, Hart M., and Anne Kusener Nelsen. *Black Church in the Sixties*. Lexington: University Press of Kentucky, 1975.

Niebuhr, Reinhold. *Moral Man and Immoral Society: A Study in Ethics and Politics*. Library of Theological Ethics. Louisville, Ky.: Westminster John Knox Press, 2001.

———. *Reinhold Niebuhr: Theologian of Public Life*. Edited by Larry L. Rasmussen. Minneapolis: Fortress, 1991.

Noll, Mark A. *Christians in the American Revolution*. Grand Rapids, Mich.: Eerdmans, 1977.

———. *A History of Christianity in the United States and Canada*. Grand Rapids, Mich.: Eerdmans, 1992.

Olson, Lynn. *Freedom's Daughters: The Unsung Heroines of the Civil Rights Movement from 1830 to 1970*. New York: Scribner's, 2001.

Paris, Peter J. *Black Leaders in Conflict: Joseph H. Jackson, Martin Luther King, Jr., Malcolm X, Adam Clayton Powell, Jr.* New York: Pilgrim, 1978.

———. *Black Religious Leaders: Conflict in Unity*. Louisville, Ky.: Westminster John Knox Press, 1991.

———. *The Social Teaching of the Black Churches*. Philadelphia: Fortress, 1985.

———. *The Spirituality of African Peoples: The Search for a Common Moral Discourse*. Minneapolis: Fortress, 1995.

Patterson, Orlando. *Freedom in the Making of Western Culture*. New York: HarperCollins, 1991.

Patterson, Orlando. *Slavery and Social Death: A Comparative Study*. Cambridge: Harvard University Press, 1982.

Paul, Nathaniel. "An Address, Delivered on the Celebration of the Abolition of Slavery, in the State of New York, July 5, 1827." In *Negro Protest Pamphlets: A Compendium*, edited by Dorothy Porter. New York: Arno, 1969.

Pinn, Anthony B. *Terror and Triumph: The Nature of Black Religion*. Minneapolis: Fortress, 2003.

———. *Varieties of African American Religious Experience*. Minneapolis: Fortress, 1998.

———. *Why, Lord? Suffering and Evil in Black Theology*. New York: Continuum, 1995.

Powell, Adam Clayton, Jr. "Black Power in the Church." *Black Scholar* 2, no. 4 (December 1970): 32–34.

———. *Marching Blacks*. 1945. Reprint, New York: Dial, 1973.

Proctor, Samuel D. "The Metes and Bounds of Black Theology." *United Theological Seminary* 96 (1992): 33–41.

———. *Samuel Proctor: My Moral Odyssey*. Valley Forge, Pa.: Judson, 1989.

Raboteau, Albert J. "African-Americans, Exodus, and the American Israel." In *African-American Christianity: Essays in History*, edited by Paul E. Johnson, 1–17. Berkeley: University of California Press, 1994.

———. "The Black Experience in American Evangelism: The Meaning of Slavery." In *African-American Religion: Interpretive Essays in History and Culture*, edited by Timothy Earl Fulop and Albert J. Raboteau, 89–106. New York: Routledge, 1997.

———. *A Fire in the Bones: Reflections on African-American Religious History*. Boston: Beacon, 1995.

———. *Slave Religion: The "Invisible Institution" in the Antebellum South*. New York: Oxford University Press, 1978.

Rahner, Karl. "Observation on the Problem of the 'Anonymous Christian.'" In *Theological Investigations*, vol. 14. New York: Seabury, 1976.

———. "The One Christ and the Universality of Salvation." In *Theological Investigations*, vol. 16. New York: Crossroads, 1983.

Rauschenbush, Walter. *Christianity and the Social Crisis*. New York: Macmillan, 1913.

Rawick, George P., ed. *The American Slave: A Composite Autobiography*. Vol. 8, *Arkansas Narratives*. Westport, Conn.: Greenwood, 1972.

Redkey, Edwin S. *Black Exodus: Black Nationalist and Back to Africa Movements, 1890–1910*. New Haven: Yale University Press, 1969.

———. *Respect Black: The Writings and Speeches of Henry McNeal Turner*. New York: Arno / New York Times, 1971.

"Reverend Wright at the National Press Club." *New York Times*, April 28, 2008.

Riggs, Marcia, ed. *The Kelly Miller Smith Papers*. Nashville, Tenn.: Jean and Alexander Heard Library, Vanderbilt University, 1989.

Roberts, J. Deotis. *Africentric Christianity: A Theological Appraisal for Ministry*. Valley Forge, Pa.: Judson, 2000.

———. "Black Ecclessiology of Involvement." *Journal of Religious Thought* 32 (Spring–June 1975): 36–46.

———. *A Black Political Theology.* Philadelphia: Westminster, 1974.

———. *Black Religion, Black Theology: The Collected Essays of J. Deotis Roberts.* Edited by David Emmanuel Goatley. African American Religious Thought and Life. Harrisburg, Pa.: Trinity, 2003.

———. "A Critique of James H. Cone's *God of the Oppressed.*" *Journal of International Theological Center* 3, no. 1 (Fall 1975): 58–63.

———. *From Puritanism to Platonism in Seventeenth Century England.* The Hague: Martinus Nijhoff, 1969.

———. *Liberation and Reconciliation: A Black Theology.* Philadelphia: Westminster, 1971.

———. *The Prophethood of Black Believers: An African American Political Theology for Ministry.* Louisville, Ky.: Westminster John Knox Press, 1994.

———. *Roots of a Black Future: The Black Family and the Church.* 2nd ed. Silver Spring, Md.: Strebor Books, 2001.

Robinson, Cedric J. *Black Marxism: The Making of the Black Radical Tradition.* Chapel Hill: University of North Carolina Press, 2000.

Rodgers, Walter. "A Year into Obama's Presidency, Is America Post-Racial?" *Christian Science Monitor,* January 5, 1010.

Rooks, Charles Shelby. "'The Minister as a Change Agent." *Journal of the ITC* 4, no. 1 (Fall 1977): 12–23.

Ross, Rosetta E. *Witnessing and Testifying: Black Women, Religion, and Civil Rights.* Minneapolis: Fortress, 2003.

Salley, Columbus, and Ronald Behm. *What Color Is Your God? Black Consciousness and the Christian Faith.* Rev. ed. Downers Grove, Ill.: InterVarsity, 1981.

———. *Your God Is Too White.* Downers Grove, Ill.: InterVarsity, 1970.

Sanders, Cheryl J. *Empowerment Ethics for a Liberated People: A Path to African American Social Transformation.* Minneapolis: Fortress, 1995.

———, ed. *Living the Intersection: Womanism and Afrocentrism in Theology.* Minneapolis: Fortress, 1995.

Sawyer, Mary R. *Black Ecumenism: Implementing the Demands of Justice.* Valley Forge, Pa.: Trinity, 1984.

Schmidt, Jean Miller. *Souls or the Social Order: The Two-Party System in American Protestantism.* Chicago Studies in the History of American Religion 18. Brooklyn, N.Y.: Carlson, 1991.

Simmons, Dovie Marie, and Olivia L. Martin. *Down behind the Sun: The Story of Arenia Conelia Mallory.* [Lexington, Miss.?]: D. M. Simmons and O. L. Martin, 1983.

Singleton, Harry H. *Black Theology and Ideology: Deideological Dimensions in the Theology of James H. Cone.* Collegeville, Minn.: Liturgical, 2002.

Smith, Amanda Berry. *Amanda Smith the Colored Evangelist.* Chicago: Christian Witness Company, 1921.

Smith, H. Shelton. *In His Image, but . . . : Racism in Southern Religion, 1780–1910.* Durham: Duke University Press, 1972.

Smith, J. Alfred, Sr. "Black Theology and the Parish Ministry." In Hopkins, *Black Faith and Public Talk,* 89–95.

Smith, J. Alfred, Sr., with Harry Louis Williams II. *On the Jericho Road: A Memoir of Raical Justice, Social Action and Prophetic Ministry*. Downers Grove, Ill.: InterVarsity, 2004.

Smith, Kelly Miller. *Social Crisis Preaching: The Lyman Beecher Lectures, 1983*. Macon, Ga.: Mercer University Press, 1984.

Smith, Theophus. *Conjuring Culture: Biblical Formations of Black America*. New York: Oxford University Press, 1994.

Smith, Timothy Lawrence. *Revivalism and Social Reform: American Protestantism on the Eve of the Civil War*. Baltimore: Johns Hopkins University Press, 1980.

Smylie, James H. "On Jesus, Pharaohs, and the Chosen People: Martin Luther King as Biblical Interpreter and Humanist." *Interpretation* 24 (1970): 74–91.

Sommerville, Raymond R. *An Ex-Colored Church: Social Activism in the CME Church, 1870–1970*. Voices of the African Diaspora. Macon, Ga.: Mercer University Press, 2004.

Speller, Julia M. *Walkin' the Talk: Keepin' the Faith in Africentric Congregations*. Cleveland: Pilgrim, 2005.

"Statement of the Black Catholic Clergy Caucus, April 18, 1968, A." *Freeing the Spirit* 1, no. 3 (Summer 1972). Reprinted in Wilmore and Cone, *Black Theology*, vol. 1, 322–324.

Sterling, Dorothy. *Freedom Train: The Story of Harriet Tubman*. Garden City, N.Y.: Doubleday, 1954.

———. *We Are Your Sisters: Black Women in the Nineteenth Century*. New York: Norton, 1984.

Sugrue, Thomas J. *Not Even Past: Barack Obama and the Burden of Race*. Princeton: Princeton University Press, 2010.

Sunnemark, Fredrik. *Ring Out Freedom! The Voice of Martin Luther King, Jr. and the Making of the Civil Rights Movement*. Bloomington: Indiana University Press, 2004.

Taylor, Gardner C. *The Words of Gardner Taylor*. Vol. 4, *Special Occasion and Expository Sermons*. Edited by Edward L. Taylor. Valley Forge, Pa.: Judson, 2001.

Terrell, JoAnne Marie. *Power in the Blood? The Cross in the African American Experience*. Bishop Henry McNeal Turner / Sojourner Truth Series in Black Religion 15. Maryknoll, N.Y.: Orbis Books, 1998.

Tesfai, Yacob, ed. *The Scandal of a Crucified World*. Maryknoll, N.Y.: Orbis Books, 1994.

Thomas, Hilah F., and Rosemary Skinner Keller, eds. *Women in New Worlds*. Nashville, Tenn.: Abingdon, 1981.

Thomas, Linda E., ed. *Living Stones in the Household of God: The Legacy and Future of Black Theology*. Minneapolis: Fortress, 2004.

Thurman, Howard. *Deep River*. Mills College, Calif.: Eucalyptus, 1945.

Townes, Emilie M., ed. *Embracing the Spirit: Womanist Perspectives on Hope, Salvation and Transformation*. Maryknoll, N.Y.: Orbis Books, 1997.

———. *In a Blaze of Glory: Womanist Spirituality as Social Witness*. Nashville, Tenn.: Abingdon, 1995.

———. "The Kingdom of God in Black Preaching: An Analysis and Critique of James H. Cone." D.Min. diss., University of Chicago, 1982.

———, ed. *A Troubling in My Soul: Womanist Perspectives on Evil and Suffering*. Mayknoll, N.Y.: Orbis Books, 1993.

————. *Womanist Justice, Womanist Hope*. American Academy of Religion Academy Series 79. Atlanta: Scholars, 1993.

Traynham, Warner R. *Christian Faith in Black and White: A Primer in Theology from the Black Perspective*. Wakefield, Mass.: Parameter, 1973.

Turner, Henry M. "The Races Must Separate." In *The Possibilities of the Negro in Symposium*, edited by Willis B. Park, 90–98. Atlanta: Franklin, 1904.

"Under Obama, Is America 'Post-Racial'?" *New York Times*, September 21, 2011.

Wald, Alan M. *Exiles from a Future Time: The Forging of the Mid-Twentieth-Century Literary Left*. Chapel Hill: University of North Carolina Press, 2002.

Walker, Clarence E. *A Rock in a Weary Land: The African Methodist Episcopal Church during the Civil War and Reconstruction*. Baton Rouge: Louisiana State University Press, 1982.

Walker, Williston, Richard A. Norris, David W. Lotz, and Robert T. Handy. *A History of the Christian Church*. New York: Scribner's, 1985.

Walton, Jonathan L. *Watch This! The Ethics and Aesthetics of Black Televangelism*. Religion, Race, and Ethnicity. New York: NYU Press, 2009.

Washington, Booker T. *The Future of the American Negro*. Boston, 1899.

Washington, James Melvin. *Frustrated Fellowship: The Black Baptist Quest for Social Power*. Macon, Ga.: Mercer University Press, 1986.

Washington, Joseph R. "Are American Negro Churches Christian?" *Theology Today* 20 (April 1963): 76–86.

————. *Black Religion: The Negro and Christianity in the United States*. Boston: Beacon, 1964.

————. "How Black Is Black Religion?" In Gardiner and Roberts, *Quest for a Black Theology*, 22–43.

————. *The Politics of God: The Future of Black Churches*. 1967. Reprint, Boston: Beacon, 1969.

————. "The Roots and Fruits of Black Theology." *Theology Today* 30 (July 1973): 121–129.

Watson, P. S. *Let God Be God*. Philadelphia: Muhlenberg Press, 1947.

Watts, Leon. "The Black Church Yes! COCU No!" *Renewal* 10, no. 3 (March 1970): 10–11.

————. "The National Committee of Black Churchmen." *Christianity and Crisis* 30, no. 18 (1970).

Wenner, Jann S. "Ready for the Fight: Rolling Stone Interview with Barack Obama." *Rolling Stone*, April 25, 2012.

West, Cornel. "Black Theology and Marxist Thought." In *African American Religious Thought: An Anthology*, edited by Cornel West and Eddie S. Glaude, 874–892. Louisville, Ky.: Westminster John Knox Press, 2003.

————. "Black Theology of Liberation as Critique of Capitalist Civilization." In Cone and Williams, *Black Theology*, vol. 2, 410–425.

————. *Prophesy Deliverance! An Afro-American Revolutionary Christianity*. Philadelphia: Westminster, 1982.

West, Cornel, and Eddie S. Glaude. "Introduction: Towards New Visions and New Approaches in African American Religious Studies." In *African American Religious Thought: An Anthology*, edited by Cornel West and Eddie S. Glaude, xi–xxvi. Louisville, Ky.: Westminster John Knox Press, 2003.

West, Traci C. *Wounds of the Spirit: Black Women, Violence, and Resistance Ethics.* New York: NYU Press 1999.

Wiggins, Daphne. *Righteous Content: Black Women's Perspectives of Church and Faith.* Religion, Race, and Ethnicity. New York: NYU Press, 2005.

Wiley, Dennis W. "Black Theology, the Black Church, and the African-American Community." In Cone and Wilmore, *Black Theology,* vol. 2, 127–138.

———. "The Concept of the Church in the Works of Howard Thurman." Ph.D. diss., Union Theological Seminary, 1988.

Williams, A. Roger. "A Black Pastor Looks at Black Theology." *Harvard Theological Review* 64 (1971): 559–567.

Williams, Delores S. "Afrocentrism and Male-Female Relations in Church and Society." In Sanders, *Living the Intersection,* 43–56.

———. "Black Women's Surrogacy Experience and the Christian Notion of Redemption." In *After Patriarchy: Feminist Transformations of the World Religions,* edited by Paula M. Cooey, William R. Eakin, and Jay Byrd McDaniel, 1–14. Maryknoll, N.Y.: Orbis Books, 1991.

———. *Sisters in the Wilderness: The Challenge of Womanist God-Talk.* Maryknoll, N.Y.: Orbis Books, 1993.

———. "Straight Talk, Plain Talk: Womanist Words about Salvation in a Social Context." In Townes, *Embracing the Spirit,* 97–121.

Williams, Demetrius K. *An End to This Strife: The Politics of Gender in African American Churches.* Minneapolis: Fortress, 2004.

Wilmore, Gayraud S., ed. *Black Men in Prison: The Response of the African American Church.* Black Church Scholars Series 2. Atlanta: ITC, 1990.

———. *Black Religion and Black Radicalism: An Interpretation of the Religious History of African Americans.* 3rd ed. Maryknoll, N.Y.: Orbis Books, 1998.

———. *Black Religion and Black Radicalism: An Interpretation of the Religious History of Afro-American People.* 2nd ed. Maryknoll, N.Y.: Orbis Books, 1983.

———. "Black Theology: Its Significance for Christian Mission Today." *International Review of Mission* 63, no. 250 (April 1974).

———. "Black Theology: Review and Assessment." *Voices from the Third World* 5, no. 2 (December 1982): 3–16.

———. "Connecting Two Worlds: A Response to James Henry Harris by Gayraud Wilmore." *Christian Century,* 1990, 602–604.

———. *Last Things First.* Philadelphia: Westminster, 1982.

———. *The Secular Relevance of the Church.* Philadelphia: Westminster, 1962.

———. "Spirituality and Social Transformation as the Vocation of the Black Church." In *Churches in Struggle: Liberation Theologies and Social Change in North America,* edited by William K. Tabb, 240–253. New York: Monthly Review Press, 1986.

———. *A Summary Report.* NCNC Theological Commission Project, Fall 1968.

———. "The White Church and the Search for Black Power." *Social Progress* 57, no. 4 (1967): 11–20.

Wilmore, Gayraud S., and James H. Cone, eds. *Black Theology: A Documentary History*, vol. 1, *1966–1979*. Maryknoll, N.Y.: Orbis Books, 1979.

Wimberly, Edward P., and Anne Streaty Wimberly. *Liberation and Human Wholeness: The Conversion Experiences of Black People in Slavery and Freedom*. Nashville, Tenn.: Abingdon, 1986.

Wimbush, Vincent L. *The Bible and African Americans: A Brief History*. Minneapolis: Fortress, 2003.

———. "The Bible and African Americans: An Outline of an Interpretive History." In Felder, *Stony the Road We Trod*, 81–97.

Wind, Renate. *Dietrich Bonhoeffer: A Spoke in the Wheel*. Translated by John Bowden. Grand Rapids, Mich.: Eerdmans, 1990.

Wise, Tim. *Between Barack and a Hard Place: Racism and White Denial in the Age of Obama*. Open Media Series. San Francisco: City Lights Books 2009.

Witvliet, Theo. *The Way of the Black Messiah: The Hermeneutical Challenge of Black Theology as a Theology of Liberation*. Oak Park, Ill.: Meyer-Stone Books, 1987.

Wood, Frances E. "'Take My Yoke upon You': The Role of the Church in the Oppression of African-American Women." In Townes, *Troubling in My Soul*, 37–47.

Woodson, Carter Godwin. *The History of the Negro Church*. Washington, D.C.: Associated Publishers, 1921.

Wright, Jeremiah A. "Confusing God and Government." Chicago: Trinity United Church of Christ.

———. "Doing Black Theology in the Black Church." In Thomas, *Living Stones in the Household of God*, 13–23.

———. "An Underground Theology." In Hopkins, *Black Faith and Public Talk*, 96–102.

Wright, Nathan, Jr. *Black Power and Urban Unrest: Creative Possibilities*. New York: Hawthorn Books, 1967.

———. "Power and Reconciliation." *Concern* 9, no. 16 (1967): 22.

Wright, Richard. *Black Power: A Record of Reactions in a Land of Pathos*. New York: Harper, 1954.

Yetman, Norman R., ed. *Life under the "Peculiar Institution": Selections from the Slave Narrative Collection*. New York: Holt, Rinehart and Winston, 1970.

INDEX

ABOUT THE AUTHOR

The Reverend Dr. Raphael G. Warnock serves as Senior Pastor of the Ebenezer Baptist Church (Atlanta, Georgia), spiritual home of the Reverend Dr. Martin Luther King, Jr. He is a native of Savannah, Georgia. His work represents his abiding commitment to Christian ministry, disciplined scholarship, and diligent struggle on behalf of the oppressed.

Made in the USA
Monee, IL
18 January 2021